Advanced Praise for
Noble Birds and Wily Trout

The brave and skillful hunter. The patient, crafty fisherman. From Pleistocene campfires and cave wall paintings to cube-farm water coolers and Instagram, stories of hunting and fishing are as old and enduring as humanity.

In *Noble Birds and Wily Trout*, Will Ryan tells these stories—our stories—with wit, wisdom, and a surgeon's touch, slicing through the static and tweezing the telling details from the great body of storytellers that arose during those transformative years between the Jefferson Administration and the Roaring Twenties, when hunting and fishing went from something done because your farm was failing and your children were hungry to a palliative for the rising middle class whose urbanized spirits thirsted for the wilder, freer, purer life of their ancestors.

Along with tales of high adventure and ripping good yarns, the new literature of hunting and fishing also set the moral tone, codified the definition of sportsmanship, and sanctified the conservation of wildlife and the environment a century before the first Earth Day.

From the generationally famous—Washington Irving and Fenimore Cooper, Teddy Roosevelt and Zane Grey—to obscure but influential writers like Aimee Morrison, Isabel Savory, and Annie Trumbull Slosson, Ryan marshals his forces and draws in readers, taking us from the Serengeti to the Himalayas, the Adirondacks to the Great Plains, along the way showing, not telling, how we modern-day hunters and fishers became who we are today.

And why, in the grander scheme of things, that matters.

—James R. Babb, Editor, *Gray's Sporting Journal*

Gray's Sporting Journal's Noble Birds and Wily Trout

Creating America's Hunting and Fishing Traditions

Will Ryan

Illustrations by Gordon Allen

LYONS PRESS
Guilford, Connecticut
An imprint of Globe Pequot Press

Lyons Press is an imprint of Globe Pequot Press.

All illustrations by Gordon Allen.

Portions of this book have previously appeared in a different form in *American Angler* and *Gray's Sporting Journal*.

Project editor: Staci Zacharski
Text design: Linda Loiewski
Layout: Melissa Evarts

Library of Congress Cataloging-in-Publication Data

Ryan, Will.
Gray's sporting journal's the great outdoors : the birth of America's hunting and fishing tradition / Will Ryan.
pages cm
ISBN 978-0-7627-8288-8 (hardback)
1. Hunting–History. 2. Fishing–History. I. Gray's sporting journal II. Title.
SK33.R93 2013
799.2–dc23
2013029124

Printed in the United States of America

10 9 8 7 6 5 4 3 2 1

Contents

Acknowledgments **viii**
Introduction **ix**

Part I—Expansion and Conservation: A Sporting Code, 1820–1895 **1**

CHAPTER 1
"Had Never Seen a Regular Angler"
Early Ideas of the Outdoors, 1810–1850 **3**

CHAPTER 2
"An Odd Mix of Slavery and Ecstasy"
The Joy of Sport, 1840–1865 **17**

CHAPTER 3
"For Body, Mind and Soul"
Everybody in the Pool, 1870–1890 **47**

CHAPTER 4
"Moved by Emotions which He but Half Comprehends"
The Meaning of Sport, 1880–1900 **66**

Part II—Sporting Traditions in American Life, 1880–1925 **99**

CHAPTER 5
"The Best of a Man's Life"
Big Game, 1885–1912 **103**

CHAPTER 6
"Deluding That Old Trout"
Fly Fishing for Trout, 1865–1912 **146**

CHAPTER 7
"What a Godsend This Sport of Hunting"
Upland Birds, 1887–1914 **188**

CHAPTER 8
"The Whisper of Wings"
Waterfowl, 1866–1923 **231**

CHAPTER 9
"Down I Went, Hat, Rod, and All . . ."
The Rise of the Black Bass, 1881–1925 **275**

CONCLUSION
"Great Sport" **305**

Bibliography **310**
Index **313**

Acknowledgments

The debts of any writer are great, and this book is no exception. A good number of folks have helped me out. A few deserve particular mention: Ron Barkyoumb, Don Bechaz, Pete Bellinger, Bob Charleston, Mark Craig, Ted Creighton, Lee Ellsworth, Frank Flack, Tom Fuller, Ken Leon, Kris Loftus, Pete Loftus, Gene Mancini, Greg McKinney, Ralph Ringer, Marcel Rocheleau, Mark Scott, Ralph Stuart, Norm Tatro, and Tony Zappia.

My friends in the outdoors press, especially Mike Toth at *Field & Stream* and Russ Lumpkin and Steve Walburn at Morris Communications, have been generous with their support and guidance.

My students and colleagues at Hampshire College have been a thirty-three-year source of new ideas, many of which are in this book. Nell Arnold, Aaron Berman, Ray Coppinger, Aracelis Girmay, Deb Gorlin, Lise Sanders, Ellie Siegel, Susan Tracy, and Stan Warner have all been nothing but a joy to work with and have taught me a great deal about writing, science, and American history.

Sarah Steadman has been both gracious and inventive in her archival assistance. Ida Hay, at the 5 College Book Depository, went out of her way to help me with research.

Jim Babb, my editor at *Gray's Sporting Journal*, and Bob Rakoff, my longtime co-teacher in the Hampshire College course "Writing About the Outdoors," deserve special mention for reading early versions of the manuscript and living to tell the tale. The manuscript only benefitted from the steady hand of Allen Jones, my editor at Globe Pequot Press.

Finally, thanks to Noreen and Brody for years of love.

Introduction

Just twenty-eight years old, Reverend William Henry Harrison Murray had recently gained the pulpit at Boston's prestigious Park Street Church. He was ambitious, but passionate as well, a sporting man by avocation, with a taste for horses and outdoor adventure. He and his wife, Isadora, had been traveling to the Adirondack Mountains for several years, staying in the Raquette Lake area, enjoying excursions with servants and guides, entertaining friends, even holding outdoor services.

Now he was back in Boston, and an acquaintance named Joseph Cook was standing in the reverend's office explaining that publishing a book with the prestigious company of Ticknor & Fields, which had offices right across Tremont Street from Murray's, could well make his reputation. Murray thought of some stories he'd begun at his previous church back in Connecticut. Written in the afterglow of his mountain trips, the tales celebrated the glory of the Adirondacks. He'd published some small installments the year before in the *Meriden Literary Recorder*. Why not try to do something more inspirational with this material?

He showed the writing to Mr. Fields, who thought the idea a fine one. On February 10, 1869, Murray signed his first book contract (with royalties of 10 cents per copy after the first thousand, 15 cents after the first five thousand).

Murray wrote furiously. His manuscript described the splendor of the Adirondacks; how to get there, manage a trip, hire a guide. What should a lady wear in the wilderness? Murray offered choices. Spectacular vistas and fish and game waited. Blackflies were largely a myth. The Adirondacks were good for the health, good for the soul. He did know how to work a congregation, after all.

Adventures in the Wilderness; or, Camp Life in the Adirondacks hit the stands on (or about) April Fools' Day 1869, and many probably thought the date appropriate. Murray's book promised adventures and, oh auntie, did he ever have them. A good example was the chapter titled "Jack Shooting on a Foggy Night," which told of Murray's night on a deer hunt. The traditional Adirondack hunting trip called for guides to paddle their sports in canoes with lights fixed to the bows. The glare of the "jack" blinded and paralyzed any deer they happened upon, at which point the happy sport shot his trophy.

Murray was all set for his big adventure, with one problem: He found the jack to be inferior. So, using an old fireman's hat as a base, he invented a jack he could strap to his head. Murray described the gizmo in lavish detail, apparently so that readers could hustle down to their basements and make their own.

As the hunt approached, Murray settled into the canoe and "touched a match to the wick." Perfect. And with that, Murray and his guide, Martin, shoved off into the Adirondack night. "Is this the same world of cities and cursing in which I lived a week ago?" Murray wondered. "Or have I been translated to some other and happier sphere?"

Before long they heard a *k-splash, k-splash* out in the fog. Murray cranked up his jack and "detected a bright, diamond-like spark. What was it? 'It may be the eye of a deer, and it may be only a drop of water, or a wet leaf.' But 'it looked gamy . . .'[and] Murray concluded to launch a bullet at it."

Blam! Murray sloshed ashore to "see what it was I had shot at. . . ." With jack blazing, he found the deer "dead as a tick!"

"He's a monster!" he called to Martin, out in the fog and paddling to shore. At that point the deer, only stunned, stood. Murray yelled out to Martin for advice.

"Get hold of his hind leg; I'll be with you in a minute," Martin hollered back. Murray "laid hold of his left hind leg, just above the fetlocks," and addressed the audience directly: "Reader, did you ever seize a pig by the hind leg? If so, multiply that pig by ten . . . lash a big lantern to your head; fancy yourself standing alone on a swampy marsh on a dark, foggy night, with a rifle in your left hand, and being twitched about among the bogs and in and out of muskrat-holes. . . ."

Then came the "heavy thud of the boat against the bank," and Murray spotted the "gaunt form" of Martin, "paddle in hand and hunting knife between his teeth, loping along toward [him]." Like a modern-day cornerback, Martin dove for the deer's legs—and missed but managed to grab the tail, and the deer, with Martin affixed, became "thoroughly roused." The bounding buck "straightened the poor fellow out like a lathe. . . . He averaged about one word to a jump. . . . The result of his efforts to express himself reached my ears very much in this shape: "Jump—*will*—you—be-e—*damned*—I've-e—GOT—you! I'll—hold-d—ON—till—your—ta-i-l—comes—off-f—*Jump-p-p*—be—D-D-DAMNED—I've—got—you-u-u."

The deer splashed into the water, where Martin gained the upper hand and, after considerably thrashing about, stumbled ashore, dragging the drowned buck behind him.

Before long the two men were back in the canoe paddling for camp. And members of the audience? They couldn't wait for an adventure of their own.

Three months after the book went on sale, readers invaded the Adirondacks like Confederate troops storming Little Round Top; afterwards they stumbled back down to civilization—scratched, bitten, and howling for the reverend's scalp. That summer proved unseasonably wet and cool, perfect for the blackflies Murray had deemed a myth. A number of tourists got lost within hours of stepping from the train. The idea of mountain vacations looked like it could use some tweaking.

"Murray's fools," as the tourists were called, drew scant sympathy from Adirondack purists, who mostly commented on how little time they needed to despoil an entire wilderness. The one point of consensus centered on the excoriation of Reverend Murray. The information on hotels, guides, and rates in the first part of the book had lent Murray's rambunctious stories the ring of truth. With little previous exposure to outdoor writers, the nineteenth-century public had no idea how to parse your basic hunting and fishing story. In other words, they actually believed him.

But the following summer, buffaloed or not, the visitors returned in greater force, and they grew in number each year afterward. One writer of the day estimated that some two to three thousand visited the Adirondacks that summer. In a 1969 essay, historian Warner Cadbury reports that the Raquette Lake House had one hundred guests in the summer of 1867, two hundred in 1868, and four hundred during the summer following publication of the book. The numbers had been increasing even before the book—a result of the expansion of the middle class that became a hallmark of the era. Murray did discover an audience, but that audience was waiting to be found. If Murray's book were a fisherman's cast, plenty of hungry trout waited in the pool.

Murray's book caught a tailwind from the emerging national sporting culture. Prior to the Civil War, America had been a country of island communities, as one historian has put it. Men hunted and fished for sport, certainly, but in smaller numbers and with little recognition. Now with the rise of media and consumerism, and improvements in transportation (particularly railroads), their activities—like so many other forms of leisure and recreation—began to take shapes recognizable across regions, even the country. The popularity of baseball in North and South encampments during the Civil War exemplified this trend. Increasing numbers of middle-class men spent their days in city offices and—surprise—suddenly found hunting and fishing appealing activities. Now if they could only figure out how to make fishing and hunting important, they could build regular outings into their increasingly circumscribed modern lives.

Murray's outdoors was dramatic, manly, heavenly—an enticing palliative to the suffocation of city living. And, he lived the dream. The reverend went hunting before services; he was a middle-class vacationer—and his readers signed on perhaps because they understood that he was one of them. Murray's book inspired sportsmen and writers throughout the nineteenth century in fact. None other than Wendell Phillips, the Boston abolitionist and reformer, wrote that Murray had "kindled a thousand campfires and taught a thousand pens how to write of nature."

Murray also prompted criticism from many who thought him nothing more than a huckster who had slipped out the side door of a Mark Twain novel. The resulting back and forth only kept the idea of a "great outdoors" in the public imagination and underscored the importance Americans had begun to attach to such adventure and stories. Murray and the writers who followed him, in effect, created and carried on a national discussion about the worth and meaning of outdoor activities. This discussion, buoyed by a rise in literacy and communication, continued through the late nineteenth and early twentieth centuries. By 1900 there were approximately 20,000 newspapers of one form or another published in the United States; the surge in print journalism was remarkable by any standard. The expectations for what the writing would deliver, moreover, increased through the period, as reflected in the saying of the time that "I only know what I read in the newspapers."

American sportsmen used the profusion of articles, stories, and books to figure out standardized methods and approaches for recreational hunting and fishing. The early anglers and hunters invested considerable energy in fine-tuning the evolving practices, worrying about whether they were effective, modern, and gentlemanly. The results were the origins of American sport hunting and fishing as we know them today.

This book returns to that body of writing, to listen to the stories in hopes of understanding what these men and women experienced, felt, and envisioned and, ultimately, what they created and revised as a result. In order to involve as many of their stories as possible, I've compressed the actual texts, summarizing and paraphrasing so that the individual tales might become a larger story that reflects the overall evolution of America's outdoor traditions from 1820 to 1920.

The story begins with the effort of nineteenth-century Americans to cast sport hunting and fishing as desirable and sustaining. If the point of the outdoor experience was to escape from society and all its rules and regulations, how could outdoor behavior be ordered so that it retained its joy, brought satisfaction and meaning, and increased the populations of fish and game that made outdoor recreation possible? If that sounds like a riddle, it was.

The story concludes with a closer look at five particular outdoor traditions: big game hunting (and a bit of fishing), bird hunting, fly fishing, waterfowling, and bass fishing. There are others of course, but these provoked the most printed "conversations" during this period and remain identifiable traditions to this day. How did participants conceive of their practices? How did they fashion and refashion them? What characteristics did they confer on the fish and wildlife they pursued? What did they make them into? Who did they become in return?

———————

A few notes about the approach. For references, I've forgone citations and listed the article, publication, and author in the text. In compressing stories, I've tried to remain faithful to the author's intent and style, though I've had to make some choices. At times I change tenses for easier reading. Where possible, I include the story's arc, as well as the various points it emphasizes. Space has ruled out a comprehensive consideration of the stories and writers, but I do hope the selection is representative of the foundation of sporting traditions in American life.

The joy of history involves how much of today's world we can see in the past. It's fun to say—look, they're just like us. But the worth of history is how it helps us rethink things we thought we knew. I hope reading this book gives you that opportunity; writing it surely has for me.

The hunters and anglers in our past are worth our time and attention, particularly if we peel back the veneer that glosses over them and try to understand them as they were, not how we'd like them to be. Sometimes what we learn about them is funny or sad, other times moving, other times less than noble. But always it is human, and more than anything else it's an homage to the power of sport—and how it provides such a meaningful, lasting place in peoples' lives. This first generation of American sports, if nothing else, left a better outdoor world than they found.

We tend to think of traditions as guideposts or practices to follow, but I would argue that they first have to be created, and that their creation involves far less inspiration and far more revision, particularly when the national culture changes the way America's did in the late nineteenth and early twentieth centuries. Writers not only "spoke" to one another in print but also sought affirmation from the larger society (and more than hunters and anglers concede). The writers in this book also needed massive contributions from those who went to the waters and woods and didn't do much reading, or were excluded from elite sporting practices. The resulting accommodations laid the foundation for the hunting and fishing we enjoy today.

In this respect, Murray's book left an early (but bold) brushstroke on the American outdoor canvas. He would be thrilled with the attention his book has received in the century and a half since its publication. He'd always sought to recast his own ambition in terms of what others desired.

The idea of a great outdoors begins, then, not in the streams and forests but in Boston offices like Murray's. Actually, it first takes shape in the imaginations of the young nation's city dwellers a full half century before the good reverend put pen to paper. It is to those beliefs and interests that we now turn.

Part I

Expansion and Conservation: A Sporting Code, 1820–1895

CHAPTER 1

"Had Never Seen a Regular Angler"

EARLY IDEAS OF THE OUTDOORS, 1810–1850

How many fishing trips over the centuries have started with a few guys sitting at a bar?

That's how one started anyway, in 1810 New York City, with its mud streets and rooting hogs, on a day when "spring began to melt into the verge of summer." The would-be anglers in the tavern had been reading Izaac Walton's *Compleat Angler*. Among them was a twenty-seven-year-old New Yorker named Washington Irving, who later described the scenario in *The Sketch Book of Geoffrey Crayon*, a collection that included such classic stories as "The Legend of Sleepy Hollow" and "Rip Van Winkle." Irving and his buddies had been "completely bitten with angling mania." Before long they grabbed their rods and dashed off for a stream near Peekskill, New York, "as stark mad as was ever Don Quixote from reading books of chivalry."

Regardless of century, every fishing party has a gear hound, and the one in Irving's group wore a "coat perplexed with half a hundred pockets," to say nothing of "leather gaiters, a basket slung on one side for fish . . . and a score of other inconveniences only found in the true angler's armory." He turned quite a few heads out in the country, where folks "had never seen a regular angler."

Like so many fishing trips, reality failed to match the imagination. The little mountain brook that pounded through the brush and boulders proved an "unfortunate place for the execution of those piscatorial tactics which had been invented along the velvet margins of quiet English rivulets." Irving hooked trees, bottom, himself—everything but a trout. Before long he settled in with Walton beneath a tree, the perfect vantage for watching his pals get skunked. A local urchin showed up with a cut stick and a "crooked pin for a hook, baited with a vile earthworm," and he absolutely slammed the brook trout.

Irving and his pals knew how to enjoy themselves, even if they didn't have the fish catching part down yet. They started with their repast, someone read Uncle Isaac's scene about the milkmaid, and Irving promptly lay back in the grass and, with "castles in a bright pile of clouds," fell asleep.

As would so many of our dearest outdoor writers over the next two centuries, Irving cast himself as more of a rube than he was. Throughout his youth he'd enjoyed hunting and fishing and had done so in the Adirondacks, no easy trip by wagon in the mud and ruts of early nineteenth-century roads. He often hunted and fished in the Catskills as well, though his facility with rod and reel remained unimpressive. Friend James Paulding called him "... the worst fisherman we ever saw." Always a city man, even when viewing the wilderness, Irving predicted the dual worlds of the nineteenth-century sportsman more than he realized.

He began to write about the story he found in his experience and, along with James Fenimore Cooper and a third, anonymous, author, left us some early impressions of hunting and fishing. Their stories point to the values, worries, and fascinations that framed the American sporting life in the decades to come.

"A Pure Serenity of Mind"
WASHINGTON IRVING

"The Angler," 1820

At the time, hunting and fishing in America received little literary attention, though as the gear hound's persona and the lunchtime rituals suggest, both activities had devotees. Irving and his friends began a publication, *Salmagundi*, and in it they observed, "The diversions of hunting, fishing, shooting, and horse-racing are enjoyed in perfection by the Americans: their forests, rivers, and lakes afford abundance of sport. . . ." (The English distinguished "hunting" from "shooting." The former involved actual pursuit of game big and small; the latter referred to wing-shooting). But like the English gamekeeper who had assisted in woodcock hunting for some forty years but had not seen anything worth reporting, Americans believed these "diversions" warranted little in the way of explicit commentary.

Only the unusual generated notice—such as when Irving and his party, canoeing in the wilds of northern New York on the Black River, happened upon a swimming doe. They shot at it, wounding it twice. They grabbed it by an ear and leg before dispatching it for good. For those of you scoring at home, that is a good deal of action from one deer. Appropriately, Irving provided observations—in a journal.

Sport hunting and fishing needed the city and its possibilities for communication. In the early nineteenth century, America remained overwhelmingly rural, with only ten cities of more than fifty thousand people. Most folks lived in one-room homes with dirt floors. Spittoons were modern conveniences. The available weaponry did not facilitate sport hunting. Among the upper classes in England, the late eighteenth century saw a rise in "shooting flying," as wing-shooting was called, but many Americans would have questioned its morality, and nearly all would have seen such an indulgence as a waste of money. People enjoyed times of relaxation and celebration but spent it in communal gatherings, not individual "diversions."

For the most part, agriculture enjoyed a respectability during the late eighteenth and early nineteenth centuries, and hunting seemed backwoods, uncivilized—"Kentuck," in the vernacular of the day. Going hunting said to the community that your farm was struggling and that you were trying to make ends meet. In *Hunting and the American Imagination*, Daniel Herman explains the state of hunting, as follows: "Thousands of Americans hunted, but not all aspired to be hunters. . . . Backwoods farmers of the colonial era regarded hunting not as a privilege but as a right; to be American was to take game without the hindrance of aristocratic game laws."

Irving and his urban friends thought differently about the outdoors. They saw the woods as romantic. In fact, even when on business in northern New York, Irving did his best to escape to the outdoors. According to one biographer, "On August 22nd [Irving's party] proceeded to Hoffman's township Lisbon, some distance toward Madrid [near the St. Lawrence River] where bonds and deeds were signed, to the weariness of Irving, who preferred the excellent fishing and shooting. . . . He wandered off into the forest, Rousseauesque in the silence of the wilderness; on one evening he fell asleep in a sawmill, and returned to find the whole party in search of him." You start to wonder about Irving and this sleeping outside thing.

Hunting and fishing memories probably sustained him when in England in 1820 and writing *The Sketch Book of Geoffrey Crayon*. The book appeared in serial installments, one of which included a story called "The Angler."

The story portrayed the best fisherman in a small English town—a man in the evening of his life, a former sailor, with many "ups and downs," including an unscrupulous partner in America and a leg that had been "carried away by a cannon ball at the battle of Camperdown." The man spent his days teaching angling to the next generation. He counted as a current disciple the son "and heir apparent of a fat old widow who kept the village inn." The angler was a graceful, human part of nature and, apparently, nobody's fool.

He enjoyed a modest but reputable station in life, "with clothes very much but very carefully patched, betokening poverty, honestly come by and decently maintained." Content and avuncular, he "took the world as it went."

His philosophy and chosen activity of angling appeared complementary. If anything, fishing allowed him a quiet heroism.

Entranced by Isaac Walton, by the beauty of angling in the garden of the old country, Irving guides the story with an easy hand—even in its concession to angling's deficiencies: "There is something in angling (if we could forget, which anglers are apt to do, the cruelties and tortures inflicted on worms and insects) that tends to produce a gentleness of spirit and a pure serenity of mind." The old man's time with nature left him a better person, made him "a universal favorite in the village . . . the oracle of the tap-room." His cottage rested "on the skirts of the village, on a green bank, a little back from the road, with a small garden in front, stocked with kitchen herbs, and adorned with a few flowers. "

The Angler had exchanged his outdoor skill for social currency. The town's gentlemen sports thought well of him, for he "had taught several of them the art of angling." He fished in spring and summer, teaching others as he did, and otherwise "employed himself at home, preparing his fishing tackle for the next campaign, or manufacturing rods, nets, and flies, for his patrons and pupils among the gentry." What was not to like about this life?

"This Wasteful and Unsportsmanlike Execution"
Leatherstocking/Natty Bumppo
JAMES FENIMORE COOPER

The Pioneers, 1823

When the next literary sensation, *The Pioneers*, went on sale in the city, the initial run of 3,500 copies sold out the first morning. The book's success confirmed the thirty-four-year-old Cooper's celebrity, and he went on to write a number of other popular frontier tales, most notably *The Last of the Mohicans*, and along with Irving became early America's leading man of letters. Both authors benefited from the beginnings of an urban culture, in evidence, for example, in New York City, which had tripled in size since the end of the American Revolution in 1783. Cooper's work presented yet another vision of outdoor sportsmen, this one largely critical.

The reading public met Nathaniel "Natty" Bumppo, or Leatherstocking as he was called in *The Pioneers*. Leatherstocking became an American archetype, probably based on Daniel Boone, as the matching phonetics and skill sets imply. A white man raised by the Indians and an expert woodsman, Leatherstocking has served as a model for weekend anglers and hunters for nearly two hundred years. These days he is most frequently referenced in humor, as in calling a friend a "regular Natty Bumppo" after he loses a nice bass at the canoe, although if it is your bass he hits with the net, say, it is acceptable to inject a favorite present participle between "regular" and "Natty."

At his first introduction, Leatherstocking offered a deep skepticism on the practice of sport hunting. The pivotal scene occurred one spring morning, when the town's inhabitants woke to find "the heavens . . . alive with the pigeons." They were so thick that "you may look an hour before you can find a hole, through which to get a peep at the sun." Before long the whole town had turned out, armed with everything "from the French ducking-gun, with its barrel of near six feet in length, to the common horseman's pistol." The townsfolk took up their positions and began blazing away, which was also when

Leatherstocking, "tall, gaunt . . . walking over the field, with his rifle hanging on his arm," made his appearance. The slaughter appalled him. His dogs picked up his disdain, "crouching under the legs of their master, as if they participated in his feelings at this wasteful and unsportsmanlike execution."

At the time, the term "pioneer," derived from French, meant "foot soldier." And Cooper described the scene as though it were a battle, with "reports of the fire-arms [that] became rapid, whole volleys rising from the plain. . . . Arrows, and missiles of every kind, were seen in the midst of the flocks." The slaughter unfolded "in such profusion as to cover the very ground with the fluttering victims."

With the sensibility of a gang of ten-year-old boys, a group of the townsfolk hit on a better idea: the local field piece. Several men hitched it to a horse and dragged it into the field. The growing crowd "filled the air with their cries of exultation and delight." They watched skyward, with one man "holding a coal of fire in a pair of tongs," and awaited a flock worthy of the firepower at hand.

"This comes of settling a country!" Leatherstocking spat.

In response to goading, Leatherstocking demonstrated his prowess, shooting a flying pigeon with this rifle. Then, he turned on his heels and headed back into the woods, explaining, "I'll go to the hut with my own game, for I wouldn't touch one of the harmless things that kiver the ground here, looking up with their eyes on me, as if they only wanted tongues to say their thoughts."

With all restraint having left the field, the citizen-soldiers fired the field piece into a swarming flock, to cheers from the onlookers.

"Victory !" shouted [one,] "victory! We have driven the enemy from the field."

Overall, though, the response was mixed. Judge Marmaduke, a local leader, said, "Like the Leather-stocking, I see nothing but eyes, in every direction, as the innocent sufferers turn their heads in terror, to examine my movements. Full one half of those that have fallen are yet alive; and I think it is time to end the sport, if sport it be." The sheriff disagreed. "It is princely sport!" he retorted. "There are some thousands of the bluecoated boys on the ground, so that every old woman in the village may have a pot-pie for the asking."

Marmaduke was the new urbanite, and in the future he would be the sport hunter. He realized the difference between morality and immorality, but often seemed swept up in the events. By contrast, Leatherstocking operated as the conscience of the story. He represented a clear upgrade on the frontiersman (or Kentuck), whom proper folks saw as those really wild men who may or may not cook their meat, depending on the kind of day they'd had. Leatherstocking hated civilization not for fear of becoming civilized himself but for what it had done to the wilderness. His self-restraint and harmonious relation with the natural world left him at odds with the larger market capitalism that was transforming the nation in the 1820s, 30s, and 40s.

Leatherstocking, in effect, responded to the new industrialism with his own version of Herman Melville's Wall Street secretary, Bartleby the Scrivener, and his famous if maddeningly polite, "I prefer not to." Both characters were "outsiders," unlike Irving's angler, who lived in the village. The difference may suggest more early tolerance for fishing, perhaps because of its longer history (in both the colonies and in England) and its gentility.

The national period of the 1820s was not only a time of new industrial horizons but also one of sentimentalism, with the American Revolution fading from memory to history, with Thomas Jefferson and John Adams dying not only on the same day but on the fiftieth anniversary of the signing of the Declaration of Independence, bringing poignancy to the sense of an era passing. Leatherstocking was a man of seventy (though his literary life, like Cooper's, was only beginning.), and Irving's angler also approached his three score and ten. The young men on the rise, who were hunting and fishing in the meadows and rivers near the Northeast's cities, could not have seen themselves in these characters. If anything, they saw restraint when they looked to their elders.

Youth and rising urban culture in fact signaled a recklessness. *The Pioneers* featured Billy Kirby, the local young hotshot who "was loading, and without even looking into the air," and being pelted with dropping pigeons. "What's that, old Leather-stocking!" he cried, "grumbling at the loss of a few pigeons! If you had to sow your wheat twice, and three times, as I have done, you wouldn't be so massyfully feeling'd to'ards the divils.—Hurrah, boys! scatter the feathers. This is better than shootings at a turkey's head and neck, old fellow."

The "sportsmen" simply lost control of themselves. Their problem became *the* problem of the late nineteenth century: How to restrain yourself, if the joy of the sporting life is to free yourself. As Leatherstocking tried to explain, the answer lies not in how but in why you draw your aim—which likewise anticipated the basic tenet of conservationists fifty years later.

Leatherstocking, by contrast, *reflected* during the hunt. He was a thinker, a philosopher, arguably the first environmentalist; he knew that progress, by definition, has both victor and vanquished. The spirituality of his sentiment anticipated the way upper middle-class sportsmen saw the wilderness by century's end. Even more, perhaps, Leatherstocking carried himself in a way that appealed to sportsmen young and old. He was understated, crusty, unerring—the ultimate radical individualist, whose response to civilization's chest beating was to hit his mark with his rifle, casually reload, and melt into the woods. Leatherstocking, in fact, did all the things that the modern sportsman imagined himself doing on Saturday morning, once he had the yard raked and his wife said he could go hunting.

"Deep, Dark and Full of Alligators"
AN ANONYMOUS NARRATOR

"Ibis Shooting in Louisiana," *Harpers Weekly*, 1853

The literary references to hunting and fishing suggest, if nothing else, that new ideas about the outdoors had begun to materialize, at least among the growing urban middle class. Paintings and prints portrayed a more benevolent landscape. With publication of *The Birds of America* as a series during the 1830s, the work of John James Audubon prompted many to reconsider the wilderness. Audubon was a scientist and artist, and he enjoyed hunting. He was not a sport hunter in the modern sense of the word, but his efforts (and promotion of his art) emphasized the beauty of the American wilderness.

David "Davy" Crockett, a contemporary of Audubon's (they were born a year apart), probably played an even greater role in piquing the public's interest in the outdoor life. Any number of Americans had risen on their rural prowess, but Crockett was the first to realize its appeal to city folks when marketed as an authentic alternative to urbane pretensions. He served in Congress and published *A Narrative of the Life of David Crockett*—all to whispers that he might some day be a candidate for president..

Unlike American politicians who have used their "humble origins" as a ruse to cover up inordinate wealth, Crockett, in fact, had risen from poverty and hardship through his own efforts. A talented, insane hunter, Crockett "took over Washington, so we hear'd tell," as Fess Parker crooned more than a century after his death. He eventually lost his seat due to opposition to Jackson's Indian Removal Act, which he correctly thought was unfair to Indians and beneficial to the rich. He tried and failed at business, in large part because he was always off hunting, and that pushed his second marriage (his first wife died) to the brink of dissolution.

Funny and entertaining, Crockett was hard wired to hunt, and, born in a different century, he'd probably have his own television show—devoted to the outdoors. Historian William Davis includes a telling little Crockett anecdote in *Three for the Alamo*. Crockett had left for Texas and the Alamo, and as he rode through frontier towns with a little band of men, he would stop and, already a national hero, be honored at dinners and whatnot. That's what the good citizens of Little Rock, Arkansas, were thinking; they probably didn't get a lot of famous visitors, let alone Colonel Crockett.

But they couldn't find him. A delegation of townsfolk basically looked everywhere. They knew he was in town because he'd already seen about a room at the Charles Jeffries' City Hotel. Finally they found him, out behind the hotel—dressing a deer he'd shot earlier in the day. A two-hundred-yard shot, he was quick to claim—and made sure everyone knew.

When not on hunting trips, politicking in cities, or riding to his destiny, Crockett did his best to also appear a gentleman (It was *David*, not Davy.) with mixed results—understandable given that in his speeches, almanacs, and books he touted himself as "half man, half alligator." He toured northeastern cities, where interest in sport hunting and fishing was greatest, drew big crowds that loved the idea of a "King of the Wild Frontier" who could tame the wilderness—a considerable shift from Leatherstocking, who wanted to keep it as it was. That idea fit more with the legend of Daniel Boone; Crockett's seemed more a part of the conquering intentions that drove Jacksonian America. By the century's end these twin ideas of an acquisitive spirit and sensitivity to nature had been forged into a foundational plank in our sporting tradition.

Crockett's death at the Alamo on March 6, 1836, added to his legend. He left his audiences wanting more tall tales about the wilderness and battles with the critters that lived there. *Harpers Weekly* certainly obliged in an 1853 piece titled "Ibis Shooting in Louisiana."

The author (who chose anonymity) claimed to be a sportsman, even though he was ibis shooting "not so much for sport, however, as that I wished to obtain some specimens [particularly the scarlet ibis] for mounting." At least he wasn't going to "et 'em", which right off set him apart from the Kentuck crowd.

Off he headed in a small skiff—your basic three-hour tour in the foreboding New World wilderness of a Louisiana bayou, the sort of place Crockett had made a career of taming. After floating some five miles, he "succeeded in bagging both the great wood ibis and the white species [and] a fine white-headed eagle (*Falco leucocephalus*), which came soaring over my boat." But the scarlet ibis eluded him—until midday, when he reached a spot where the bayou widened and was "deep, dark and full of alligators." He spotted a small flock of the scarlet ibis on a sand bar, and sculled to within range and let them have it with both barrels. The smoke lifted. Ibis down.

He hopped out of the skiff to collect his prize. As he turned to head back, he saw his rookie error: In his enthusiasm he'd failed to ground the boat. It had drifted off, and now he was on an island, surrounded by a swampy mote. He didn't know how to swim. Even if he could, alligators waited. No one knew his whereabouts.

He survived for a couple of days on ibis; then, when one of the alligators got too close, he shot it—and chowed down on some alligator tartare (which probably explains the anonymity). Between the sunburn, mosquitoes, and odor from the alligator carcass, the island began to feel as though it could use another room.

Then, inspiration. He'd nudged the carcass off the island with his gun, and . . . it floated. What "of its intestines—what if I inflated them? Yes, yes! Buoys and bladders, floats and life-preservers!"

He killed and eviscerated another alligator, extracted the intestines and inflated them with a bone from the picked-over ibis and outfitted himself with "life preservers." He waited till the hot hour of the day, when the gators took their siesta, and paddled around the bend to get his boat and before long was "sculling with eager strokes down the smooth waters of the bayou."

The story not only managed to reference America's past but also synthesized Crockett and Audubon in a contemporary approach. Early writers such as William Bartram, who traveled the South at the end of the previous century, had some florid bouts with gators, ". . . with open jaws, and belching water and smoke that fell on me like rain in a hurricane." But the anonymous narrator boldly followed Audubon's naturalist path into the wilderness, noting, "The simple habitants of the village I had left knew me not . . . [they] fancied me a strange individual; one who made lonely excursions and brought home bunches of weeds, with birds, insects and reptiles." His whole point of hunting was to gather a specimen for taxidermy.

If the purpose borrowed from Audubon, the story ended up pure Crockett. In the seventeen years since Crockett's death, his legend had continued to grow, with the heroic frontiersman shinnying up trees a hundred feet tall; aiming at a rock with his rifle to split the ball in two and thereby kill a bear and moose with a single shot (according to Constance Rourke's version of the myth in *American Humor*; the Disney storybook illustrates the twofer as a bear and a panther); starting fires by rubbing his knuckles together; and strolling around with a piece of sunrise in his pocket. In fact, if Crockett were marooned on a Louisiana bayou, the idea of inflating alligator intestines would hardly even qualify as a tall tale, seeing as how he was half alligator to start with.

For an urbanizing society interested in what happens when modern sensibilities encounter human-less nature—an idea more famously explored in *Moby Dick* (1851) and *Walden* (1854)—the Jurassic enemy provided a perfect edginess to the naturalist's terrain. The anonymous narrator lacked the self-irony (and the vision) of Melville and Thoreau, seeming instead a bit old-fashioned, rendered with a certain aristocratic innocence. In fairness, Ibis Man had little time for literary contemplation. He mostly scurried about trying to survive, befitting a wilderness sojourn in which you are up to your waist in alligators.

CHAPTER 2

"An Odd Mix of Slavery and Ecstasy"

THE JOY OF SPORT, 1840–1865

The third week of November 1864 brought a flurry of news regarding the destiny of the republic: Abraham Lincoln reelected president; General William Tecumseh Sherman and his army, sixty thousand strong, marching on Savannah. The Civil War ground on, approaching the end of its fourth year.

Wilkes' Spirit of the Times, a national weekly published in New York City, devoted its November 19 issue to those developments and included reports and other articles on various topics, among them a story on duck hunting by a New York City merchant and ship captain named T. Robinson Warren. As his article indicated, a sporting duck hunt had a particular and identifiable narrative—even at this early date.

In its twenty-fifth year of publication, *Wilkes' Spirit of the Times* enjoyed a circulation of approximately twenty thousand readers. (The publication had begun as *Porter's Spirit of the Times* but existed under a number of banners, going through owners like Lincoln went through generals.) Most readers were wealthy upper-class sports. When Warren described the hunt's preparation, he appears to do so in anticipation that his readers imagined organizing sporting ventures at their houses.

"Last week, having a little spare time on our hands, we resolved to go down to Barnegat Bay and have a shot at the ducks," Warren began. He informed the family of his plans, which induced some responses that appear familiar even today. For example, "our better half" imagined "a week's rollicking, unbecoming a pater-familias." The children, by contrast, were thrilled. They knew the drill. They all began to "quack" and "honk" and raced to dig out his boots and gear. And with that, Warren set out "by rail and stage to Tom's River, where, having had a capital feed," and crossing the bay to Bill Chadwick's house, he found a "goodlie company of gunners assembled."

Warren and his companion ducked into a "little low bar-room" that "looked cosily familiar to us." He recognized the various hunters, libations appeared, and pre-hunt chatter ensued. In time they turned in and "had hardly, as we thought, got to sleep, when . . . a rough shake of the shoulder" woke them for breakfast. Sunrise found the hunters "comfortably sitting in our blind, with our guns at halfcock, waiting for a flock of ducks." From then on, the undertaking turned rough and manly and filled with the echoes of the sea—perfect tonic for a harried nineteenth-century financier.

Warren's article gives us an interesting picture of how the sporting community saw itself in the midst of the crisis of the union. If the idea of "spare time on our hands" feels a bit cavalier, it is important to note that men of Warren's standing typically hired a substitute to serve in the military, often one of the poor Irish immigrants. Warren's life existed above the affairs of state, which permitted plenty of time for hunting and fishing. As his story detailed, Warren had considerable success in Barnegat Bay with numerous black ducks, canvasbacks, redheads, and broadbills—without a mention of the war. Outdoor recreation, which draped itself in patriotism by the time of World War I, began well outside the realm of politics and nationalism during the Civil War.

In the mid-nineteenth century, if the sporting life said anything at all, it spoke to a man's character. This definition reflected the important early influence of British sensibilities. Upper-class Americans (such as Warren) living in the Northeast and Southern planters, in particular, saw themselves as more English than American. They read the dashing tales of Sir Walter Scott. The British attitudes, the ways things were done, the social interactions— all held a regal appeal. In England one's social class was a given and worn proudly. Upper-class Americans, or those who wanted to be, did their best to adopt the old country's sensibilities as certification of their breeding and character. Establishing one's individualism, through the voluntary submission to hardship, was step one in becoming a member of the pan-Atlantic club of gentlemen sports.

"Gave Them Such a Broadside"
COLONEL PETER HAWKER

The Shooting Diary of Colonel Peter Hawker, 1893

Peter Hawker was one of the most influential nineteenth-century British sports. Shot through the thigh while serving under Wellington in the Peninsular War, he survived to marry twice, father four children, compose music, command militias, write books, and (especially) pursue waterfowl. He organized his rural English community into a disciplined company of waterfowling soldiers, ready to chop through ice, slop through mud, and sail through storms—all so that the hunt might go on. Hawker owned an arsenal, from his nineteen-pound "shoulder" gun to punts, including his favorite, a two-hundred-pound, eight-foot double punt gun capable of throwing a pound of shot from each barrel. He was the world's first famous duck hunter.

Hawker owed his literary legacy to *Instructions to Young Sportsmen* (first published in 1814, with ten editions through 1854), the most influential hunting book of its day. Hawker also kept a shooting diary (which was originally published in 1893 as *The Shooting Diary of Colonel Peter Hawker*), and that writing reveals a more candid angle on his sport—the sort of conversation engaged in once the children put the candle out and went to sleep. Hawker had a voice that has echoed in duck blinds across the years: Hunt constantly, regardless of conditions or numbers of ducks; complain about sickness and the work that has piled up around the home; develop a colorful string of invectives to characterize the competition, then hire the best of them (James Reade) for your guide. The entries spanned a half-century, beginning with comments on a snipe hunt in September 1802 and ending in mid-July 1853, just three weeks before his death. Noted English waterfowler Sir Ralph Payne-Gallwey edited this particular edition of the diary. Payne-Gallwey thought Hawker a bit egotistical, though I find him more forthright than anything.

The events of the following passages took place in Keyhaven, located just southwest of Lymington in southern Hampshire, across from the Isle of Wight on the western coast.

Getting home from duck hunting in mid-nineteenth-century England was no gimme, even for war-hero aristocrats. As Hawker wrote, "I had afterwards to ride from Warren Farm to Keyhaven, about 14 miles, and among unfrequented marshes and bogs, where I had never been before, in the most miserable night I ever weathered; it was so dark, I literally could not see my hand before me." Wind and hail made matters worse.

Hawker had his "19-lb. gun and an immense quantity of ammunition to carry," and his "old blind mare" was not exactly a Budweiser Clydesdale. Hawker secured his gear to her saddle and sloshed with her through the bogs. At one point he had to "anchor her with the shot belt" so that he could wade back in the water and search for his gun, which he finally found and fished out.

A couple of weeks later he had the same problem "and fell about a dozen times from the tops of the banks down into broad ditches full of water." Again the gun and ammo were the villains. He "wandered all over the enclosures for several miles, and once lay down where some sheep had been penned, to pass the night." When the rain let up, he stumbled through a field, found a road, then a farmer, who blessed him with a couple of pints and pointed him in the general direction of home. For all his faux whining, Warren misses no detail. It is as though he somehow enjoyed being so annoyed. Perhaps he thought the hard work was part of the equation. Duck hunters have always seen unearned suffering as at least vaguely redemptive or, in what modern psychologists would call magical thinking, at least more likely to bring them waterfowl in days to come.

So it was that April 17 at Keyhaven brought "magnificent weather" with "fowl pouring in by thousands." But luck eluded him again. This time he "flashed in the pan at about 1,000 widgeon; again at as many geese; and, after drawing and squibbing, flashed again at a splendid hooper close to me." Like any waterfowling day breaking bad, this one only got worse: "To complete my sorrows I found my lock broken, and had to leave all my sport and go off with my gun to Lymington."

His guide/assistant/buddy James Reade, who, in a busman's holiday, went out by himself while Hawker went to Lymington, didn't fare much better, in spite of "wallowing about in his mud sledge from the break of the Sabbath till daylight." Reade fired the punt three times and "came in with 17 widgeon, and . . . 5 more dead [found] after breakfast."

Back from Lymington, Hawker realized that the birds had arrived with the cold weather. After hunting all day, he snatched a quick break "to refresh myself and wipe the gun" but then "Off again at ten, out all night. . . . My cap froze on my head, and it blew a gale of wind; but I had so much to do that I perspired the whole time, except at intervals when my hands were so frost-bitten that it was with the utmost difficulty I could grope out of the traps to load, and particularly to prime the gun."

Hawker's help didn't fare any better, as "the man who followed me to retrieve my dead birds fell overboard, and was obliged to go home in order to avoid being frozen to death." As a result his ducks "fell into hands of the lee-ward shore hunters, who lurk about after gunners as vultures follow an army." The commoners were the bane of Hawker's existence, and he blamed his bad luck on them whenever possible. This entry is typical: "Out from nine at night till one; had a glorious chance spoiled by a wretched tailor of a fellow spitting off his popgun, but, the tide being slack, I had no other chance for a shot."

But on this particular night that didn't matter. The weather had brought the birds. Hawker approached the waterfowler's delirium: "The labour of working for the fowl was an odd mixture of ecstasy and slavery. I brought home, shot on the spot and caught on the ice at daybreak by self and helpers, 69 widgeon and 1 duck, making in all 101 widgeon and 4 ducks and mallards, besides the 6 plover and the old coot, in eighteen hours, as I was out from past twelve in the day till six the next morning."

Three hours of shut-eye, and the colonel was "off again." This time the wind "froze the oars as we rowed." The prize awaited: "Saw seven splendid hoopers!" With shallow water beneath the boat, "Reade had to steal overboard and shove the punt with his chest while I crept 'abaft' to give her life forward." They got to within 130 yards of the swans; and, "having shifted my common shot to some glorious pills for them, I tried my luck." His first "barrel missed fire by the lock cover catching the cock," but his second didn't, and "these huge monsters began to flap and sprawl. But I gave them such a broadside as they little expected." Hawker recorded that "I never made so splendid a shot in my life." Reade performed expertly after climbing back in the boat, "'shipping sail' and 'cutting off' one of my birds that was only winged from going seawards . . . one of the most finished maneuvers I ever saw." They reached the swan just "in time to blow out his brains with the cripple stopper before he reached some breakers that would have swallowed us." Hawker ended up with three swans.

Nine years later they were still at it: "Lovely weather. Pumps and water jugs frozen, and a furious easterly gale." Perfect.

Hawker did not give his whereabouts, but Reade "was out yesterday, his gun missed fire three times; and once he was so eager to pull off his worsted glove to shoot, that he seized it with his mouth, and literally pulled out one of his teeth, which fell into the punt." At least he didn't drop it overboard. That could have spelled trouble.

"Angle a Little in Their Peculiar Manner"
GEORGE TATTERSALL

The Sporting Review, 1839

English travelers to America found themselves stunned at the bounty of the land. Their general opinion of Americans tended to be favorable, though some couldn't get past the coarseness of the colonists. The novelist Frances Trollope probably spoke for a number of visitors when, after traveling aboard a steamship during the 1830s, she famously proclaimed, "For myself, it is with all sincerity I declare, that I would infinitely prefer sharing the apartment of a party of well-conditioned pigs."

One of the earliest English travelers who wrote of the outdoors, and who shared Mrs. Trollope's acerbic tone, was a sport and writer named George Tattersall. He fished throughout the South and then back north to the shores of the Great Lakes. Tattersall wrote a series of articles titled "Fishing in the North American Lakes and Rivers" that appeared in the October 1839 issue of *The Sporting Review*, a British publication (and subsequently appeared in the Spring 2003 issue of *The American Fly Fisher*, with an introduction by fly-fishing historian David Ledlie), and in general left impressed with neither American anglers nor their fish, much preferring the streams of Britain, where the open, uniform flows favored fly fishing.

Tattersall conceded that a few "do angle a little in their peculiar manner," that is, by cutting "fishing poles" from "their adjoining woods." They used twine for line and for bait, most any small creature at hand. The farmers on Lake Ontario speared fish in the bays in the spring, though they seemed to prefer netting, given its efficiency. But it was not clear that they much enjoyed "this species of night fishing . . . while the water is still so very cold . . . and did so not for entertainment but for gain."

Tattersall described the fish available, citing the basses and the whitefish as the greatest delicacies (over perch and walleyes, interestingly enough, neither of which he mentioned). He described at some length ice fishing for pickerel, detailing how the natives made a version of a tip-up. After cutting through the ice, the inhabitants placed a piece of board or shingle over the hole, with a long stick inserted in one end (that was lying on the ice), and the line attached to the other end (positioned over the hole) and a hook baited with a minnow or piece of pork. "When the bait is but slightly molested" the shingle "is seen to shake." If the pickerel grabs it, then the stick flies straight up (Flag!) and may even keep "bobbing up and down in a very interesting manner."

Tattersall's assessment of ice fishing fit with Hawker's idea of sport being a mix of hardship and excitement: "After the disagreeable operation of cutting holes though the ice, when it is probably a foot thick, and baiting all the hooks with the thermometer at zero—when the angler has got thirty or forty lines prepared in this manner, and the pickerel are in the right humour—there is no lack of either sport or exercise in running from line to line, as you witness the various sticks put in motion by the biting of the fish."

Brook trout fishing, by contrast, was too easy, particularly in areas newly settled. In those places, "the trout, with which nearly all streams are abundantly supplied, are literally so tame that neither science nor cunning is requisite to take them in any quantity." Tattersall caught thirty score in a day. He and his assistant could barely dress them all, and the trout took any fly he cast. They were too tame for good sport, and "where no skill or science is necessary to ensure success, angling, like any other diversion where the feelings are interested and excited, loses its chief, its most delightful charm." Fly fishing for trout was the equivalent of "pearls before swine," a phrase he in fact used.

"A Britisher with a Bird Gun"

PARKER GILLMORE (UBIQUE)

Gun, Rod and Saddle, 1869

Like Tattersall, visiting Englishman Parker Gillmore found bounty and ignorance in North America. But he told a different story in "A Big Buck," a chapter
in his book *Gun, Rod and Saddle*. Turned out a snowstorm stranded Gillmore
in, of all places, the land of Lincoln. The scuttle in the local tavern revolved
around a certain big buck that had eluded all the local hunters. Gillmore was
unimpressed, even when "one regular old leather-stocking, whose opinion was
always listened to with the reverence due to an authority" crowed that "the bullet would never be moulded that would tumble him (the buck) in his tracks."

The next morning, Gillmore was enjoying a pipe and figuring out how
to get on with his travels "for there was absolutely nothing to do but eat and
sleep, unless the prices of pork, corn, or wheat had possessed an interest."
A teamster entered the tavern, asking to borrow a rifle because a "big buck
had crossed the road about a mile off, and gone into the Squire's corn. (Every
person in Western America is either Squire or Colonel.)" And with that Gillmore tamped out his pipe, slipped off to his room, and collected his 10 bore.
He sneaked out to the road—and sure enough struck the tracks of a big buck.

Gillmore's inside joke with his audience is that he knows more than the
colonists but condescends to them so they don't realize it. He vowed "to show
the neighbours that a Britisher was good for some purposes." He followed the
track with confidence and made it partway across the field before hearing a
commotion and the voices of some locals who, as far as he could tell, were
"encouraging a dog to hold a pig."

Gillmore hurried into a thicket and took a stand, one barrel loaded with
buckshot, the other with a slug. He knew "The noise of the men, dog, and
porker" would send any deer running, let along an "old stager" like this one.

Sure enough, along came the buck. Gillmore steadied himself, and when
an eighty-yard crossing shot presented itself, he squeezed the trigger and hit his

target. He smoked a pipe, followed the tracks a short distance, and found the buck dead.

Later that day, and "in the most ostentatious manner" in front of the full bar (presumably around happy hour), he "ordered a team to be got ready in the morning to bring in the big buck." As for the Americans? They were stunned, and "old leather-stocking, *sotto voce*, remarked that I had not been reared on the right soil to be able to come that game." The next day Gillmore returned to a cheering tavern with the buck. "I don't know what the world was coming to, by G-d," allowed old leather-stocking, "when a Britisher with a bird gun could kill the biggest buck in Illinois."

Like Tattersall, Gillmore was trapped less in a natural wilderness than a cultural one. Unlike Tattersall, however, Gillmore was able to identify that a sporting subculture was in place, however naïve and braying that community might be, and join it, which suggests how much the American sporting life had developed in the quarter century between Tattersall's visit and Gillmore's book (and Warren's article, for that matter). Not that Gillmore didn't enjoy the extra opportunity his success presented—namely, turning the tables on that tavern full of loudmouthed colonists. Finally.

"Sportsmen of a True New England Stamp"
SIR CHARLES LYELL

A Second Visit to the United States (vol. 1), 1849

You wonder what sort of impact tales like Hawker's, Tattersall's, and Gillmore's had on hunting and fishing in America. The stories probably did give wealthy American sports a path forward, one that distinguished them from those they saw as the rabble on the sidelines. These examples offered wealthy sports a way of explaining why sport mattered. (The English upper classes fished and hunted, so such activity must be important.) Beyond that, the answers seem murkier. Could such early sport be said to make men manly? Or did it simply confirm the manliness that a man already possessed? The former would be taken up in the years at the end of the century, but for now the latter seemed more on people's minds.

In the early and rapidly evolving definition of sport, the one certainty seemed to be that the main purpose could not be for the procurement of food (even though the reputations of our most esteemed game animals today are almost always traceable to how good they are to eat). Hunting (or fishing) for food signaled a lower social class, which kept practitioners with such designs out of the gentlemanly aspiration track, and therefore the early sporting crowd as well.

These matters appear clearer in retrospect. At the time, the definition of sportsman tended to blur around the edges. Moreover, while attributing a single motivation to any behavior can be historically reassuring, reality was probably a good deal more complex and dynamic. Even today, most of us go hunting or fishing for two or three or even more reasons—that we know of. Consider when you've arrived late from hunting or fishing and face the inevitable, "What on earth possessed you to stay out fishing until now?" The standard reply—"I don't know"—is sometimes actually the truth.

What about back in the day? A good example comes from the description in the journal of touring Englishman Sir Charles Lyell, who in October 1845 stopped at a "decoy pond" in East Weymouth, Massachusetts, where hunters had killed a total of eight geese. "Swimming in the middle of a sheet of water was a tame goose, having one leg tied by a string to a small leaden weight." Near it was "a row of wooden imitations of geese." Between the honking and decoys, migrating geese couldn't stay away. When they landed "they [were] shot by sportsmen of a true New England stamp, not like the Indian hunters, impatient of a sedentary life or steady labour, but industrious cobblers, each sitting all day at his own door, with his loaded gun lying by his side, his hands occupied in stitching russet brogans or boots for the southern negroes." The goose, it turned out, "may fetch in the Boston market, in full season, two and a half dollars—the value of a dozen pair of brogans."

In other words, as Lyell emphasized, these hunters were shooting the geese for business, and should not be castigated for their idleness. They were not ne'er-do-wells, not backwoodsmen nor Indians, not Southern slaves hunting for their table, but industrious townspeople in obvious possession of middle-class virtue. And, I suspect, they found themselves quite aroused by a descending flock of Canada geese.

But was it sport? And were they sportsmen? Probably not in the Hawker, Tattersall, Gillmore, English gentleman sense of the term. Such stand hunting retained a communal feel, harkening to the pre-industrial pace of life. The depiction also reflects the sectional differences that existed in the antebellum years in America, not simply in politics or ideology but also in attitudes about the idea of leisure time—a new concept that was worming its way into daily life. A Southern planter could flaunt his leisure as a sign of his aristocracy, while a Northern middle-class artisan might have had to be more circumspect about how he spent his days out of the shop. The national culture in the years following the Civil War homogenized these differences—to an extent.

"Manly and Exciting"
ELISHA LEWIS

The American Sportsman, 1857

Sir Charles Lyell operated as an anthropologist, and his journal entries ended up revealing the difference that existed between hunting and fishing in print and in practice. He was literally describing the way people not of his class hunted. The hunting at the decoy pond in East Weymouth—as Lyell emphasized—hardly represented the range of harvest methods employed at the time. Some men pursued game for sport, shooting ducks on the wing; others pursued game to eat it, and they snared and netted their quarry. A good example of the range in fishing appears in George Tattersall's report, with farmers who speared and netted their fish and anglers who fly cast for them, perhaps in the same bay

American writers naturally took less of an anthropological view, and told stories of their own adventures. In the 1850s most of these printed articles and stories, of course, focused on sporting methods. Their readers were from the upper and upper-middle classes, individuals who actually had the time on their hands to make hunting and fishing into a problem to be solved, or a challenge to be met.

With their English role models in mind, wealthy Americans had begun reframing their activities (in print anyway) in the 1830s in *The American Turf Register,* a periodical largely devoted to horseracing. Each issue contained a brief article or two describing a hunting or fishing trip—prairie chicken hunting in Illinois, for example, or trout fishing, often in Cumberland County Pennsylvania. These observations often appeared next to articles on badger hunting or some other equally unseemly "diversion."

The general public continued to see sport hunting and fishing as frivolous at best, and the number of men actually engaging in these activities was small. Far greater quantities of fish and game were netted, snared, speared, sacked, clubbed, and ground swatted than were shot over pointing dogs or hooked on flies. At the same time, however, those writing about hunting and fishing treated their topics as if the methods were rendered from years of experimentation, with approaches that had been in practice for a time; an *American Turf Register* article on using a dog to toll canvasbacks and redheads is a good example. The writer noted that a dog with a reddish body and bushy tale (perhaps because it looked like a fox) was typically preferred. The tradition was already in place, in other words, and the new members of the club were basically signing on to it.

The internal enthusiasm and external skepticism may have given the early sporting culture a certain definition, developing as it did during a time in history when Americans began organizing themselves, be they philosophical groups such as the Transcendentalists, utopian societies such as John Humphrey Noyes's Oneida Society, or even larger groups such as the Masons. *Porter's Spirit of the Times* (the forerunner of *Wilke's Spirit of the Times*) joined the *American Turf Register* in becoming available to enthusiasts in 1839, and together these two papers created a source of identity for American sportsmen.

These men, as with T. Robinson Warren, lived in New York, Philadelphia, Baltimore, and in the South, where the plantation system provided slaves to help with the hunting and fishing excursions and where planters did whatever they could to be seen as gentlemen. They hunted deer, driven by hounds, and fished for bass. One particular Southerner, a Carolina planter named William Elliot, published an 1846 book titled *Carolina Sports by Land and Water; including Incidents of Devil-Fishing, Wild-Cat, Deer and Bear Hunting, etc.* A Harvard-educated congressman from South Carolina, Elliot told of rip-roaring adventures with his dogs, horses, and slaves. He hunted wildcats and speared devil rays, but deer were his favorite quarry.

In the North—New England, Pennsylvania, and southern New York, Long Island in particular—anglers fished for trout, and their efforts revealed the earliest organization, with rod makers, clubs, and recognized experts.

Northern sports also trained bird dogs and hunted woodcock and grouse and bobwhite quail. ("Partridge," as quail were called in the South, were favorite quarry of planters like Elliot). Duck hunters not only kept their communal stands, but those with money began to travel. Early waterfowl hunting's destination was Chesapeake Bay, where canvasbacks, redheads, and black heads (scaup) blanketed the bays each autumn.

With communication and transportation—the wellspring of a sporting community—in their earliest forms, it wasn't like the boys were lining up to head for Chesapeake Bay. And, perhaps as a result, some writers began to wonder exactly what kind of men these American hunters were. Elisha Lewis, writing about duck hunting in *The American Sportsman*, emphasized its "merits as a manly and exciting sport." Lewis hoped that with the "opening of new steamboat and railroad routes, our pleasure-loving and novelty-seeking people will flock to the secluded haunts of the wild fowl much more generally than they do at present." Lewis worried that "this sport, at present, is almost entirely confined to the hands of those who follow the occupation of killing wild fowl not from motives of pleasure or healthful recreation, but as a means of subsistence for themselves and families." Lewis avoids trashing market hunters, but he does take pains to distinguish a sportsman from those who needed the meat for food or money.

For gentlemen interested in securing and retaining a certain class standing, the last thing they needed was to be seen as hunting because they had to. And even at this early stage, gentlemen hunters (in print) avoided rabbit hunting. To call a man a "rabbit hunter" was similar to calling someone today a "couch potato" or a "real slug." Most proper folks still suspected that hunting and fishing amounted to cover stories for drinking and gambling. Character mattered.

If hunting and fishing were to gain participants, they had to *build* character, not sap it. As if to emphasize the manliness of sporting pursuits, Lewis advised the sportsman to keep "the elements at defiance, and resort to every expedient to keep his powder dry, his gun from rust, and his own person from the effects of the cold and rain to which he will often be exposed during these excursions." In addition to layers of clothes, the sportsman needed "a flask of good spirits," which "should be resorted to as seldom as possible; for the use of liquor during active exercise often creates an unnatural thirst, which, if indulged in to an extent sufficient to produce a flush on the cheek or a glow on the body, will most assuredly make the eye uncertain or the hand unsteady."

"Heat of the Moment"
JOHN KRIDER AND H. MILNOR KLAPP

Krider's Sporting Anecdotes, 1853

Books such as *The American Sportsman* offered instruction and encouragement. But a fellow did not just walk out the front door, grab his decoy sack and shotgun, and start pounding canvasbacks. Arranging such expeditions required initiative and resources. Out of this need emerged a pillar of the American sporting experience: the sporting goods store—your one-stop source of material and gear and information regarding where to go and who might help once you get there.

Sporting retail had originated with the colonial angler, who had to buy his horsehair lines somewhere—generally in Boston, New York, or Philadelphia. The eighteenth-century sporting goods entrepreneur favored a mobile operation, meaning he would buy from a maker and open a temporary stand, which he would fold up at the end of the day. Records show that a Philadelphia tavern owned by Edward Pole served as one of the earliest fly-fishing shops, in operation even as Washington and the lads were cornering Hessians out on the Yorktown Peninsula.

The 1850s brought increasing numbers of permanent retail endeavors. John Krider's store in Philadelphia, The Sportsman's Depot, is a good example. Like his customers, Krider was a man on the rise. An ornithologist (he was an avid taxidermist and significant contributor to the Academy of Natural Sciences in Philadelphia), he trained dogs, built guns, and hunted every day he could. A farm boy who apprenticed at a Philadelphia gun shop at age thirteen and owned the shop by age twenty-six, he also possessed a fair business acumen. His personality was such that his customers formed their own sportsmen's club, and his store became one of the best-known sources for hunting equipment and fishing tackle in the nation through the mid-nineteenth century—a place where, in the words of fly-fishing historian A. J. Campbell, writing in *Classic & Antique Fly Fishing Tackle: A Guide For Collectors and Anglers*, ". . . anglers met to mull over subjects ranging from artificial flies to

artificial fish hatcheries." Krider understood the importance of keeping a recognizable profile in the new print media, and he began his own publication,
Krider's Sporting Anecdotes.

Just as Krider the storeowner knew his customers, Krider the writer
knew his audience, as reflected in a story he published about canvasback
hunting near Havre de Grace on Chesapeake Bay. The bay's rail link to urban
areas allowed the sports to travel there of course, but it also fostered market
hunting, the human by-product of which was a guiding community, which in
turn could service the visiting sports. Krider's store—for that matter, Krider
himself—could inform any customer on this hot spot, say nothing of supply-
ing them with the gear they needed. Krider's story could fire readers (and
potential customers) with desire to go duck hunting soon. In years to come,
businesses outsourced this role to outdoor writers; but for now, Krider kept
the operation in-house.

This particular story was an "as told to" venture, with Krider's fellow
Philadelphian H. Milnor Klapp doing a good deal of the heavy phrase-turning.
Krider and Klapp had been partridge hunting when a friend invited them to his
new forty-foot scow that had room for sleeping, eating, carving decoys—even
space for a "helmsman and a boy" to hunt for the "far-famed" canvasback. The
guides, experienced baymen, made setting decoys an art, and Krider sighed
at the naturalistic genius that emerged from time in the marsh—the "old duck
hunter," venerable even at birth.

Before stepping into his sinkbox, Krider offered obligatory excuses for
himself and partner, noting how "years had intervened since we had drawn
trigger on wildfowl." And wouldn't you know it, they screwed up their first
shot. The ducks came in, and an anxious Krider sat up and shot the first
duck as it swam in the decoys, the second on the wing, and then struck out
with the second gun on the other two. He castigated himself, noting, "In fact,
gentle reader, in the inexcusable heat of the moment, a great blunder had
been committed in shooting at the ducks in the water"—not for reasons of
fair chase but because he could have gotten all four if he had taken the outside birds first.

The hunt went swimmingly after that, however, with plenty of shooting. A long lull prompted the group to begin to pick up the decoys, which, of course, is when the ducks started flying. Krider complained about the cold: "Taking up some two hundred decoys on a cold, blustering evening is rather tedious and benumbing work to a novice"—an odd sentence (he's the sport, after all) until you realize that as early as the mid-nineteenth century, old duck hunters had figured out ways to get newcomers to pick up the decoys.

After the hunt Krider repaired to Baird's Hotel, where duck shooters gabbed about "the exploits of the day." A city fellow, Krider seemed to remember that he was in the company of real duck hunters, "men [who] were both fishers and fowlers . . . well informed on all matters connected with their business—sometimes even acute, and some of them realize handsome profits in their hardy and exciting pursuits." They were market hunters, in other words, and in time they became the sworn enemies of sport hunters, but for now Krider needed them and their help in order to hunt. In his generosity—or perhaps to show that he was himself an insider—he called them "expert shots" and noted their resourcefulness, as some of "the poorer inhabitants train their large dogs not only to retrieve ducks, but to assist in bring in quantities of driftwood 'for winter fuel.'"

The baymen in the smoky tavern certainly had the on-the-ground info on duck hunting, but Krider had something more: He got to decide what it all meant—the hunting, the bonding, the humor, the feats of shame and skill. This country mouse–city mouse division of participants characterized the American outdoors at least until the years following World War II. The locals were experts during the hunt, but once the decoys were wrapped, the ducks dressed, and the guns put away, they lost their leverage. What happened had become Krider's story to tell. Now he was the man.

His rendition followed a generous arc as he took a one-down position, noting the challenges of the sport, understating his own "manliness," and, as a travel writer, using his trepidations, whether actual or fabricated, to connect with his audience. He was a city man talking to other city men. A transitional figure, writing in the naturalist-anthropologist travel-writing tradition of Bartram,

Wilson, and Audubon, he added a retailer's eye toward the inventory back in the store, cheering on, it is fair to say, the growing sport-hunting community. By situating his wonder at the new world exotica within a respectful, nostalgic rendering of duck hunting's protocols and exhilarations, Krider no doubt struck a chord in his urban, middle-class audience—like him, but a generation removed from the farm. And in lifetimes to come, thousands found themselves inexplicably drawn to this liquid frontier, where baymen are persnickety about decoy placement, city sports blow easy shots, and the ducks start flying as soon as you pick up the decoys.

"Nothing but His Sport"

WILLIAM HENRY HERBERT (FRANK FORESTER)

*Frank Forester's Fish and Fishing of the United States and
British Provinces of North America*, 1850

Two distinct threads appeared in the growing American conversation about hunting and fishing. One was the "how to git 'em" (you can *do* it) of Krider's piece, as well as the writings of Peter Hawker and Elisha Lewis. But there was also a romantic school, influenced by Sir Walter Scott's chivalrous tales of Ivanhoe and other knights. Capt. Mayne Reid, an Irish writer who spent nearly twenty years in the United States and served in the army during the Mexican war, wrote for a youthful audience and followed a similar romantic path. *The Boy Hunters*, a tale of three lads who braved bears and Indians to try and bag a white buffalo, exemplified his rip-roaring romantic adventures, enriched with realistic natural descriptions. As historian Douglas Brinkley argues in *Wilderness Warrior*, this twin focus of high drama and realistic description made Reid an important influence on later conservationists who read his books as youths during the antebellum period. But Reid also added to the growing enthusiasm for the outdoors in the 1850s.

Of all the antebellum writers, the most influential was William Henry Herbert. Like Reid he had a foot in both the romantic and the how-to, conservationist worlds too, although his legacy owes more to his early promotion of those latter ideals. In the late 1840s he began publishing outdoor books (under the pseudonym of Frank Forester), typically with a general instructional form that catalogued the fish and game of the country and laid out the accepted approaches and methods for their pursuit.

A Cambridge-educated English aristocrat exiled by his family, Herbert started a new life when he arrived in New York City in the 1830s. He hit the ground running, proving to be a prolific writer and editor. But his personality contained a darker, mercurial element, and he also wrote pieces of high drama, such as the romantic story "A Fatal Salmon," a sort of Lord Byron goes a-fishing. The tale took place on a morning when "all nature was alive and joyous [and] the air was vocal with the piping melody of the birds." Young Jasper St. Aubyn leapt through "the fresh mountain air, with a foot as elastic as that of the mountain roe." Jasper dressed the part of romantic hero, wearing a close-fitting jacket and tight hose of dark green cloth, with a broad leaf hat with "a single eagle's feather thrust carelessly through the band." But he was no common fellow. His rustic dress belied a "fine intellectual face" and "gentle birth."

The river's cascading flows offered "as striking and romantic a scene as ever met the eye of a painter or of a poet." Entranced by the tumbling, dangerous water, Jasper followed the faint deer trail, bounding along the shore, "leaping from rock to rock, alighting on their slippery tops with the fine agility of a rope dancer." His manliness showed up, interestingly, through his daring behavior, not in the feats of strength common to Paul Bunyan or Mike Fink. Such a description would render Jasper coarse and lower class, hardly befitting a fly fisherman—even at this early point.

Jasper landed one salmon of twenty pounds before tying into a much larger fish that tore through a narrow chasm. Thrilled, "and thinking of nothing but his sport, he dashed forward. . . . Leap after leap he took with beautiful precision, alighting firm and erect on the center of each slippery block. . . ." Jasper brought the salmon under control—until a "female shriek" from a nearby garden distracted him and in the drink he went. His "last glance fell upon a female form wringing her hands in despair on the bank." He slipped beneath the surface, "the vital spark . . . faded into darkness—perhaps was quenched forever."

Sport, pursued properly, called on a man to do what he must. The thought of his own safety never crossed Jasper's mind. Nor should it. All that mattered was his manhood—the equivalent of his honor, really: Any activity that allowed an individual to demonstrate that element of his character became valuable, essential, one could argue.

But the activity had certain ground rules. If the fish called for the angler to choose safety or engagement, he had to select the latter—without a thought.

The ibis hunter figured out how to circumvent danger. The new sport searched for it. Otherwise he might as well go rabbit hunting.

In an America where dueling still occurred, where a congressman caned into unconsciousness a senator in his chamber in order to uphold family honor, in which citizens girded for a great Civil War, such behavior only brought angling and hunting into the realm of respectability.

That was one side of Herbert, or Forester. The other side showed in his more prescriptive writing about how to hunt and fish, and in particular his prescient awareness of the fragility of the natural resources of fish and game. Herbert rose to leadership in the early sporting community in New York City; he argued for habitat preservation and the regulation of hunting, and against market hunting and commercial harvest "for the benefit of fat, greasy merchant princes." A chapter on woodcock hunting in his 1853 book, *American Game In Its Seasons*, exemplified his early articulation of what became the conservation ethic.

Summer "cocking," in particular, provoked his ire. After introducing the reader to the natural history of the woodcock, Forester explained his "very strong desire to see summer woodcock shooting entirely abolished." Otherwise, he predicted, in less than twenty years, "the woodcock will be as rare an animal as the wolf . . . so ruthlessly are they persecuted and hunted down by pot-hunters and poachers, for the benefit of restaurateurs and of the lazy, greedy cockneys who support them." (In spite of their small size, woodcock fetched $1 per pair in the New York City market in the 1870s—the same as a pair of canvasbacks.)

Herbert doubted the efficacy of any such legislation, even if it were passed, for "too many even of those who call themselves, and who ought to be, true sportsmen, are selfish and obstinate on this point." Moreover, other problems prevented the enforcement of such a law—namely, the fact that "so vehemently opposed are all the rural classes." (A migratory bird, the woodcock was hunted somewhere every month of the season. In a addition to July hunting, firelighting—clubbing them at night under torchlight—was a popular means of harvest.)

Herbert saw sportsmen as the saviors. He lobbied for a mid-September season opening, when dogs won't tire "and the sportsman can do his work too, as he ought to do it, like a man, walking at his proper rate"—not skulking or lagging like a rabbit hunter, in other words, but moving manly, athletically, like Jasper.

In the "oh, well" rule of early conservationist writing, after a valiant plea for its elimination, Herbert launched into the best approaches for summer "cocking." He rued the loss of some of his favorite gunning pals and the railroad's destruction of the best covers around New York. In other words, like Krider, he described the shooting culture as though it already had a long tradition.

Herbert himself was a tortured soul, whether because of his exile, what he considered to be a failed writing career, or the extent to which conservation practices were ignored. In any case, widowed in 1848 and divorced by a second wife, perhaps at the mercy of an unresolved past, he became increasingly despondent and shot himself in a New York City hotel in 1858.

"To Enhance His Enjoyment"
ROBERT BARNWELL ROOSEVELT

Superior Fishing, 1865

The next generation of conservationists would champion Herbert's ideas. He had been the first to connect the sport of hunting and fishing with a devotion to wildlife. One became the reason for the other. That formulation also had a more immediate impact and inspired other writers and sportsmen of his day, the most significant of whom was Robert Barnwell Roosevelt, uncle of President Theodore Roosevelt. An important member of the New York City sporting set that included Herbert, Roosevelt was an all-round sportsman and writer, particularly dedicated to fishing. His first book, *The Game Fish of the Northern States of America and the British Provinces (1862)*, with its "scientific" and sporting instructions on topics ranging from fly tying to fish culture, was the first American publication of its kind. *Superior Fishing* (1865) and *Game Birds of the Coasts and Lakes of the Northern States of America* (1866) made important marks too. A man of science, letters, and law, congressman, ambassador, conservationist, sportsman, writer, satirist, and reformer, the bespectacled, bearded Roosevelt succeeded Herbert as the best-known sportsman of his day. He became a larger-than-life reformer, who in time brought government into the business of trying to regulate fishing and hunting.

RBR, who lived in the brownstone next door to young Theodore, was not only a devoted angler and hunter but also loved animals in general, and he was out of the box about his commitment to their well-being. He and his wife, Lizzie, maintained a home featuring a German shepherd that dined at the table with the family, a fashionably dressed monkey that leapt about the Victorian decor, and a cow that grazed in the backyard. Neighbors eventually forced the cow's eviction, and, as Theodore's sister Bamie remembered, the poor animal became so frightened that it refused to reenter the house (the only way it could be removed from the backyard) and finally "had to have its legs bound partly together and its eyes blindfolded and then be dragged out." One can only imagine the impression such scenes made on Theodore, or Teedie, as the family called him.

Robert Roosevelt's disregard for social correctness also extended to his attitudes toward the conventions of marriage. Roosevelt had a reputation for handing out bright-green gloves as "presents" to women with whom he had been intimate. His rakish activities were but a foreshadowing of more permanent transgressions. In fact, he led a double life; just blocks from his brownstone, he kept a second family with Minnie O'Shea Fortescue, whom he married in 1888, a year after wife Lizzie's death.

In the middle of it all, Roosevelt loved angling and hunting—and science too. Charles Darwin's *On the Origin of the Species*, published in 1859, had already begun to reshape writing about the natural world, and Roosevelt took pains to bring scientific concepts to bear on the matter of fish, in particular. Roosevelt also believed in having a good time, and if Herbert remained a bit on the stuffy and fatalistic side, RBR was more like the friend your mother told you never to play with. In his idea of sport, daring and excitement certainly revealed one's manliness, but they also led to a good deal of fun. And his definition of "fun" had a certain elasticity, extending far beyond the adolescent thrills of Captain Reid or the romantic sacrifice of Scott or Herbert.

"Point Judith," a chapter in *Superior Fishing*, is a good example of Roosevelt's notion of sport, beginning with the getting there part. He conceded that it can be "a long, weary, and dusty ride by the way of the New Haven and Shore Line Railroads to Kingston" but that the inconvenience may be worth it if "a pretty little widow, with hazel eyes, is found waiting to drive over to the South Pier in the stage, and you are the only other passenger."

Roosevelt's audience apparently excluded husbands and family men in general. (Maybe they hid their books under their mattresses.) After all, he wrote that if you are lucky, "the driver may happen to be a little tight, very sleepy, and wholly unobservant of what is passing in the back of his vehicle," for "hazel eyes, white teeth, rosy lips, soft hands, and a slender waist are very bewitching in a close carriage of a moonlight night, with a preoccupied driver." And in case readers of the day were unsure of what Roosevelt was really trying to get at, he added, "If you happen to be riding alone with a pretty widow, and something suggests love-making, and her merry laughter slowly dies away into a gentle smile, and the smile fades into a look of sympathetic feeling, that you have to draw very near to see, till you feel her palpitating breath upon your cheek, and her hand trembles when by the merest accident you touch it, and the ride occupies an hour or more, you may, before the South Pier is reached, almost forget that you are married." OK?

Roosevelt directed the reader, as did Krider, to a particular spot—in this case a house kept by one John Anthony. Here sportsmen could get everything they needed for the expedition, "except the wherewithal to quench their thirst." Roosevelt had an abiding interest in the biology of fishes, much as Herbert did in the ways of woodcock and other game birds. He urged anglers to be scientific about their approach. He speculated on the serendipitous nature of the Gulf Stream and how the weather can influence bass, some of which reach fifty to sixty pounds.

Again, the fishing, as in Forester's salmon story, tested the manliness of the participant. "The waves will come rolling in, streaming out in the wind like a courser's mane, with snowy crest, and breaking with thundering roar they will sink back seething with foam . . . and if you are not on the watch will lift you in their embrace and fling you torn and wounded down among the sharp-pointed rocks."

Different species deserved different treatment, and it was the sportsman's responsibility to be knowledgeable: "If the blue-fish comes, and he does not carry away your hook at the first snatch, reel him in as quickly as his indomitable pluck and vigor will permit. He is not game when you are bass-fishing." If even less-noble species such as "the ungainly flounder" hit your bait, "lug him out by main force, treating him, though excellent to eat, like the vulgar commoner he is."

Roosevelt marked a new synthesis in American writing about the outdoors. He insisted upon knowledge and skill like Forester, included specific travel information like Krider, and wrote in a voice that imbued the American sportsman with competence and courage. These heroes did not fashion water-wings from alligator intestines; Roosevelt's anglers actually lived and died.

He told of two anglers fishing from a large rock when one hooked a striper of seventy pounds or more. With tide running and wind whipping, the angler finally muscled in the fish. Just then "a gigantic wave, rolling in unheeded, caught the preoccupied fishermen unawares, engulfed them in its green waters, flung one down bruised and sore, and carried off the other who held the gaff, and was nearer the brink, into the deep water beyond."

One of the most popular after-dinner speakers in New York, Roosevelt could ladle it on: "Poor fellow, he could not swim, and the terror of approaching death passed across his features as he looked up beseechingly and tried to cling to the steep and slippery rocks." The surging seas carried him like a toy, eventually tossing him up on the jagged rocks. The man's friend had the stringer with a dead striper on it, and he flung it to the man and maneuvered him in "to the shelving rocks, and twice during a lull [the drowning man] could have climbed them in safety, had not his strength been too greatly exhausted." The man's friend drew him in, "called to the drowning man to cling fast with his hands for a moment, and rushed down to seize him." But when he relaxed the line to reach for the man, the water carried him out, and in washed "a tremendous wave, resolute to devour its prey . . . it rose above points . . . it dashed in flying spray high . . . its crest gleamed and hissed, and with one mad leap it sprang over the intervening ledges and threw itself upon the fishermen with fearful power. . . . The line was broken, and man and fish were swept away together."

Roosevelt seemed to clear his literary throat. "Danger never deterred a sportsman," he explained, "but rather seems to enhance his enjoyment." In this respect, striper fishing at Point Judith offered the perfect sport, as "there is just sufficient risk and enough cold water to make fishing from the rocks a pleasurable excitement. The fiercer the storm and the wilder the water the better the fishing, and if he does perish it is in a good cause, and he has the sympathies of all his ardent brothers of the angle. . . ."

Roosevelt added another dimension to the adventure–natural history travel piece: What happened upon arrival at home mattered. Angling could give you an actual leg up in the world. So have your fish "nicely packed in ice." That way you have proof "of the large fish you captured and enormous ones you lost, of the dangers you ran and how beautifully you cast, and your friends that receive of the game will believe in you."

To be sure, the actual sporting practices and methods awaited some fine-tuning, but the broad principles were falling into place. The sport should be joyful, should involve hardship, risk, or challenge; the participant should face and solve the problems bravely and honorably, preferably (thoughtfully, apparently, if he is British). His style, the way he acts, matters greatly, and for that reason the sporting life is not for everyone. Subjecting oneself to the above conditions must be voluntary.

Roosevelt was a public figure. His involvement suggested that outdoor sports were beginning to be normalized, were taking their place alongside team sports and spectator sports, both of which were exploding in popularity. Hunting and fishing represented one set of many different "leisure activities," and like an increasing number of Americans, he saw no irony in using the two opposing words to mean one practice.

The outdoor sports are very old activities, with centuries, even millennia, apt measurements of time. The British and Americans did not invent hunting and fishing. But men like Roosevelt showed how much fun these activities could be. It should come as no small surprise that a lot of others wanted in on them too.

CHAPTER 3

"For Body, Mind and Soul"

EVERYBODY IN THE POOL, 1870–1890

C harles Stevens and his wife left Boston for Maine on a Monday evening in early June, sometime in the 1870s. They planned to fish for trout in the Rangeley Lakes, a premier sporting destination of the era.

The Stevenses took a steamer to Portland, where they boarded a train for Rumford. On that train Mr. Stevens, a businessman and writer, had his initial interaction with a Mainer, which he recounted in his 1881 book, *Fly-Fishing In Maine Lakes*. At the time Stevens may have been dreaming of the region's big brook trout.

"Goin' a-fishin?" came an inquiry, along "with a poke on the left shoulder." The jab had come from "a rural specimen of the *genus homo*" sitting behind him on the train. "What der yer 'spect ter ketch?"

"Any thing, sir, that will rise to a fly; wouldn't object to a salmon, but will be content with a trout," said Stevens.

"Rise to a fly! I guess if they rise to flies you'll see lots of fish."

"Oh! Then trout are plenty this season, are they?"

"Don't know nothing about trout, but flies air. Where yer from?"

"Boston."

"Where yer going?"

"Upper Dam, Richardson Lake."

"Sho! She going too?" referring to Mrs. Stevens.

"Yes."

"Fishing?"

"Certainly."

"Gosh! Cummin' all the way from Boston to go a fishin'. Not in them clo'es, is she?"

Stevens and his wife assured the man that "our fishing-outfit was quite different from our present dress," and that they were used to fishing in the woods. But as Stevens recalled "the idea of our "cummin' all the way from Boston to go a-fishin', and she goin' too," had a noticeable impact on the man, and he promptly "lapsed into profound meditation." He sat in silence till the train reached its destination some hours later and Stevens heard him say to a woman seated across from him:

"Jess think of it! He said they'd come all the way from Boston to go a-fishin'."

As it turned out, scenes such as this one would be repeated all over the country during the 1870s. Small-town folks who had seen—if not been—fishing and hunting all their lives couldn't believe the fuss that now accompanied such ordinary activities. Well-to-do people from the city couldn't wait to go themselves. They wanted to be "sportsmen" (and women). Children, women, and men from every walk of life all went to the woods and waters with old and new ideas. In short, Americans hit the outdoors, as if they were third graders on recess.

"Give Him the Butt!"

Luke, the guide

CHARLES DUDLEY WARNER

In the Wilderness, 1878

In one particular way, the rush to the outdoors followed the stories of Irving, Cooper, Krider, Forester, Roosevelt, and others. That is, the new enthusiasm originated not in the marshes, uplands, streams, and lakes of the countryside but in the offices and homes of eastern cities. City living sent folks back outdoors, re-creating the experience as a positive venture in renewal—and not simply idleness or a sign you had too much money and no place to spend it.

City residents experienced a nostalgic pull for several reasons. The longing for a time from before had real legs thanks to the horrid destruction of the Civil War. The nostalgia had pernicious manifestations in the South in the "Lost Cause" sentimentality that fueled the brutal racial repression of Reconstruction. The nostalgia also manifested in the rise of Northern city suburbs and their "rural ideal," as historian Sam Bass Warner has called it. Throughout the country the longing the for pre-sectional times of Crockett and Audubon drew Americans to a range of outdoor activities, including not just hunting and fishing but also canoeing, sailing, hiking (or tramping, as it was often called), camping, skating, and riding.

This nostalgia was not simply a matter of a "cultural trend" and general response to the war and industrialism. Many of those in the new middle and upper-middle classes had their own personal rural origins. The Civil War had wrenched their lives out of the tracks, at the least. These folks certainly intended to succeed in the future, but they understandably felt wistful about their childhoods too. Outside felt like the place where Americans belonged, if for no other reason than that was the place Americans had been.

Whereas upper-class men previously had to worry about convincing people that vacations were good, the dynamics shifted in the years after the Civil War. With an entire generation of middle-class fellas no longer clearing woods and clumping behind a plow and mule but sitting behind desks ciphering, many worried that the United States would become a nation of damn sissies. Actually, concerns over loss of masculinity had been around ever since the city began to grow. As early as 1819, former president Adams had written to former President Jefferson, "Will you tell me how to prevent riches from producing luxury? Will you tell me how to prevent luxury from producing effeminacy intoxication extravagance Vice and folly?"

William Henry "Adirondack" Murray's *Adventures in the Wilderness; or, Camp Life in the Adirondacks* with its tail-grabbing hunting adventures and wilderness advice, certainly provided an answer. And his was only the opening salvo in a barrage of publications and books urging Americans to improve their health by getting outside. The exhortation of mid-twentieth-century mothers to their children to "Go play outside!" probably had its origins in the pulpits and pamphlets of the mid-nineteenth century.

Minister W. C. Prime, in *I Go-A-Fishing*, an important book published in the wake of Adirondack Murray's manifesto, opined, "The summer vacation, which is about the only recreation that an American professional or business man allows himself, is apt to be wasted entirely by the want of mental refreshment which can not be found in the ordinary resorts of summer pleasure-seekers." Fishing was what men needed "for body, mind and soul," for "there are many who would find this the true rest and recreation. And . . . you will [also] find, as Peter found, that you are drawn to it whenever you are weary, impatient, or sad."

Middle class men and women not only heard the message, but as historian Cindy Aron explains in *Working At Play: A History of Vacations*, were able to go "because of the changes in the nature of middle class work during the last half of the nineteenth century. The growth of large corporations, mass retailers, and expanding government bureaucracies brought with them the demand for an army of white-collar employees. Clerks, salespeople, bookkeepers, and mid-level managers joined the professionals, school teachers, and small entrepreneurs who inhabited the ranks of the expanding American middle class." With the leisure time such jobs allowed, these individuals were all headed to the nearest trout stream, duck blind, or campground—whatever got them outside and kept them busy. The caveat was that the vacationers had to return as better citizens and workers, not simply stumble back into the office with world-class hangovers. As Stevens, Prime, Murray, and many others would respond, "Then get yourself a fishing rod (or shotgun)"—and Americans did just that.

The flurry of books and publications confirmed that readers couldn't get enough of the new outdoors religion. And Adirondack Murray, in particular, responded in kind, touring the Northeast throughout the nineteenth century, throwing out the lifeline to half a million men and women. If his sermonizing had taught him anything, it was how to reframe his personal passion as everyone's salvation. Prime's incantation that "the outdoors is good for you" was right in Murray's wheelhouse, and he sold north woods vacations like they were steps on the stairway to heaven.

Murray's zealotry, coming as it did in an age of hucksterism, scandal, and skepticism, prompted many writers to question the reverend's truthfulness. None did so with quite the charm and lasting effect of Charles Dudley Warner in his book *In the Wilderness*, which was serialized in *The Atlantic Monthly* in 1878 as "The Adirondacks Verified." Warner was a neighbor and friend of Mark Twain and his coauthor on *The Gilded Age*. In one particular essay, "A Fight with A Trout," Warner poked fun at Murray's tale of trout fishing.

In *Adventures in the Wilderness*, Murray had not only written breathlessly of deer hunting but also of trout fishing, in particular an evening trip to Nameless Creek, where "the setting sun yet poured its radiance though the overhanging pines, flecking the tide with crimson patches and crossing it here and there with golden lands . . . as far as the eye could reach, the air was literally full of jumping trout."

Murray, being Murray, hooked multiple fish on every cast. At one point "four gleams of light crossed the pool and four quivering forms, with widespread tails and open mouths, leaped high out of the water." Murray's guide,

John, pointed out a spot near a patch of lily pads. Murray cast, and "The flies, in response to the twist of the pliant rod, rose into the air, darted forward, and, pausing over the lily-pads lighted deftly on the water." A two-pounder took the fly—or one of them—and after a fierce battle, John slipped the net beneath it.

Murray made another cast, "and the three flies leaped upward and ahead. Spreading themselves out as they reached the limit of the cast, like flakes of feathery snow they settled, wavering downward" and a trio of two-pounders leapt into the air and struck the flies in synchronicity, as if they'd been trained at SeaWorld.

The fish plunged for the lily pads, then turned and steamed straight for the boat. "Give 'em the butt!" called John, and Murray obliged handsomely. Within forty minutes he landed some one hundred fish, fifty of which were in the two-pound class. Hoo boy.

Warner began his scathing response by cautioning his upper- and middle-class *Atlantic Monthly* audience that "the trout is a retiring and harmless animal, except when he is aroused, and forced into a combat; and then his agility, fierceness, and vindictiveness become apparent." No one, he noted, visits "the lonely lakes of the forest without a certain terror." Anyone who read about fishermen developed an "admiration for their heroism."

Warner claimed to have loved his own Adirondack trip, explaining that the fishing would have been great if the state of New York would stock some trout in the waters. The deer hunting would have been good too, if "previous hunters had not pulled all the hair and skin off from the deer's tails." Conditions were such now that visitors were "hourly pained by the sight of peeled-tail deer mournfully sneaking about the wood."

Warner and his faithful guide, Luke, sneaked off one morning for the lake, and "each of us carried a boat, a pair of blankets, a sack of bread, pork, and maple-sugar; while I had my case of rods, creel, and book of flies, and Luke had an axe and the kitchen utensils."

Bearing their loads cheerfully, the pair tramped five miles through a cedar bog, ending up at Unknown Pond. The water boiled "bubbling and breaking, as if the lake were a vast kettle, with a fire underneath." Surprising? Hardly, as a "sportsmen will at once understand me when I say that the water *boiled* with the breaking trout. . . . They seemed to be at play rather than feeding, leaping high in the air in graceful curves, and tumbling about each other as we see them in the Adirondack pictures."

Warner selected a fly, noting that "it requires some training on the part of the trout to take to this method. . . . No sportsman, however, will use anything but a fly, except when he happens to be alone." Warner added that the fly fisherman's equipment was of the greatest delicacy. The leader was "made to order from a domestic animal with which I had been acquainted. . . . The interior of the house-cat, it is well known, is exceedingly sensitive."

Luke paddled Warner about the pond, but they found no fish. Warner worried that the trout may have been "too green" to understand their own role in all this. "After studying the color of the sky, of the water, and of the foliage, and the moderated light of the afternoon," he changed flies and tied on "a series of beguilers, all of a subdued brilliancy, in harmony with the approach of evening."

Warner's second cast produced a splash, and, skilled as he was, Warner "did not need the unfeigned, damn, of Luke" to confirm that he hooked Luke's felt hat "and deposited it among the lilies." From there the fishing picked up. "Three trout leaped into the air. He hooked a trout that, feeling "the prick of the hook, was off like a shot, and took out the whole of the line with a rapidity that made it smoke."

"Give him the butt!" yelled Luke. As Warner explained, that was the typical remark in such a fix. Warner "gave him the butt; and, recognizing the fact and my spirit, the trout at once sank to the bottom, and sulked. . . ." Warner reeled up, which enraged the trout so much that it then charged the boat.

"Look out for him!" cried Luke, as the trout flew through the air. Warner dove to the bottom of the boat and "gave him the butt again; a thing he seemed to hate, even as a gift." The trout charged again, and "Luke, who was used to these encounters, having read of them in the writings of travellers he has accompanied, raised his paddle in self-defense. The trout left the water about ten feet from the boat, and came directly at me with fiery eyes, his speckled sides flashing like a meteor."

When Warner came to, Luke was gaffing the trout at the boat-side. After he had got him in and dressed him, the trout weighed in at three-quarters of a pound. Fish always lose by being "got in and dressed." It was best, Warner advised, to weigh them while they were in the water.

As anglers themselves, readers of fishing stories eventually figured out (duh) that a catch of four foot-long brookies was in reality closer to three eight-inchers—and a fourth that could have been a trout or a chub but fell off at the bank. Eighty years later, a Santa Claus look-alike outdoor humorist named Ed Zern explained the ancient communal of all anglers: "Fishermen are born honest, but they get over it."

The larger point was that readers still devoured Murray as if they wanted both adventure *and* fun in their outdoor tales. Could having fun be more important than being honorable and brave? Sometimes?

Everyone knew that on balance, people had more fun outdoors than in. Three years after Warner's satire, Charles W. Stevens mentioned Murray multiple times in his book on Maine, as did many outdoor authors during the nineteenth century. Murray's problem was the absence of any self-irony in pursuit of something as small and "innocent" (a characterization that shows up frequently in the literature) as a trout. Other writers often noted its absence. In describing a tussle with a trout some fifteen years later, author Lewis France wrote, "While I was doing this [fighting the fish] I remembered having read a whole column of imagination, written by somebody named Murray, wherein he described his 'happiness' under like circumstances." France vowed not to repeat the mistake. Murray's florid descriptions could have been one of American fly fishing's first clichés. But the readers didn't care, even if the writers did.

For the reading public, the fact that Murray had really been there mattered more, and they were inclined to cut him some slack. By the new century, publications vied to call themselves the "been there" magazines. Editors touted the extent to which their writers actually spent time in the field and, at least to an extent, gave up on their telling the truth. If nothing else, all the hubbub—"the controversy"—only meant free promotion for a growing industry that was built around people taking to the outdoors.

"A Fisher o' Men"
Jimmy Whitcher
ANNIE TRUMBULL SLOSSON

"Fishin' Jimmy," 1889

Tourism became important as rural communities found themselves eating the dust of the great industrial expansion in the years following the Civil War. Maine was the new destination with trophy brook trout, for instance, but sportsmen went west to Colorado too. The quail hunting of the Old South drew many, as did the bass fishing in Florida.

Railroads revolutionized transportation, magazines did the same for communications, and both permitted regions to market themselves. As the din and grime of industry came to dominate southern New England, for example, the boundaries of "classic" New England moved north into Vermont, New Hampshire, and Maine, where towns had been emptying as fast as kids figured out which way was south. Desperate for some sort of economy, northern New England states designed aggressive tourism campaigns to package the desolation as nature and promote their region as the "real" America. Soon every town had an "Old Home Week," and the north country vistas became the "real" Yankeedom, with terrific hunting and fishing by the way.

The desire for such authenticity can be seen in such a variety of sources as Charles Dudley Warner's title (*The Adirondack's Verified*), the rise of realism in journalism, and the new fascination with photography. Rural areas were the home of "real" American life. The city certainly wasn't, what with the parade of changes in transportation, communication, and residents, with their babble of tongues, vices, and customs. The belief in the realness of country life made it the center of an ideal world promising a soothing, predictable reality.

One example of this cultural longing was the Local Color Movement, a literary school in which books and stories used a natural setting, regional idiosyncrasy, and local dialect to venerate the disappearing small-town culture. Joel Chandler Harris, Sarah Orne Jewett, and Mary Wilkins Freeman were well-known local color writers. (Other authors—Mark Twain, for example—were influenced by the movement, if not in theme or form then at least in setting and characters.) The genre revolved around children, old men, and widowed women—a reflection of the Civil War's dreadful toll on the nation's adult men, a factor only reinforced by the hundreds of thousands of men missing limbs who haunted the American landscape. But the genre also represented a reaction against the city's allure, and above all a disavowal of romantic and national impulses, perhaps even of virility as well—all of which had sent American boys and men to their deaths. The old-fashioned virtues of simple country folk found literary life. Canned or not, the plots played well to the ambivalence of a modernizing society—and drew trainloads of Americans to the outdoors in search of nirvana, most clearly captured in the twenty-first-century slogan of Maine's license plate: "The way life should be."

Fishing and hunting stories with their natural setting, their centrality of wildlife and the rural way, road the wave of this rediscovery of the real America. Perhaps the classic local color outdoor story is "Fishin' Jimmy," a profile of Jimmy Whitcher, a lifelong fisherman from a small town in the hills of northern New Hampshire, written by Annie Trumbull Slosson.

Largely forgotten today, Slosson was an important American writer and scientist at the end of the nineteenth century. Born in 1838 to the Connecticut Trumbulls, she attended the Hartford Female Seminary, developing a progressive religious philosophy and an interest in nature. She ended up a sister-in-law to W. C. Prime (of *I Go A-Fishing* fame), who encouraged her to write a story about the White Mountains, where both families summered. The result was one of American angling literature's enduring tales.

Fishin' Jimmy was as plain as New Hampshire dirt. He'd lived in the same village his entire life. His life work was to teach children how to fish, which left him a place in the collective heart of the community.

Jimmy was the best fisherman anyone had ever seen. An instinctive naturalist, he had no idea that "the yellow spatterdock was *Nuphar advena*, but he knew its large leaves of rich green" sheltered bass and other fish. One time Jimmy guided a famous botanist searching for a rare plant, explaining,

"There's a dreffle lot o' that peppergrass out in deep water there, jest where I ketched the big pick'ril. . . . I seen it nigh a foot high, an' it's juicier and livin'er than them dead sticks in your book."

He knew "the phoebe, the jay, the vireo, all these were friends, familiar, tried, and true to Fishin' Jimmy." He saw bears, foxes, deer, moles, mice. "Nobody don't see 'em but fishermen," he said. "Nobody don't hear 'em but fishermen."

One day Jimmy heard a preacher tell of how Christ had called out to fishermen. Something clicked inside Jimmy, and he later remembered how "The min'ster said [Christ] jest asked 'em to come along with him; an' they lay down their poles an' their lines an' everything an' jined him." Jimmy found his calling.

One time, a little French Canadian girl was orphaned when her mother, "an unknown tramp," died by the side of the road. Townspeople discovered the child "clinging to her mother's body." She "fought like a tiger" when folks tried to take her away.

Who ya gonna call?

A short time later, Fishin' Jimmy and the waif could be seen sneaking along the local stream, each with a pole in hand, trying to catch some trout. The urchin "chattered in her odd patois," while Jimmy responded in his "broadest New England dialect." Fishermen both, they understood each other, though Jimmy later admitted that he found it "dreffle to hear her call the fish pois'n." But that was after she had been cured and packed off to Bethlehem (actually a nearby New Hampshire town) to live with a family.

As Jimmy aged, he developed a deep attachment to the writer's dog, Dash. The two of them formed a predictable sight on the stream or in a boat, with Dash barking away at fish for Jimmy to catch. Frail, "nigh on to 70" Jimmy would hurry over as best he could and make a cast.

One summer day, a severe thunderstorm blew in and stranded some boys who had hiked up a mountain. Now was Jimmy's chance. He'd always wanted to be a fisher of men. As he said before heading up, if I "couldn't be a fisher o' men, mebbe [I] knowed nuff to ketch boys."

The boys in fact made it back, but Dash, who'd gone along with them, remained up there and had gotten himself into a fix, slipping down a cliff. Jimmy found the dog and looked down on him from above. Dash gazed back up "whimpering . . . holding up one paw helplessly. Was Dash not a fisherman? And fishermen, in Fishin' Jimmy's category, were always true and trusty." So Jimmy climbed down in an attempt to help him but fell in the process, severely injuring himself.

Later, with Dash at his bedside, the community gathered round, Jimmy was taken to heaven. "Here I be, sir! It's Fishin' Jimmy, ye know, from Francony way; him ye useter call James when ye come 'long the shore o' the pond an' I was a-fishin'. I heern ye again, jest now an' I straightway f'sook my nets an' follered."

The rest was garbled. "But the words were not for us; and we did not know when he reached the other bank."

In a sense, "Fishin' Jimmy" was Washington Irving's "The Angler," picked up from across the Atlantic and dropped off onto the thin soil of New England years after the Civil War. Jimmy's wisdom emanated from his intimacy with nature, like American heroes from that earlier period—David Crockett and Jonathan "Appleseed" Chapman, for example—but his reward had less to do with a place in American history and more with an opportunity to be "nearer my God." Understandable: Given the horrific scars of the war, patriotism, any hint of chauvinism, held little appeal. Salvation was another matter. If fishing as an allegory for "throwing out the lifeline" seemed heavy-handed, it is worth noting that angling emerged from the tale as a positive, almost beatific pastime.

Here was a Leatherstocking Christ, so humble his best friend was someone else's dog, so committed to others that he ran a free after-school program, and also took in any homeless immigrant youths that happened by. If nothing else, his life provided a strong spiritual message to the American public about the worth of the outdoors and the character of outdoorsmen. Jane Addams might run the Hull House for poor children in Chicago, true. But Fishin' Jimmy did much the same in the tag alders of northern New Hampshire.

American religious favor was turning from traditional Calvinism to a Protestantism based on humility and good deeds. Such a portrayal as Fishin' Jimmy certainly advanced the goodness of people with passion for hunting and fishing. Such spiritualism lifted the general social purpose of the outdoors—to help people feel and be better. Hunting and fishing in America enjoyed a deep connection with religion from this period on. Having the Lord's blessing for outdoor undertakings represented an important step in the integration of hunting and fishing into the larger American society.

"What Shall We Do with This Boy?"
Mrs. France (the author's mother)
LEWIS B. FRANCE

With Rod and Line in Colorado Waters, 1884

In many ways, middle-class Victorians discovered childhood—at least with respect to the idea that school, manners, play, and other aspects of youth should be geared toward preparation for adulthood. Although proper folks had grown accustomed to the idea that adults could be trusted in the out-doors, they were not so sure about children. Fishin' Jimmy's presence helped of course. But what about when he wasn't around—and the likes of Huck Finn were? The outdoors came to occupy a gray area in child rearing. It couldn't be cuddly and soft like a child's bed. It still had to have an element of risk in it; otherwise it would lose its defining distinctiveness.

This tension figures prominently in the beginning of the book *With Rod and Line in Colorado Waters*, published in 1884. Author Lewis B. France recalled wistfully his own childhood, "forty years ago—a big slice off the long end of one's life!" He'd been fishing off a pier all day, and now, with the shadows lengthening, he headed home. "A little fellow, barefoot, coatless and with a ragged straw hat," he had "a string of perch as long as his precious body" to go with the two-and-a-half-foot eel bringing life to the mass of fish flesh. He trudged home contented, for "what ten-year-old could boast comparison, as with the day's trophies over his shoulder."

His mother was appalled when he landed in the kitchen. "Court was at once convened."

"What *shall* we do with this boy?" she asked, thinking aloud. His fate, she decided, should be a bath and some clean clothes. Then she noticed his leg. "What is that round your leg?" she asked.

When informed that it was an eel skin and that its function was to "keep off cramp," [so that he wouldn't drown if he fell in] she called in some reinforcements, namely her husband, who told the boy, "go bring me your fishing tackle," which he did. His father inspected it with obvious disgust and threw it all in the stove. When young France started to cry, his father reassured him that he was only doing so because the tackle was inferior. He would buy him the best. When his wife protested, his father responded that he was a boy once too.

Such was the way so many writers of the 1880s and 90s remembered their youth. The content of the nostalgia mattered, and it seems particularly telling in this situation—namely the boy, being a boy, was tsk-tsked by his mother (and to a lesser extent by an African-American servant or slave—probably the latter, as the scene occurred in Maryland, a slave state—who is also a part of this scene, though in the background; in his memory she ran some interference. Dad understood what was going on. Whereas mid-nineteenth-century parents might have worried that their boys spent too much time playing with the likes of Huck Finn, late-nineteenth-century dads, anyway, worried more that they would end up like Becky Thatcher.

Whether such a scene actually happened is less important than how a writer in the 1880s remembered it in print. It says much more about tensions of the end of the century than viewpoints of the antebellum period. The key then was for the boy to be just manly enough to worry his mother, but not to the extent that he defies his father. The dad circumvents trouble by sticking up for his boy—all of which the African-American slave understood, as she did the initial aligning with the boy (mostly by not piling on with the mother). And in these ways did hunting and fishing contain both rebellion and affirmation, and fortify the individual by allowing him to challenge (and thereby become a man) and to strengthen the community, since Mom had to approve given her husband's stance, which in turn strengthened the nuclear family and made it the pillar of the middle class. Adults wrapped the experience in the nostalgia that appeared in so many of the paintings and art of the time, with boys walking to and from the fishing hole. So ubiquitous was this image that by the middle of the next century, the barefoot boy playing hooky and going fishing stood as one of America's enduring clichés.

But that was in the future. For now, as rural work and the Civil War faded in memory, and urban living cushioned the bumps and bruises of frontier boyhood, the new generation's masculinity offered an additional source of worry: They'd be wearing skirts. The rise of athletics and team sports—college football, in particular—emerged in part from this concern. Boys had no war to toughen them as the preceding generations did. And though the idea itself came out of Oliver Wendell Holmes Jr., and other men who in fact had served in the war, others who had not (and perhaps for that reason) worried even more. Theodore Roosevelt Sr., a wealthy businessman from New York City, was a good example.

His two boys, Theodore and Elliot, concerned him—each for different reasons. An underdeveloped body and asthma crippled Theodore. He responded to his father's injunction to build his body by devising a strict regime of physical fitness, hiking, rowing, riding, and boxing. The athletically and scholastically gifted Elliot struggled at St. Paul's prep school in New Hampshire. When blackouts and headaches forced his withdrawal, his father sent him off to stay with an officer he knew at Fort McKavett in Texas in hopes that it might invigorate him. That was a considerable journey for a fifteen-year-old boy in 1874 and indicated, if nothing else, a tremendous belief in the power of the outdoors.

Initially the cure worked. Elliot's newfound confidence showed through in a letter to Theodore in which he described a frontier turkey hunt in what could be called the voice of brotherly excitement. He gushed that "the long-rolling plains of Western Texas" were nothing less than "a sportsman's paradise" with the crests of rolling hills revealing "an endless vista of . . . billowy-looking prairie." After a long day's journey, Elliot and the older men and soldiers finally arrived at the "pecan-tree forests," the roosting place of that "king of game birds, the wild turkey." That night they shot countless birds off the roost.

The toughening-up part, what we would call the outward-bound experience, took place the next day. With greyhounds and horses, Elliot and the men searched for turkeys in order to flush and chase them down. Three of the great birds roared out of a brushy draw—and the chase was on. "It was whip and spur for a mile as hard as horse, man and hound could make the pace," wrote Elliot.

They flushed the turkeys again, and this time the birds flew but a short distance before hitting the ground and running ahead of the hounds and, as Elliot puts it, "Now came the sport of it." The greyhounds bunched behind one bird, different hounds taking turns at leaping and lunging at the turkey for some time, with "their clean, cruel fangs" while "the brave old gobbler . . . rose just out of reach. . . ." Finally one hound, the oldest, "again made his rush, sprang up a wonderful height into the air, and cut the bird down as with a knife. . . . The astonishing springs of a greyhound who is an old hand at turkey coursing will make are a constant source of surprise and wonder to those fond of the sport." If the description seems to fall a bit below our contemporary bar for fair chase, we should recall that in the pre–Little Bighorn West, sportsmanship hinged mostly on the dangers facing the hunters. More to the point, the outdoor life appeared to be reconstituting Elliot's personality and determination. He hardly sounded like a boy beset with panic attacks in prep school.

But Texas proved the high point of Elliot's life. He returned from the West, ready to start anew, only to find his father terminally ill and Theodore at school in Cambridge. Elliott cared lovingly for his father until he died, and the loss flattened him. By age twenty he was drinking heavily, while TR was storming through the halls of Harvard. Growing up, Elliot had always been the better hunter, horseman, and sportsman; but now TR emerged, stronger in every sense of the word. Off to India, Elliot had adventures befitting a Roosevelt but could never work his notes into a book. Perhaps as encouragement, TR dedicated *Hunting Trips of a Ranchman* to him. (The book included this letter describing the turkey hunt.) This effort failed, like many others, and in less than ten years, Elliott drank himself to death. His legacy was weakness and debauchery in a family of drama and achievement, his only contribution the children he left behind—a daughter, Eleanor, and a godson, Franklin. All of which makes his letter, written in that full-throated Roosevelt voice, so noteworthy: If Elliott's failings consigned him to the wings, this one time his adventure earned him center stage. This one time, anyway, he lived life to its fullest. This is who he could have been, and the outdoors brought that out in him.

TR probably knew as much. Before long he was insisting that the outdoors could cure not only an individual but also an entire nation.

CHAPTER 4

"Moved by Emotions which He but Half Comprehends"

THE MEANING OF SPORT, 1880–1900

One day in the 1830s, while in England working on *Ornithological Biography* (the sequel to *Birds of America*), a middle-aged John James Audubon took a break to write a sentimental story about his early days back in Henderson, Kentucky, on the Ohio River. (It later appeared in *Delineations of American Character and Society*; the excerpt referenced here is included in *The Gigantic Book of Fishing Stories*.) Audubon felt at home in Henderson, whose few inhabitants brought his young family bacon and flour. "Our pleasures were those of young people not long married," Audubon recalled, "and full of life and merriment."

To supplement his larder, Audubon ran a trotline for the four different species of catfish swimming in the river. Like so many catfish stories that would flow from the pens of American writers in the next 180 years, this one included a comment on the cat's wholesale feeding habits. In Audubon's tale, one bewhiskered fellow, hooked on a set line in the rapids below Tarascon's Mills, had ingested "the greater part of a suckling pig."

For everyday bait, however, Audubon and other local anglers preferred live toads, which were common in the spring months. He used a stone for an anchor and set the line by rowing the stone across the river and dropping it near the opposite shore. Audubon extolled the trotline's efficiency: "The trot line is in the river, and *it* may patiently wait, until I visit it toward night." In the meantime, rather than stand there fishing like some village idiot, Audubon could grab his gun and go hunting—which, unlike *fishing*, he apparently did enjoy.

In the ninety years between the spring of the toads and turn of the new century, many elements of the American sporting scene changed—but none more than the essence of Audubon's recollections, namely the reason a person might fish (and hunt). The *process* of fishing—the very part that Audubon happily skips out on—became the defining aspect of the sport, as it would for hunting as well. It was the *creel* or *bag* that lost value, which would have no doubt left Audubon and his Henderson neighbors scratching their heads.

Fair chase not only served as the new crucible of sport's thrills and stories, it led to the meaning that outdoor experiences claim today. By the 1870s and 1880s, there was really no other choice. The sporting writers of the day—particularly Theodore Roosevelt Jr. and George Bird Grinnell—reframed scarcity as a challenge and did their best to cast the activities as ones worth doing. It was the most important conceptual shift in the history of American outdoor recreation. The destruction of water and forest habitat, the increased efficiency of market hunting and fishing, and the explosion of interest in recreational hunting and fishing by the middle class had the cumulative effect of vaporizing native stocks of fish and game. If the worth of sport continued to be calculated in poundage or numbers, before long there wouldn't be anything left to catch or kill.

How did sportsmen think about the decimation of fish and wildlife? Whose fault was it? What earlier ideas did they use to coat their own newer, radical thinking with the veneer of tradition? How did they think about the fish and animals that they lost and saved? How did they rethink the idea of scarcity so that it could help make hunting and fishing not only permissible but desirable?

These questions dominated the sporting community in the years after the Civil War, although the devastation of native stocks was not a new phenomenon. As early as the 1840s, in *The American Angler's Guide*, the first book on fishing in America, John J. Brown noted that "the overarching banks of your favorite streams conceal your spotted friends no longer." Netting "by mercenary fishermen, who, in season and out of season take large and small (for all is fish that comes to their net) is one cause."

But a deeper cause, clearer in retrospect, was the governing sensibility about hunting and fishing in pre-sporting America: Git 'em before someone else does. Even visiting Englishman George Tattersall found himself in the embrace of this way of thinking, explaining how he and other anglers often tried to catch all the fish in a stream, more or less because they were there and just kept biting.

The same mentality continued in the post-war era, as Ed Van Put describes in "The Beaverkill: Preservation and Posting," which appeared in the fall 1996 issue of *The American Fly Fisher*. George W. Van Siclen, a founder of the Beaverkill Club, sent a letter to *Forest and Stream* in 1878, notifying all that the upper Beaverkill was off-limits to public angling. The final straw had occurred one day the previous summer when he was fishing and "there came down from 'Quaker Clearing' three men on a buckboard, and they boasted of 'over 400 trout.'" Van Siclen could not see where they had so many "stowed away . . . [until] they opened a twelve-quart butter firkin and showed me the poor little things. They claimed 400, and I guess they told the truth. I think not one of the 'fish' was over six inches long." The upshot was that Van Siclen and others purchased the rights to the upper Beaverkill and made the waters private. They remain so to this day.

For reasons having to do with political philosophy and general geographic space, Van Sicklen's response did not serve as a general solution to wildlife deprivation in America. The inclinations of the men on the buckboard did become the problem, however, and it extended far beyond a couple of backwoods anglers. It characterized the entire society's attitude toward native resources. Such a belief system had profound systemic implications, as the rise of an industrial strength market-hunting systems, thanks to improvements in refrigeration, transportation, and weaponry, all made possible the large-scale killing, processing, and marketing of upland game, ducks, and big game.

One example: the obliging and delicious golden plover. As early as 1821, Audubon attended a shoot involving two hundred men who accounted for an estimated forty-eight thousand plovers. But their abundance was such that they could absorb the pre-industrial harvest. That changed after the Civil War, as the number of hunters increased and weapons improved. With the decline of the passenger pigeon in the 1880s (they went extinct in 1914), upland plovers drew the full attention of market hunters, who shipped them to urban markets. The 1918 Migratory Bird Act halted the plover's decline, and their population eventually stabilized, although the upland plover (or sandpiper, as it is called today) continues to face problems of disappearing habitat in the twenty-first century.

All wildlife faced threats from the growing commerce of the expanding population. A good example was the increasing popularity of feathers in women's hats. Many of those feathers and skins came from non-game species (the ibis was a favorite), but the overall bird slaughter was hardly discriminatory. The expanding urban markets for food and fashion ensured growing profits. The unrestricted slaughter of all fish and wildlife that could be eaten, worn, or rendered into fuel was just a start. The deforestation of land and damming and polluting of rivers made sure their populations could never rebound— and meant that all wildlife suffered. For native species, with no regulations to restrain their harvest, these were dark days.

Increasingly sport hunting writers took pains to condemn "pot" hunting and market shooting, citing both as activities unbecoming gentlemen and dangerous to sporting pursuits. Casting the issue of commercial hunting and fishing as the good guys (sportsmen) versus bad guys (market hunters and commercial fishermen), however, disguised the fact that market hunting represented an entire system involving hunters, buyers, shippers, owners, and consumers. Like any sort of nefarious pyramid, those at the bottom took the risk and got the bad name; those at the top banked the money.

In truth, market hunting included far more gray area than black and white. Market hunters worked as guides during the fall and spring migrations. Who else could ensure that the sports got some shooting? Duck hunting in the shore areas around New York typically involved a headquarters boat, a tender boat, a sinkbox or permanent blind, a retriever, a set of decoys (with some live ones, depending on the setup), and, by the end of the century, bait. The pre-hunt preparation was not an errand the businessman-sport might handle on his lunch hour.

In fact, sport hunting often needed a market itself. As George Reiger, longtime *Field & Stream* conservation editor, wrote in *Wings of Dawn*, a history of American waterfowling: "On another occasion . . . Judge H. A. Bergen, tended by Richard B. Hamel, killed 98 black duck, 64 broadbill and one gadwall between 9 a.m. and 1 p.m." Clearly Judge Bergen, corpulent as he might have been, did not eat 154 ducks.

One of the least-appealing aspects of the wildlife crisis was the inclination of wealthy sportsmen to pin the blame for the destruction of fish and wildlife on everybody but themselves. Northern sports emphasized the threat posed by increasing numbers of immigrants. In the South, ex-planters blamed the newly freed African Americans, particularly for the decline in quail numbers. Wealthy sports around the country picked up this mantra. In *American Game-Bird Shooting* (1910), George Grinnell wrote, "A chief danger to the quail of the south is the non-enforcement of the game laws, and the market shooting by negroes, many of whom gun persistently almost the whole year round and are excellent shots." However, most other writing of the day claimed the exact opposite (see chapter 6), noting that it was in the South that the quail populations were strongest. Quail populations showed their greatest declines, on the margins of the quail range, where African Americans were fewer in number. African-American hunters and anglers (of whom there were many, particularly in the rural South) and poor white outdoorsmen generally pursued rabbits, squirrels, possums, raccoons, and, for fish, catfish and panfish—quarry that were considered less sporting but whose pursuit (particularly with inferior weaponry and tackle and limited access to private land) was more likely to result in food for the table.

And the whole country blamed the Indians.

Such blaming and stereotyping were essential elements of the larger upper- and middle-class white Protestant cultures of the late nineteenth century—no more mean spirited in the matter of who was to blame for declining stocks of fish and game than they were in any other element of American life, from education to housing to employment to team sports to common stereotypical constructions in print and visual media. Further, these prejudices were certainly not limited to wealthy sports in the United States, as Kipling's exhortation to "Take ye up the white man's burden" surely reminds us.

In truth, the problems of fish and wildlife stemmed from the shrinking habitat, a burgeoning market system, and the growing outdoor participation of all Americans. The middle class in particular read their Murray, and their numbers filled the fields and streams. And these new sports did not suffer for proper gear. Sears and Roebuck catalogs now reached every town. In the cities, department stores increasingly included sporting goods departments. Hunters and anglers were better equipped than ever before.

As twenty-first-century inhabitants of planet Earth, it's easy to see the nineteenth century as a time before technology dominated our lives and reality lasted longer than a twenty-four-hour news cycle. But in hunting and fishing, anyway, that is simply not true. Constant and significant technological change dominated the latter part of the nineteenth century. Nearly all the technological foundations of modern fishing—bait-casting rods and reels, bamboo rods, trolling and bait-casting, modern artificial lures and fly types (streamer, wet fly, nymph, dries, and poppers)—had been either invented or rounded out by this time. There are some significant exceptions—spinning reels and plastic baits, for example—but the foundations seem to have been in place by the 1920s.

The Victorian period was equally conducive to the development of modern hunting equipment. A man could have begun bird and duck hunting with a flintlock shotgun in the decade before the Civil War, for example, and closed out his career in 1902 with John Browning's humpback auto-5. The time span of this change is stunning, particularly when you consider how little the basic technology of the autoloader has changed in the century since.

Such improvements in firearms and ammunition had significant implications not only for the rise of middle-class enthusiasm for hunting but also for the future of game stocks. The same was true of fishing tackle and angling, though the change may not have been so dramatic, at least in terms of capacity for increasing the harvest. (It was hard to improve on the efficiency of nets and trotlines.) But new gear certainly made it easier to "take up" hunting and fishing as an adult. More people now had more access to newer equipment—and the constant prodding of media to get it and use it while there was still something left to git.

The final point to consider is the attitude Americans held toward the loss of wildlife. Most folks with any common sense resigned themselves to it—loss had been the experience of their lives. Be it the slaughter of war, the genocide of Native American tribes, or even the end of shad and salmon runs and the clearing of forests, loss had been their story. It was reflected in the sentimentality of the popular culture. In a remarkable bit of historical irony, the last herds of buffalo were killed by native peoples hired by the railroads—the hope being, in some official quarters, that as the Indians killed the buffalo they would also be killing themselves.

With such cynicism running government, with the commercial interests locked into place with the market system, with an advertising-magazine partnership recruiting more outdoorsmen and women by the day, the annual harvests of fish and wildlife only intensified. The land's native fish stocks, the waterfowl and birds, the deer, elk, and buffalo, barreled straight toward oblivion.

"The Means More Than the End"
ROBERT BARNWELL ROOSEVELT

Superior Fishing, 1865

George Bird Grinnell and Theodore Roosevelt were the two most important men in the American conservation movement. But the foundation for their influence actually began a generation earlier with Roosevelt's uncle, Robert Barnwell Roosevelt.

Robert Barnwell Roosevelt loved fishing and hunting. But there was more to him than indulgence. Barnwell's audacity and ebullient personality, his love of being the first to do something—be it the first Roosevelt to drive an auto or, at age thirty-three, the first American to publish a full-length book devoted to fishing—also made him the perfect individual to raise the banner of fish and wildlife in mid-nineteenth-century America. In particular, Roosevelt was able to use the strength of his personality to raise awareness of the plight of the nation's fisheries.

An example: Robert Roosevelt recruited Seth Green, the best fish culturist in the country, to help figure out ways to artificially propagate fish species decimated by commercial fisheries. Green, a more even-keeled, humble man, made an excellent teammate for the bombastic Roosevelt, whose motto was "Up guards and at 'em!" and who beat everyone to the punch. He'd earlier changed his middle name from "Barnhill" (after his mother) to "Barnwell," before political opponents could make hay of its connotations of manure. And it was probably well that he did, as he loved the battle. He rallied many to the cause of fisheries preservation, originated the first state fish commission (New York), and led it for twenty years.

In addition to the rousing style apparent in the Point Judith story—one that blended personal narrative, instructional advice, observational authority, and wildlife advocacy—Roosevelt introduced concepts of sportsmanship and conservation and tried to fuse excitement and restraint. This became the template for George Grinnell, Theodore Roosevelt, and other later conservationists. He emphasized that the sportsman "must look beyond the mere result to the mode effecting it regarding, perhaps, the means more than the end." This attitude would free sportsmen from their natural enemies of indolence and intemperance and mark them as a race of braver, stronger men, immune to the softness of modern city life. True, a man might be swept to his death fishing from that rock, as he wrote in his story of fishing at Point Judith. Oh well, as long as "it is in a good cause." Plus, he'll have "the sympathies of all . . . ardent brothers of the angle." He argued that sportsmen had a duty to their quarry, their "fellow creatures." Americans at the time considered fish and wildlife as either food or competitors for food; they really didn't have a third category for wild creatures. But Roosevelt did. The "fellow creatures" concept represented only one of his radical and critical first steps in saving wildlife from destruction.

In short, Robert Barnwell Roosevelt prompted a different way of thinking about the outdoor experience: If you wanted more people out there (and a good number in the nascent sporting community did, for philosophical and economic reasons) but you also wanted to build up the fish and game populations, both humans *and* fish (and game) had to be synchronous parts of the same overall system. There had to be a few rules. At the time, there were not very many.

And that was the gauntlet that one day Robert Barnwell Roosevelt's nephew, Theodore, and George Bird Grinnell so famously took up. But their famous partnership got off to a rocky start.

The problem? The mixed review that Grinnell, editor of *Forest and Stream*, gave Roosevelt's book *Hunting Trips of a Ranchman*. Grinnell praised the book's "freshness, spontaneity, and enthusiasm." But he upbraided Roosevelt for his tendency to generalize on limited data and observations—on antelope for instance. At the time, in 1886, Roosevelt was mostly known for being the twenty-five-year-old nephew of Robert Barnwell Roosevelt. True, the younger Roosevelt was a naturalist, author, and civil service director—a rising star in his own right. But he was by no means the man we look back on today. He was just starting out—and not pleased with any criticism from the older and esteemed Grinnell.

Roosevelt marched down to *Forest and Stream*'s offices and insisted on seeing the editor. Grinnell agreed to meet him. At first glance the expectation might be for fireworks, for the two men couldn't have appeared more different. Deliberate and learned, Grinnell was a jug-eared, mustached, wire of a man, inclined to listen carefully and respond with self-effacement. Roosevelt—a bespectacled, toothy, chest-first, stake-out-the-territory fellow—was speaking as he walked in the room. But Grinnell had an easy way about him, one that offered a soothing front for a prodigious intellect. Roosevelt believed in the honor and power of ideas and wanted the older man's approval. The two met for hours, reviewing the book point by point. They ended the meeting colleagues and friends.

They were, in fact, similar—each from long-standing wealth; each ivy educated (Grinnell at Yale; Roosevelt at Harvard); each a mediocre classroom pupil and brilliant field researcher; each a poor shot who loved hunting; and each a steel-willed, passionate lover of the wild. It was on the latter point that the two would combine and convince anglers and hunters to change the way they saw their place in the wild world.

"The Killing of the Game Is a Mere Incident"

GEORGE BIRD GRINNELL

"Climbing for White Goats," *Scribner's Magazine,* May 1894

Anthropologist, historian, naturalist, and editor of *Forest and Stream*, George Grinnell combined a scholar's mind with a boy's enthusiasm for the outdoors. A patrician lineage granted him access to power, but he wore his privilege lightly, his personal authority untainted with pretention. Born in 1849, Grinnell grew up on the grounds of the Audubon estate, roaming the woods with the great man's grandson, studying with his widow, Lucy. In spite of a year's suspension from Yale and a record of a gentleman's C's, Grinnell finagled his way on to a trip West with esteemed archaeology professor O. W. Marsh. Grinnell returned in body, but the adventures stole his heart.

An example: Attached to an army expedition deep into Indian country, the twenty-year-old Grinnell and a pal volunteered to kill ducks to feed the regiment because doing so meant a day-long jump-shooting trip. The boys shot ducks, got lost, started a prairie fire, backtracked twenty miles down the creek they'd just hunted, spent the night, awoke with hair still on their heads, and the next day relocated the regiment (which had presumed them dead).

Grinnell returned to the West the following summer, joining eight hundred Pawnees on their last buffalo hunt. Two years later he rode with Custer in search of Black Hills gold, before turning down the general's call to join his '76 Bighorn tour. In the meantime, Grinnell accepted the invitation of editor Charles Hallock to prepare a nature page for the new weekly, *Forest and Stream*. Several years later, in 1880, with the Grinnell family building a stock position in the publication and editor Hallock drinking heavily, the *Forest and Stream* board of directors "appointed" Grinnell editor. It was then, at age thirty-one, Yale PhD in hand, that George Grinnell began his life's work.

As author Michael Punke details in *Last Stand*, the fight to save the buffalo dominated the first fifteen years of Grinnell's time at *Forest and Stream*. He wrote countless editorials (as well as feature articles in other publications) advancing their cause. A talented organizer and tireless politicker, Grinnell pushed hard for the preservation of Yellowstone Park as a protected area (for buffalo, in particular), and the effort left him in a stalemate with powerful railroad interests that had their own designs on the territory. With the countdown to the buffalo's extinction under way, *Forest and Stream* reporter Emerson Hough exposed the release of a notorious poacher. Public outrage broke the legislative impasse and prompted the passage of The National Park Protective Act, which provided enforcement teeth to Yellowstone's game protection. President Cleveland signed the bill in May 1894.

That same month, Grinnell's article "Climbing for White Goats" appeared in *Scribner's Magazine,* and its publication in a general-interest magazine reveals the way he tried not only to spread the gospel of sportsmanship but also to articulate a new, less-consumptive way for the entire society to embrace its wild creatures. Grinnell reimagined sport hunting, embodying the new conservation ideas and showing them in action. He used himself as a subject, disclosing his own foibles as a way to balance any preachiness that might be lingering around such high ideals.

More than anything else, Grinnell showed that white goats had worth of their own—and that its origin lay not in their worth to us but in their own being. They had a scientific standing. The white goat "really . . . is not a goat at all, but an antelope—the analogue and not distant relative of the European chamois." To be sure, the white goat "has horns and a beard," and as a result "the western American, with his faculty for seizing on any salient characteristic, has called it goat." Its white coat proved a boon—not to us for our use but to the animal, in its high peak habitat, where snow, or patches anyway, exist nearly year-round and "it is mere accident if a white animal is seen by the hunter."

Thanks to the influence of Charles Darwin's *On the Origin of the Species,* Grinnell, both Roosevelts, and other conservationists worshipped the workings of the natural world, which they saw as beauty in action—and they tried to get the rest of the country to share that joy, to understand the innate, non-utilitarian value of all creatures. Grinnell, for instance, described the shaggy exterior of the animal's coat and the fine undercoat, explaining that "the long, coarse top-coat sheds the rain or the snow like a thatched roof while the under coat is thus protected from the wet and keeps the heat in and the cold out." The goat was a microcosm of our larger natural system, and for that reason it deserved our respect and study.

The white goat had its own character traceable to its own doing. It was pugnacious and, like any animal, made the ultimate use of its habitat. "The white the goat is the plodder" and when "alarmed [the] goat starts straight for the mountain-top at a rate which seems slow, often no more than a walk, but which is so steady and continuous that it soon carries the animal out of the way of danger." The goat seldom spooked "and seems to regard one from beneath its eyebrows." When it did sense danger, "it moves off either slowly pulling itself up over the rocks, or if the way is level, going with a swinging, sidelong gait, which reminds one of a pacing dog." The white goat's sure-footedness was due in part to its physiology, its "large hooflets." But it was also due to training. In fact, "Kids which have been captured when very young and kept in captivity have been observed to play at rolling down steep banks, repeating the tumble over and over again, as if practicing for the falls which they might be obliged to take later in life." In a sense, white goats embodied the very authenticity that people took to the woods to find.

Grinnell argued that these qualities made hunting the white goat a true challenge, "man's work." To pursue them in their habitat required "muscle, nerve, and experience in mountain climbing . . . for the labor of reaching the animal's home is extremely arduous." You had to be the goat, in other words. Or at least try.

Grinnell conceded that the shooting part was often the easiest aspect of the hunt, "for they are gentle and unsuspicious." But the unwritten is what matters here: It was not the shooting of the goat that made the sport; it was the process of entering and traversing the goat's habitat that elevated the hunter. A sportsman *became* real; he didn't start out that way. It was not a matter of vaunted status guaranteeing access; a man acquired the status he deserved through his behavior and dedication.

Grinnell detailed two hunts that occurred within a couple of weeks of each other, including "hand-over-hand work" on climbing. He confessed it hard to understand how any animal, "unprovided with hands or wings, could have ascended" these areas. The men inched along ledges but "two or three inches wide," and hugged rock walls, "clinging with tenacious grip to projections hardly large enough to support the finger-tips, our feet resting on little roughnesses in the rock which barely supported the toe." Grinnell admitted that "some of the work was trying to the nerves."

Eventually the men spotted a goat and, with the wind in their faces, made a successful stalk and shot and killed it. After skinning the animal and cutting up the meat and packing it, they descended to camp but came out on the wrong side of the valley and had to retrace their steps. Five hours of hiking later, "much of it in the dark—down ledges, among fallen timber and through swamps," they spied the firelight of their camp. It had been a long day.

A week or so later, another incident exemplified the rare self-consciousness Grinnell was able to exhibit on a hunt. "We approached [the goat] very cautiously from above, keeping the rock between it and ourselves, and tiptoeing along as quietly as possible over the clinking shale. When we were within perhaps ten yards of the rock, the goat walked from under it, on my friend's side." Grinnell's friend fired three times, and "The goat was mortally hurt, but at first kept its feet and ran." Below them the gulf was two thousand feet deep. The goat fell, regained its feet, but then began to slide into oblivion.

As it did, Grinnell becomes both writer and subject. As writer he tells us, "In vain; with staring eyes it looked toward the brink before it, holding back with all its might bracing itself, with stiffened outstretched legs, while still it slipped and slid onward toward the verge of the cliff." He puts himself in the picture, as subject, narrating from the scene: "We watched it with hearts full of pity now, although—so full is man of contradictions—we had felt no pity when the bullets struck it. A moment more and it had reached the brink and disappeared . . . into the abyss." The beauty of Grinnell's story is not only that he expresses and shows his empathy but that he reflects as it unfolds. No doubt he saw it as a teaching moment—using his own vulnerability to make the point.

Grinnell emphasized that "the killing of the game is a mere incident of this climbing for goats." The wonder of the hunt is the "freedom of the mountain life [and ultimately] the joy which comes from the surroundings. . . . The lofty mountains uplift the soul and the man lives in a mental atmosphere above that of his everyday life. . . . His companions are the changeless peaks, the far-reaching snow fields and the blue ice rivers. The voices that speak to him are the hoarse bawling of the mountain torrents, the shrill scream of the winds throwing themselves against the peaks, the thundering report of the moving glaciers, or the long drawn road of the snow slides. From lofty pinnacles he looks down on mountains and valleys and lakes, far below him, and is thrilled by feelings he cannot put into words. The very air he breathes is instinct with the solemn spirit of the mountains, and he is awed by its inscrutable mysteries.

"Moved by emotions which he but half comprehends, he rejoices in each varying aspect of the scene. . . . On these heights he exults alike in the sunshine and in the storm, for he has found nature pure and untouched, and for the time has become a part of it." When humans hunted with thoughts on matters apart from the pounds or numbers, this was the outcome—a stronger, deeper, more lasting awareness of their role in the larger system of all living things.

You can't help wonder to what extent the political slime on the ground, with the political work to pass the legislation on Yellowstone, inspired Grinnell to pine for the purity of the altitudes. The article certainly posed a counter-narrative to the destruction of the buffalo, and the submission of self to the quarry's world represented a clear departure from the conquest narrative that "settled" the frontier. The new sport hunter searched for the experience that might uplift his interiority, not his landscape or finances. Grinnell's genius was to make the joy of hunting the engine of conservation and articulate how one depended on the other. The key seemed to be restraint in killing and excess in muscle and nerve, a formula Christian America well understood. In our day, empathy for wildlife has been enlisted as a reason not to hunt; Grinnell believed it the very reason a person should. In so doing the hunter became "moved by emotions he but half comprehends" and not only appreciated nature but "for the time [had] become a part of it"—a goal we continue to pursue whenever we step into the outdoors.

"The Countless Camps He Has Made"
THEODORE ROOSEVELT JR.

"The White Goat," *The Wilderness Hunter*, 1893

If self-effacement and a studied response came naturally to Grinnell—like so many men of letters, he lived a life inside his own head in addition to the one he walked through every day—such a demeanor proved more elusive to his young friend, Theodore Roosevelt Jr. He was nothing if not a man of action, though it should be noted that he had been preparing all his life to become an authority on wildlife. Some folks considered his early devotion excessive— the cook, for instance, who announced that either the woodchuck went or she did, after Teedie ordered the slain rodent boiled with fur *on* so that he might examine *Marmota monax* in its natural detail. Before politics intervened, biology was his career path, ornithology his true love.

Like his Uncle Rob, TR was never one to hold his tongue, as was the case in his first meeting with Grinnell, but he never stopped learning either. If Grinnell was conservation's great teacher, Roosevelt was almost certainly its greatest student. He read everything, observed everything, tested everything. He defended strongly his beliefs and sought out people like Grinnell who knew more than he did. He constantly reevaluated his approaches. Effective arguments changed his mind. Such flexibility was absolutely vital, for the plight of American conservation was a dynamic situation, with different species in trouble, different regions under siege, different politicians in the tank, different interests clashing. It is interesting to look at Roosevelt's evolution, which is certainly evident in his writing. If he didn't hold his tongue, he didn't disguise his thinking either. His interest in discussion and debate played an important part in keeping his mind open.

Roosevelt's friendship with Grinnell had an important impact on this thinking, if only by forcing him to expand his field of vision to include the entire scientific community. A final influence on Roosevelt in the aftermath of *Hunting Trips of a Ranchman* was John Burroughs, a renowned naturalist who believed that all wild fauna and flora had worth. Roosevelt admired Burroughs's strong convictions, his immersion in the wild, the purity of his thinking.

Another frame of reference was Roosevelt's emotional constitution. Above all, he was a man of deep attachments to the American landscape— that was the most important part of his life in the 1880s. More than anything, he taught American readers how much a person could be enriched by his connection with nature. TR's love affair with the West became the great example for all sportsmen. If Grinnell felt his emotions shift through his hunt for white goats, Roosevelt allowed the outdoor experience to absolutely change—some would say, save—his life.

In the West, Roosevelt could both imagine himself in a resonant past and lose himself in the natural world. He had moved out there in 1883 when, as a newly married New York assemblyman, he had experienced the sudden, eviscerating loss of both his mother and his wife, each dying in his arms on the same day in the same house. He had been west on a trip with his brother, Elliot, several years earlier and found the land entrancing. Alone, wracked with grief at age twenty-five, he'd headed to the badlands and took up cattle ranching. He survived—thrived, in fact—eventually remarrying and writing *Hunting Trips of a Ranchman*.

TR's third book on hunting, *The Wilderness Hunter*, appeared in 1893 and shows the influence of ideas from Burroughs and Grinnell in a maturity and a reverence for the actual process of hunting that is simply not apparent in his earlier work. The trip description that follows, found in the chapter titled "The White Goat," probably took place in August 1889 in the Big Hole Basin in the heady early days of the Boone and Crockett Club, the conservation organization he created with Grinnell.

The new TR begins with a profile of his companion, "a friend of many hunts, John Willis, a tried mountain man" who "possessed that inexhaustible fertility of resource and unfailing readiness in an emergency so characteristic of the veteran of the border." Willis was a strapping ex–market hunter who claimed he taught TR to be a man. When they met years later, Willis reputedly called him "Theodore" (not "Colonel") and made fun of his pot belly. Others in attendance gasped, until TR roared with laughter, responding that he thought he'd taught Willis to be a Christian. The moment underscored features that balance Roosevelt's bravado; history might remember him as the ultimate individualist, but he was at his core a relational man who developed lasting friendships with his outdoor companions, regardless of their social class.

As in so much of TR's writing, he first paid homage to those who had come before him—not simply Willis but in the sacred western land itself. He passed a site of the soldier's fight with Native Americans, in this case "the Battle Ground, where a rude stone monument commemorates the bloody drawn fight between General Gibbons' soldiers and the Nez Perces warriors of Chief Joseph." He had only recently been working on his four-volume *The Winning of the West* and was more than ever certain of how hunting represented in miniature the larger victorious movement of White America to control the continent.

At the same time, new social elements showed up in his writing. TR was learning, perhaps as a writer, perhaps with experience, perhaps through his friendship with Burroughs and Grinnell, the worth of printed self-effacement. At one point the team of horses and supply wagon broke through the ice, and, with the wind whipping, an "absolutely unruffled" Willis began "perseveringly whistling the 'Arkansas Traveller.'" Later, still working, "when we were up to our waists in the icy mud, it began to sleet and hail, and I muttered that I would 'rather it didn't storm'; whereat he stopped whistling for a moment to make the laconic rejoinder, 'We're not having our rathers this trip.'"

After a day or more of hard work, the party approached a small stream, bordered "by mountains and the dense coniferous forest. They pitched a tent and built "a big fire of crackling, resinous logs." They covered the supplies with a tarp, arranged pine boughs for beds, erected platforms to dry meat, and "In an hour or two we had round us all the many real comforts of such a little wilderness home."

Roosevelt took a break to philosophize, and it is worth considering his ideas in light of the ones that Grinnell composed (at nearly the same time) about the beauty of the mountains at the end of his white goat story. The influence of Burroughs also seems to show: "Whoever has long roamed and hunted in the wilderness always cherishes with wistful pleasure the memory of some among the countless camps he has made. The camp by the margin of the clear, mountain-hemmed lake; the camp in the dark and melancholy forest, where the gusty wind booms through the tall pine tops; the camp under gnarled cottonwoods, on the bank of a shrunken river, in the midst of endless grassy prairies—of these, and many like them, each has had its own charm. Of course in hunting one must expect much hardship and repeated disappointment; and in many a camp, bad weather, lack of shelter, hunger, thirst, or ill success with game, renders the days and nights irksome and trying. Yet the hunter worthy of the name always willingly takes the bitter if by so doing he can get the sweet, and gladly balances failure and success, spurning the poorer souls who know neither." Of note might be that while Grinnell's point centered on how a person is moved by site or experience, Roosevelt's focused on creating a settlement, thinking back on other such settlements, and how his trip recapitulated the larger conquest and settlement of North America.

Roosevelt celebrated camp life, and the overall atmosphere starts to feel more like a cul-de-sac in Southport, Connecticut, than it does the Big Hole Mountains. A curious black bear cub "thrust its sharp nose through the alders a few feet from [Willis], and then hastily withdrew and was seen no more." And there were "smaller wild-folk" that were even easier in their camp presence; "the gray moose-birds and voluble, nervous little chipmunks made themselves at home in the camp. Parties of chickadees visited us occasionally." The smaller wild creatures filled in the tapestry of the outdoor experience, helped *you* feel at home *there*. Again, the point was not that readers were going to go white goat hunting, necessarily, but that a universe of wildlife existed everywhere. It was up to you to enter it, up to you to keep it alive and well.

As for the white goat hunting, Willis and Roosevelt scouted the peaks in front of them and "reckoned that the trip would take three days." They tramped all the first day, Roosevelt killing some spruce grouse for dinner with a stick—including one that "was partially saved from my first blow by the intervening twigs; however, it merely flew a few yards, and then sat with its bill open—having evidently been a little hurt—until I came up and knocked it over with a better directed stroke." It is difficult imagining Grinnell writing that sentence. But Roosevelt plunged ahead, called the spruce grouse "marvellously tame and stupid," and noted how "a man who has played much base-ball need never use a gun when after spruce grouse." In part, such a characterization fits with Roosevelt's belief in the survival of the fittest idea, in which he is the fitter.

But the description also distinguishes Roosevelt from Burroughs and Grinnell, both of whom reflected almost instinctively on their choices. Roosevelt's unguarded and uncensored self drew people to him, allowed others to see themselves in him, made him such a great companion, whether in print or in person. As Roosevelt's friend and diplomat Cecil Spring Rice later said, one must never forget "that the President is about six." And the exuberance and joy were here in the voice, and his reader never forgot that hunting and fishing were supposed to be fun, supposed to be somewhere to get carried away. You sense that at times like this, TR imagined he was camping with his children and growling like a bear or doing whatever it took to hear them squeal in glee while the log fire spit and crackled.

But there was still the matter of the goats the next day. Before long, the angle of assent steepened. Then the men headed upward "and passed a day of severe toil in climbing over, the crags . . . and when we got high among the peaks, where snow filled the rifts, the thinness of the air forced [TR] to stop for breath every few hundred yards of the ascent." They spotted some goats to stalk. They climbed over a mountain, and in the reverse of Grinnell's narrative, they eased "*down* from ledge to ledge. One would hold the guns until the other got safe footing, and then pass them down to him.

A goat, unaware of their presence, came into view. TR didn't see it for a moment, but then he spied it, "feeding on a terrace rather over a hundred and twenty-five yards below me." Like so many others taking a downhill shot, Roosevelt fired high. His "second bullet went through its lungs; but fearful lest it might escape to some inaccessible cleft or ledge [he] fired again, missing; and yet again, breaking its back. Down it went, and the next moment began to roll over and over, from ledge to ledge." Eventually, the goat lodged in a small evergreen, and TR had his trophy.

That night, after packing the meat down, after TR missed a shot at an eagle (but killed a goshawk), the hunters cooked some young spruce grouse for dinner. Then they promptly got lost heading back to the main camp and wandered around for twelve hours without food before finding it. In all, an excellent adventure.

To borrow a phrase from the 1970s, Roosevelt was in touch with his own feelings when in the outdoors. In reporting on them, he could be annoyingly self-congratulatory, but, as in this story, he could also be charmingly unaffected. What an open self he presented when in the woods, but what a fierce advocate of conservation he became when he returned home. These twin features became the model for the new sportsman, who went outdoors for the joy of the experience rather than the weight of the creel or game bag—and did his best to make sure the experience would remain joyful for those who followed.

TR was thirty-five years old when *The Wilderness Hunter* appeared, and this excerpt makes him seem older than his years. He appears to be writing about something else—the moments in time, the landscape, the special bond he would always have with the West, where he went following the deaths of his father, mother, and wife.

Now, a decade later, he was remade, with a family, including two new sons, and literary and political reputations, older certainly than his actual age of thirty-five. If anything, the mountain goat tale traces the arc of the Western experience that gave him a new lease: wading through mud, leaning on a few friends, building a wilderness home, ascending the peaks . . . and heading home again. Engaged with a true sporting spirit, outdoor trips can provide a narrative for how a person heals too.

"A Mass of Feathers and Bones"
GEORGE BIRD GRINNELL

American Duck Shooting, 1901

The transformations experienced by Roosevelt and described by Grinnell certainly set the bar for the collective aspirations of sportsmen who read their work. As continental populations of fish and wildlife continued their decline, such writing helped keep the pressure on legislatures to regulate the seasons and bag limits, as well as enact more forward-reaching laws such as the 1894 legislation protecting Yellowstone and the New York state laws protecting the Adirondacks.

Americans had historically resisted legislation that governed their interactions with the natural world. Understandable. Hunting and fishing provided a chance to break free of society. Fusing excitement and restraint provided an attractive resolution: It gave hunters and anglers a manly way to enter and love the outdoors—and remain on the side of the future of wildlife. A connection to the past also mattered because it certified outdoor sport as intrinsic to the country's American-ness, even if such a past was imagined and such a tradition was in fact created and constantly revised—as Grinnell and Roosevelt were busy doing.

Either way, connection to a mystical past was vital. Grinnell and Roosevelt did the only sensible thing: They enshrined hunting's past in the form of the Boone and Crockett Club—and used it to make money for wildlife's future. They hoped the group would highlight the crisis of wildlife and involve, in a more concerted fashion, the wealth of other like-minded individuals in conservation. The original roster of twelve members shows them to have both wealth and prominence in the sporting community. By its presence on the public and political scene, by connecting the power in society to the vulnerability of the country's wilderness, the club marked a milestone in the crusade for wildlife.

For Grinnell, Roosevelt, and others, this was an age of action. Being a sportsman came with responsibilities for the health of the populations of wildlife. Changing matters wasn't just a question of philosophizing but of actually doing. A good example of this concept in action, and how the men intended to use it, came in Grinnell's opposition to the spring shooting of waterfowl.

In the Northeast black ducks were the most important species of waterfowl, but they were not killed in big numbers like mallards were in the Midwest and South. The problem in the Northeast was one of many hunters killing a few birds each, not fewer hunters killing big numbers each. The implementation of a twenty-five-bird daily bag limit, which had an effect on the harvest of mallards, pintails, and various divers in other regions, would have no impact on black duck harvest. The way to limit black duck harvest was through the seasons.

Grinnell was always willing to take a one-down in a swap for a changed mind. As he wrote in *American Duck Shooting*, he learned his "lesson on this subject in Connecticut." The particular winter in question (1875–76) was so cold that "almost all the feeding and drinking places" had frozen over. Grinnell finally found a spot where several hundred black ducks were coming into an open spring at night, and he arrived at dark and shot several. But "when I got these birds in my hand I found them a mass of feathers and bones, for the breast muscles had shrunk away from starvation, so that it hardly seemed that the birds could fly." He was appalled and "show[ed] the birds to a number of local gunners, all of whom agreed that it was a shame to shoot birds that were having so hard a time, and no local gunners shot Black Ducks again that winter."

This anecdote represents the new attitude of Grinnell's generation toward government. The cynicism of the Gilded Age was giving way to progressive politics, a time when "shoulds" changed to "coulds." Grinnell, Roosevelt, and their colleagues thought they could change minds, particularly with regard to the importance of restraint as an element of the sporting creed. They believed that not only sportsmen could be educated to do the right thing but market hunters as well. As Grinnell explained, "I believe that if the unprejudiced opinions of marketmen could be taken on this point they would agree that birds shot in New England in winter and spring are too thin in flesh and too fishy in flavor to be a popular food, and the average gunner—if the matter were brought to his attention and explained to him—has too much sense of fair play to wish to destroy the birds under such conditions."

Whether Grinnell was actually right is hard to say. But laws did start to change, and with their enforcement, so did behavior. States began requiring licenses and hired game protectors. Some states outlawed market shooting, and the Lacey Act of 1903 outlawed the sale of illegally shot game. But these laws had little teeth, since wide-scale enforcement was difficult at best. Then in 1913 the Weeks-Maclean Bill conferred responsibility for management of waterfowl (and other migratory birds) on the federal government. However, enforcement remained a problem until the United States and Canada signed a treaty that included management of the migratory continental birds, at which point matters assumed a more concrete form. The Federal Migratory Bird Act of 1918 effectively ended spring shooting and market hunting, and when conservation officer Ray Holland arrested the Missouri attorney general in 1919 for violations and the matter went to the Supreme Court, the federal government's right to manage these matters became the law of the land. Bag limits were set at twenty-five per person (many states already had such limits).

As Grinnell implied in the above formulation, things got tougher when the fish or game in question was not some handful of feathers and bones but a more toothsome creature. In many ways, that had been the basis of "value" in all fish and game and, arguably, the reason populations were in such trouble. The idea that animals had value apart from what humans might subscribe to them was not only important but radical—particularly since market hunting (and fishing) played such an important role in commercial life at the time.

Nevertheless, the idea gained traction from the larger Darwinian notion that we are all creatures in a system. Emotionally, as both Grinnell and Roosevelt showed, hunting (and fishing) began with entering the wild universe of creatures, in which the human was a stranger, less equipped, for example, to negotiate cliffs than the goat or, to go back to Robert Roosevelt, to navigate in the ocean shoreline than the striped bass. Entering that universe and engaging a sporting experience on those terms rendered him open not only to the adventure of Adirondack Murray but also to change—in Grinnell's words, to be "moved by emotions which he but half comprehends." Animals were more than potential dinner. The better they were on their own, the better we became from their pursuit. In the end, we needed them a good deal more than they needed us.

"They Floated and Made Love"

H. S. CANFIELD

"The Death of the Red-Winged Mallard," *Outing*, January 1900

This slope can get slippery. Throughout the late nineteenth and early twentieth centuries, articles and stories abounded describing the rich interiorities of wildlife. Books such as *Black Beauty* and *Call of the Wild* romanticized animals, providing them with an emotional complexity that enthralled Victorian readers. Roland Pertwee's famous story "Fish Are Such Liars" poked fun at this idea, with trout bragging about how many anglers they had deceived. Other stories were anything but satirical.

In January 1919 *Outers' Recreation* published a story titled "Lucy, That Old Mallard Hen," about a hen mallard, winged by a hunter, that in turn (somehow) had the bad wing chewed off by a muskrat but managed to survive the winter, raise a brood, and find a home in the barnyard of the hunter who shot her in the first place. Thanks to her, the hunter was able to start a world-class duck farm and save himself and his family from financial ruin. That is one heroic hen mallard.

What the stories had in common was that they tried to get people to care about animals as something other than objects. Writer H. S. Canfield's "The Death of the Red-Winged Mallard," which appeared in the January 1900 issue of *Outing*, ratcheted matters up a notch, but did so in a different way—staying with the hunter's point of view, only presenting him as ignorant of the sanctity of wildlife until a series of strange encounters with a particular duck.

The story involved a good-hearted Texas market hunter named Robert Lee Briggs, who caught sight of very large drake mallard with bright red wings that was too intelligent to be shot. Brigg devoted his days to trying to kill that mallard, letting his market hunting business go all to hell in the meantime. He fashioned perfect blinds out of the weeds that mallards loved; he tried his best calls—one, his "swaller call," imitated the cluck of a mallard swallowing an acorn; another said, in mallard talk, "I have found a wonderful new kind of food in great plenty. Come and have a lot of it." He sent letters to all his duck hunting buddies, asking for advice, but only one wrote back and that was to find out "where he got his opium."

Briggs pursued the red-winged mallard for five years, and during that time the drake took a mate. Briggs watched them paddle about safely out of range, where "they floated and made love." Eventually Briggs managed to kill the hen. The next day he laid her out in front of his blind, and the heartsick red-wing drake, his "wife" floating, decided on a hero's death. Briggs obliged, as the drake hovered over the hen, shooting him through the head, throat, and heart. Briggs later told the tale to his buddies by the wood fire, even showing them the body of the red-winged mallard. But it was an empty, perplexing moment for Briggs, and "he felt hurt because the men did not praise him."

Such a story would be unimaginable in today's outdoor press. But the sport hunting community of 1900 welcomed challenges to the market system's premise that wild animals were only objects to be killed at will. Into such a world, on the first month of the new century, was "Red Wing" sent, a mystic mallard, an embodiment of all that was duck—a winged savior destined for unearned suffering that just might absolve wildlife killers of their sins. A Pilate in canvas, Robert Lee Briggs was almost certainly getting more than his fair share of the blame, even if his hands *were* bloody.

What animals could and could not do eventually became the subject of a national debate between sentimentalists such as Ernest Thompson Seton, future Scout leader, and realists such as Burroughs and (then President) Roosevelt. Could woodcock fashion casts from mud to heal their broken legs? Did crows send their young to school? And so on. For now it may be worth noting that the lead story in Seton's popular book *Animals I Have Known* (1898) told of a cunning, heroic wolf, Lobo, who eludes his captors until they kill his mate. In his grief, Lobo returns to the spot where he last saw her, and, well, we can imagine how it goes from there.

Of all the Nature Faker controversies, as the dispute came to be called, the most heated surrounded the Reverend William J. Long, a brilliant scholar and prominent minister and one of the most eminent—and imaginative—nature writers of his day. Handsome and mercurial, he suffered from periodic episodes of hysterical blindness and always seemed to be battling some sort of orthodoxy. He didn't hesitate to respond to Roosevelt and Burroughs when they questioned his anthropomorphic depictions of animal behavior, sightings that included foxes crossing railroad tracks to kill pursuing dogs, wolves rescuing children, crows trying one another in crow court, and so on. Burroughs and Roosevelt had many questions, mostly barbed: Why was Long always the only one to witness these remarkable behaviors? Because, Long retorted, Roosevelt was so busy killing animals that he was unable to see them as anything but targets.

The Nature Fakers debate ended in 1907 with Roosevelt bloodied and Long discredited—but not before it inspired a spirited public discussion regarding the place of wildlife in the modern world. Long's books, read in homes and schools across the land, have continued to influence our understanding of animals ever since. Roosevelt even read the stories to his children (as fables); Ronald Reagan remembered Long's *Northern Trails* as his favorite childhood book.

Interestingly, Long enjoyed shooting and in fact wrote for *Outing* about such topics as hunting the auerhahn, a rare German grouse. It might seem odd that a writer with Long's views would be welcome in the signature outdoor publication of the time; but sport hunters of the day would probably have thought it odd if such a writer were not. After all, sportsmen functioned as the ecologists of their day and loved to study questions of animal behavior and sentiment. Moreover, as excessive as Long's views were, he erred on the side of animal nobility and intelligence. Most sport hunters believed that commodifying wildlife posed a far greater threat to their sport than did telling a few stretchers about how smart a fox was. In fact, in the article on hunting the auerhahn, Long emphasized that a man can be both hunter and a naturalist—just not at the same time. In the future he planned to return to German woods without a gun so that he could study the bird's mating display. Long would be the first to observe the behavior and report on it, as "no human eyes have yet seen it." TR must have loved that one.

"Human Wits against Wildfowl Instinct"
J. R. BENTON

"A Winter Day with the Ducks," *Outing*, December 1897

Conferring such value on animals did a great deal for sport hunting and fishing. Sportsman could reframe "scarce" as "rare" and allow the various species of fish and wildlife to take on value apart from their meat. For the auerhahn hunt, for instance, Long traveled to Germany to shoot a single grouse. The problem with "rare" was that it conferred little on the pursuer. It had more of the "white elephant" to it. Better were concepts such as "elusive" or "exhaustive," as in the case of the white goat hunts, which allowed the hunters and anglers to derive affirmation from their choices and efforts during the hunting or angling excursion.

The limitation of those constructions came in their relevance to the experiences of middle-class readers, who were the ones taking to the woods and waters in great numbers. As much as TR or Grinnell might write helpful how-to tips for stalking white goats or, for that matter, how big-game anglers such as Charles Holder might explain how to handle a tuna's first run, most Boston cost accountants were not measuring their dens for white goat rugs or wall space for stuffed bluefins. Their fish and game opportunities were far more humble, even if their ardor received an initial stoking from grand tales of the Rocky Mountains or Pacific Ocean.

Increasingly, stories of challenging outdoor trips came to center on the less-exotic, even formerly undesirable species closer to home. The native brook trout, for example, had disappeared from most rivers and streams close to cities. (Brown trout, stocked in 1883, would be more common after the century's turn.) But bass were quite available, and increasingly stories of fishing for them appeared in the magazines and books around the turn of the twentieth century.

As for hunting, the pickings were slimmer. Thanks to land clearing and market hunting, white-tailed deer had disappeared from New York and New

England by the 1890s, except in the central Adirondacks and northern Maine. Throughout the region, grouse were depleted, pheasants yet to be stocked. Migrant, bottom-shelf waterfowl such as fish ducks, old squaws, whistlers, and buffleheads escaped the evisceration of local flora or hunting pressure and were, so to speak, the only "sporting" game in town for many Northeastern hunters. This fact is reflected in a lively piece published in the December 1897 issue of *Outing* titled "A Winter Day with the Ducks."

J. R. Benton's tale began with a couple of central facts: The shooting was difficult, and there wasn't a whole lot of it. Otherwise, what a day to be alive. Benton and his buddy have plans to jump-hunt a river, the challenge being that "the birds, naturally shy, have been trained by the experiences of autumn and early winter until they are almost unapproachable."

The limited number of ducks and their wariness heightened the men's desire to get one. As it did to Roosevelt and Grinnell, the hardship only quickened their step, for it was January cold in nineteenth-century New York, and "the creaking snow and tingling air confirmed the thermometer report of 'five below.'" The sport was a joyful test pitting "a day's trial of human wits against wildfowl instinct."

The morning opened with a heavy mist due to the cold air. By a millpond they jumped eight ducks, and with four collective barrels, they got one. One fish duck in the bag.

The remaining ducks set in a quarter mile downstream, and Benton decided to try and flush them, while his buddy stayed in hopes they would come back. Benton walked the quarter mile, then stooping, slinked along. He dropped to his hands and knees before eventually falling to the snow and "lying flat and crawling like a snake." As Benton admitted, "It was cold work, but I cautiously wriggled along until within fifty yards of the stream; then I leaped up and ran swiftly towards the birds, or rather toward the place where they had been." Turned out they were way upstream and flying away. As Benton watched the ducks disappear, he "really began to realize that it was a cold day."

The men jumped and shot one bufflehead the rest of the morning and then heard or saw nothing for the afternoon except for one hound (heard), one fox (inferred from tracks), and one snowbird flock (positively identified). Early on in the hunt, Benton claimed to have been delighted that "the shooting is most difficult." Maybe. But you sense that he had darker thoughts by late afternoon. Benton and his partner faced the emptiness and bleakness of no more ducks, no more chances. What would he give up to see a duck? He seemed to be a praying man; maybe a small vow. . . . Dots on the horizon. A flock of fish ducks materializing out of the heavens, flying the river past the two men. They shot—and, yes, two more in the bag. Merganser stew tonight.

They are now in cruise control, crunching across the snow, whistling their way home, until they take a shortcut across the ice, as though they have never heard of Jack London or building fires in the winter. Upon the bordering snowbank they experience a "sudden yielding sensation, a quick implosive movement" and "descend through three feet of exceedingly cool water on the way down." The men stand in shock, "while the chill liquid gurgled cheerily into [their] boots."

As if to echo Roosevelt standing waist deep in icy water on the way to white goat hunting, Benton's companion "grimly remarks that there were several ways of going ducking, and [they] were trying them all on." They step lively, matching their "gait to the musical accompaniment of the water sloshing in [their] boots." Three fish ducks and a bufflehead—it doesn't take much to make the sportsman of 1897 happy. Audubon would have no doubt suggested a trotline.

Part II

Sporting Traditions in American Life, 1880–1925

One evening in the summer of 1899, a nattily dressed, twenty-four-year-old financial clerk named George La Branche, cast fruitlessly over some trout swirling at the surface of the pool where Mongaup Creek joined Willowemoc Creek in the Catskill Mountains. Actually, the evening was no different from others. Every night the trout rose regularly, while La Branche drifted various wet flies past their noses. He later wrote "that their constant rising to everything but my flies exasperated me to the point of wishing that I might bring myself to the use of dynamite."

La Branche remembered an article he'd saved from the *Fishing Gazette* (a British publication) on the very topic of rising trout. Later that night he studied the article and made some adjustments, which involved "doctoring" the wet flies so that they had upright wings. La Branche returned the following evening—only to find "a boy disturbing the water by dredging it with a worm." La Branche "lured away [the lad] with a cake of chocolate." Before long, the fish began rising.

He cast, and the fly drifted toward the fading rings—and disappeared in a bubble. As La Branche later wrote, "Instinctively I struck, and to my astonishment found that I was fast in a solid fish that leaped clear of the water. The leaping of this fish was a new experience, as I had never seen a trout jump as cleanly from the water." It turned out to be a rainbow (La Branche's first). American fly fishing would in many ways follow a similar trajectory.

Several years later, William Harris' *The Basses: Freshwater and Marine* (1905) included a chapter titled "Bass in the Beaverkill," written by well-known angler Louis Rhead. Like La Branche, Rhead enjoyed fishing the Catskill rivers, but for bass as well as trout. Whenever he fished the Beaverkill for bass, often from Junction Pool downstream to Cook's Falls—about twenty miles down the Willowemoc from where La Branche fished—he could "fill a basket." He used flies, but if they were refused, "young lampreys may be dug out of the sandy reaches of the river side." The lampreys "afford the best . . . fishing"; i.e., the quickest way to get a bass on the hook.

La Branche, by contrast, returned night after night to the difficult fish, hooked by their indifference. His response was to find an article about how to catch them; Rhead was to start digging too, though with a shovel.

Figuring out how to fool the trout was the fun part. But with bass, anglers focused more on where (possibly, how) to find them. Their ambivalence was to be circumvented; the fun started once you had them on the line.

These different traditions have, in the century since, come to define angling for trout and bass. Their origins, as well as those of the traditions of hunting for birds, waterfowl, and big game, are the subjects of Part II.

The American sportsman was an active participant in this development. He (and, to a lesser extent, she) had choices of publications and books to read, places to go (and by the end of the period, choices in how to get there and where to stay), types of equipment to use and different ways of acquiring it (should he tie his flies or buy them?), types of quarry to pursue, and various methods to use. He had licenses to buy, outfitters to consider, dog breeds to mull over, boats to rent, time to allot to his various outdoor indulgences. All of which suggests that the American sportsman of this period was first and foremost a consumer, often conspicuous, hardly reluctant, alternately groomed and teased by many of the same private and public operations lurking about today. He or she enjoyed the identity that came with the various forms of participation in the sporting life. (Oh, so you train bird dogs?) This section of the book looks at the various elements in that identity and considers the ones that men and women adopted and rejected as they created the traditions of their favorite sports.

The stories in Part II also tell us a good deal about the essence of the various quarries these men and women pursued and how the hunters and anglers arranged their particular outdoor experiences—not only to give sportsmen and women the biggest creels and bags but also to provide the participants with the fullest meanings. What were the tensions within each sport? What did men and women want the sport to be? In short, what traditions emerged from these various outdoor activities? They created the outdoor world we enjoy today.

Finally, these stories reflect the cultural tensions of the time and as a result become history themselves. As the larger society changed, sometimes at a dizzying pace, the outdoor adventures and activities did so as well. At times hunting and fishing predicted social trends, gave them the space to occur more dramatically than they might have otherwise.

These are the attitudes expressed in print. What anglers actually did was a different question. The example of contrasting tales of glory on the Willowemoc and Beaverkill offer a good example. Smallmouth bass can certainly develop an indecipherable case of lockjaw; unlocking the mysteries of their behavior became one of angling's great joys. And a good many trout fishermen over the past 115 years have flipped rocks in search of bait to use when flies didn't work or, like my Great Uncle Frank, tipped their Royal Coachman with a half garden worm, "just to sweeten it a little." The point is more that the printed portraits of the two species took different paths, and following those paths led to different traditions surrounding the fish and the fishing.

CHAPTER 5

"The Best of a Man's Life"

BIG GAME, 1885–1912

Twenty-five-year-old Theodore Roosevelt and his companion, Frank Merrifield, looked down at the "huge, half-human footprints." They seemed to be staring back up at them. Grizzly. A big one. As Roosevelt later wrote, the tracks "gave me rather an eerie feeling in the silent, lonely woods, to see for the first time the unmistakable proofs that I was in the home of the mighty lord of the wilderness." That night, "a ruder noise—a kind of grunting or roaring whine," woke them. The men grabbed their rifles to give chase, but it was too dark.

The next morning, Merrifield and Roosevelt followed the grizzly's trail and found the remains of a black bear they had killed the day before; *remains* being the operative word, for "the grizzly . . . had utterly devoured the carcass, with cannibal relish."

Merrifield and TR followed his trail "over the soft, yielding carpet of moss and pine needles." As Roosevelt recalled, "every little sudden noise sent a thrill through me. . . . Two or three of the ravens that we had scared from the carcass flew overhead, croaking hoarsely; and the pine tops moaned and sighed in the slight breeze—for pine trees seem to be ever in motion, no matter how light the wind."

They fought their way through the thatched branches and "crossed what was almost a breastwork of fallen logs." Merrifield sank to a knee and, "his face fairly aflame with excitement," turned to Roosevelt. TR "strode past him" and "there, not ten steps off, was the great bear, slowly rising from his bed among the young spruces." The bear apparently heard the men but could not identify them. Roosevelt drew a "bead fairly between his small, glittering, evil eyes [and] pulled the trigger. Half-rising up, the huge beast fell over on his side in the death throes, the ball having gone into his brain, striking as fairly between the eyes as if the distance had been measured by a carpenter's rule." Roosevelt noted that "the whole thing was over in twenty seconds from the time I caught sight of the game; indeed, it was over so quickly that the grisly did not have time to show fight at all or come a step toward us." Any disappointment quickly gave way to other feelings: "It was the first I had ever seen, and I felt not a little proud, as I stood over the great brindled bulk [later estimated at 1,200 pounds], which lay stretched out at length in the cool shade of the evergreens."

For Roosevelt this was an important moment. Courage was a part of his constitution, and testing it mattered to him. This story appeared in *Hunting Trips of a Ranchman*, written when TR was twenty-five and with no military service to claim. Nor could he reference his father, Theodore Sr., whom he deeply admired but who had hired a substitute during the Civil War out of deference to his Southern wife, Mitty. And though Theodore Sr. had performed a valuable service in helping institute a pension system for Union soldiers, his civilian status weighed on his son. Killing a bear at ten paces didn't erase his embarrassment, but it was a step in the right direction. Placing his life in a precarious situation was essential if he was going to encourage readers to try it for themselves.

Hunting Trips of a Ranchman, his first hunting book, blended Roosevelt's reverence for America's frontier-military past with knowledge of wildlife and wired it all with his joy of the hunt. The chapter on grizzly bears was certainly a rousing Roosevelt exhibition that began with a salute to his predecessors, explaining that the sport was certainly very much safer than it had been at the beginning of the nineteenth century. "The first hunters who came into contact with this great bear . . . belonged to that hardy and adventurous class of backwoodsmen which had filled the wild country between the Appalachian Mountains and the Mississippi." They handled their bears with small-bore rifles that "had done excellent service as military weapons in the ferocious wars that the men of the border carried on with their Indian neighbors, and even in conflict with more civilized foes, as at the battles of King's Mountain and New Orleans." But these guns were light weapons for the job at hand. After all, "the grisly [was] a beast of far greater bulk and more savage temper than any of those found in the Eastern woods." Small wonder the bear developed such a fearsome reputation.

At the time TR wrote about the grizzly hunt, he was only a couple of years from starting what would become his most ambitious work, the four-volume *The Winning of the West*. You can sense that germination in this story as he treads silently through the dangerous woods. The grizzly hunt reveals a foundational element in the big game tradition—the importance of the hunter facing down the fearsome, adventuresome, and exotic. This particular tradition extended to the corners of the earth, followed the "explorer" impulse of the turn of the twentieth century, and usually included some element of conquest, the hunter representing his government or people as a wilderness soldier. The civilizing influence must never shirk; otherwise savagery wins. But wilderness must be preserved—as test grounds to keep civilization strong.

Dangerous game was one important path in American big game sports. The second main path celebrated the white-tailed deer. This tradition developed later, because excessive hunting and loss of habitat had devastated the continental deer population. Whitetails had numbered thirty to forty million at the time of European contact, but dropped to as low as three hundred thousand by the turn of the century. Deer hunting, that timeless index of the continental bounty, retained a fervent following, even with the season closed for years in certain states that today have herds of deer eating flowers in backyards. As the deer began to come back, their hunting likewise began to acquire definition and tradition through an increase in the number of stories and articles.

First, the corners of the earth.

"On the Frontiers of Savagery"
WILLIAM WILLARD HOWARD

"Hunting the Jaguar in Venezuela,"
The Century Magazine (illustrated monthly), July 1897

Hunting for dangerous game attracted increasing numbers of upper-class hunters in Western nations in the late nineteenth century. The sport often seemed a corollary to the general exploration inherent in imperialist expansion. It would be a stretch to call big-game hunting patriotic, but the thinking did go something like this: Any game animal with sharp teeth represented the danger of the wilderness, which in turn meant *a danger to* the civilized world, and could therefore use some taming and Christianizing—at the least. The following story about jaguar hunting in Venezuela, which most Americans saw themselves as more or less owning, since it was in our hemisphere, followed such a trajectory, with a bit of role reversal along the way.

"Hunting the Jaguar in Venezuela" no doubt enjoyed an enthusiastic audience. With the North American frontier officially "closed" as of 1890, the curtain had lifted on a second act of virgin land—this southern expanse bursting with lushness and diversity and ferocity, governed by a noble elite, guarded by a legendary aboriginal population. Latin America comprised a hemispheric Eden, bathed, as one cultural historian has put it, "by some of the waters of the same flood that had driven Noah on to his ark," visited by the first Europeans. Their descendants, the contemporary elite of Spanish heritage, known for their elegant demeanor and internecine throat slashing, had many admirers among wealthy American sportsmen, including George Bird Grinnell, who, for example, characterized one well-born Mexican gentleman as having "the polish and suavity of a real hidalgo." TR, for his part, noted that "in civility and courtesy we can well afford to take lessons from them."

But things did not begin auspiciously for the expedition, which had been well publicized. Howard's hunting buddy got cold feet—brought on by dinner the first night, explaining with "perhaps unnecessary vehemence," his disgust with iguana. Howard believed his companion's return prudent, for traveling in the Americas did not seem propitious for any man who would "turn his back upon the great lizard of the South."

Howard's contact was a certain general sequestered for reasons having to do with "the benefit of his health, and the incidental protection of his neck." The general would have loved to have joined Howard on his excellent spear-hunting adventure, but he was on Injured Reserve with "an unhealed wound on his left arm." There seemed no point in delaying, Howard realized, for "Possibly the general's cousin, twice removed, would have died, or his brother-in-law's father would have taken the fever, if the unhealed wound had not been convenient."

The general pointed Howard to a certain skillful, loyal native named Terife who'd served as his guide during the recent "revolution which had caused the general's retirement to Cucuta." Howard was taken aback upon meeting Terife, for he "was only a Guajira Indian, and a half-breed at that, and the general was about as proud a man, even in defeat and exile, as one would expect to find on the frontiers of savagery." But Terife's knowledge of the wilderness and wildlife quickly gained Howard's confidence.

So it was that several days later, in the pre-dawn darkness, Howard was following at Terife's heels as he stole along a faint trail, the native guide's only armaments a short spear. Many native people in South America hunted jaguars, but typically with the seven- to eight-foot "long" spear, which was planted in the ground as the jaguar began its spring so that the jaguar impaled itself upon completing the leap. Terife belonged to the northern hunters who used the short spear, a four-footer. "Anybody," word on the jaguar circuit had it, "can hold a spear so that a tiger will jump on it, but only a Guajira [like Terife] can use the short spear." Bunch of pantywaists, those southern jaguar hunters.

In the blackness, "the vines and branches were wet and suggestive of reptiles . . .Terife paused, held up a warning finger, and said, 'Quiet. . . .'" As light spread over the jungle, he dropped off Howard on a rock cropping and melted into the jungle in search of the jaguar. Howard glanced around, noticed tufts of hair and bones, and realized that he was sitting on "a lookout used by tigers when lying in wait for their prey."

Howard sat and kept watch. "The stillness, the loneliness, of the forest had something of the foreboding of evil in it . . ." He heard the raucous calling of birds. Terife materialized. The tiger was near, he told Howard, who found himself exhaling in relief "that it was no worse, although what could be worse in these tropical solitudes than a tiger, and a big tiger at that, I was not prepared to say."

Terife stood in the path, adjusted his kerchief, and rechecked the spear point. Watching Terife, Howard thought of a Roman gladiator waiting for the lion. Only in this instance the cruel emperor who has him fight for viewing pleasure "was a curious American who had risked his own life, and the life of an honest Indian, merely that he might write the story afterward for the entertainment, not of the lords and ladies of the blood-stained Colosseum, but of kindly men and women in Christian America."

The flock of call birds, circling above the jungle, worked its way closer. Any second. Suddenly a flash of yellow and brown! Terife slumped. The tiger had seen him and turned away.

They tried without success the next morning.

Then, the third morning, the tiger returned. He padded down the path, "a great brown-and-yellow beast, spotted and ringed with black." He glanced "upward at the screaming birds." He was "king of all beasts south of the Isthmus of Darien, and matched in ferocity and courage only by the wounded grizzly bear of North America." He knew he was beautiful.

Suddenly he stopped, paw raised. He had seen the hunter. Slowly now, head slung low, he eased closer. Terife waited, "a sort of bronze image that might have stood neglected in the wilderness since the days of the Chibchas whom Quesada conquered" in the sixteenth century.

Crouching, the tiger halted, "his giant muscles quivered in tense knots, his red tongue curled stiffly between his keen fangs, his tail thrashed viciously, and his spotted skin moved in bristling waves of anger, as a quick squall races across standing grain." What to make of the still creature in front of him? He sniffed at his feet. And "Like a steel spring the great beast recoiled. The strange, still thing was flesh and blood." He pulled back, gathered himself and . . .

Terife whisked his kerchief from his neck and tossed it in front of the cat. The square of white cloth fluttered through the air. The jaguar lifted its upper torso and pawed at it playfully. Terife jammed the four-foot spear into the jaguar's exposed throat—and released it. Tiger and spear rolled in the dust, blood spurting. He was dead.

Howard knows all this, not because he saw it but because he was told it. After light had come, he'd ventured forth from camp and "found Terife . . . beside the vanquished jaguar." Terife told him about the encounter in all of its detail, at which point Howard "leaned across the stiffening body of the tiger, and grasped his hand."

It was now Howard's exotic story to tell. Numerous reviews heralded this tale, with *The Literary News*, for example, calling it "a thrilling story." Credit Howard with stepping aside so that the reader could join the intrepid guide on the path and, even more impressively, credit him with creating a narrative persona that became the perfect foil to Terife's heroism.

Howard told the truth about who was brave. Sailor, adventurer, writer, editor, businessman, he served humanitarian causes throughout his life, playing important roles with the Red Cross in Cuba and Galveston and later during World War I. Some observed that Howard ended up benefitting financially from many of his "altruistic" efforts (through gaining the trust of beleaguered locals and buying land at reduced prices, according to one historian). If so, that lay in the future. For now he seemed without apparent agenda, poking fun at himself wherever possible.

To be sure, Howard fitted Terife with the obligatory stoic demeanor and bronze features and mystical hunting prowess. The native was stealthy, unerring, philosophical, embodying the mysteries of the jungle, materializing and disappearing as easily as another man might turn his head. For Americans who had just finished eviscerating the wilderness and native peoples of the lower part of their own continent and were finding themselves nostalgic, Terife was a canning jar full of 100-proof. He speared jaguars. And not with some wussy eight-footer, the spearing world's equivalent of an unplugged 10-gauge. His favorite chillin' rock was the front porch of the jaguar's house. (Can Pooh come out and play?) American men—Howard's readers—spent their weekends afield trying to sneak a taste of wildness into their cubicle selves. In the meantime, a few printed moments of waiting for the jaguar with the heroic Terife, while the white sport is back in bed, offered the literary equivalent of attending one of Buffalo Bill's Wild West shows, or perhaps even mounting an imaginary savagery-taming expedition, albeit from the comfort of the living room while waiting for dinner.

"Slid into Eternity"

ISABEL SAVORY

A Sportswoman in India, 1900

Among the most intrepid of the explorer sports was a young English woman named Isabel Savory, who traveled throughout India and wrote about her adventures in *A Sportswoman in India*, a book read avidly on both sides of the Atlantic.

Born in Surrey in 1869, Miss Savory came into wealth upon the death of her father in 1886. In preparation for this book, she traveled through India for a year, unescorted in a party of family and friends. (One historian counts the person referred to as S. as her husband, but there is no evidence of marriage in the available documents pertaining to her life; it is more likely that S. is her brother.) Savory the explorer had media appeal. The following appeared in *Literary World:* "To picture Isabel Savory think of a slight girlish figure, with a sweet, gentle, demure, feminine face, surmounted by a huge cork helmet of the most domelike height and eaves-like breadth, and supported by a man's shirt, collar, necktie, and coat, with lower garments which the frontispiece leaves largely to the imagination with room for uncertainty as to whether divided skirts or baggy pantaloons are the finality; a woman who justifies cigarette smoking by her sex, and herself apparently enjoys the unwomanly indulgence. . . ."

Savory the writer had many fans as well, particularly middle-class women. Considerable acclaim greeted the publication of *A Sportswoman in India*. *The Daily Chronicle* opined, "No better-written book of Indian sport has come our way through 10 years. Boar, bear, tiger—this gallant sportswoman faced them all." Savory's favorite, by her own admission, was the boar; she couldn't get enough pig-sticking, as it was called, and devoted the first chapter of the book to its thrills. This was not your mother's travel writing.

From several weeks of serious pig-sticking—think polo with spears and boars rather than mallets and balls—to camping and hunting across the subcontinent in a turn-of-the-twentieth-century version of *Planes, Trains and Automobiles*, Savory knew how to get the most out of a hunting vacation. A particularly revealing passage occurs in chapter IV, titled "Chamba into Kashmir." At that point in the narrative, Savory's party included another female traveler, M., the above-noted S., and innumerable servants (though no "lady's assistant").

Savory was a competent, self-aware hunter and an even better narrator. Thoughtful: "Women do not shoot with their husbands and brothers nearly as much as they might do . . . [and] in the present day, when so many of them care for a free life, I wonder that the majority of those should still live a conventional one." Self-aware: One must be "the right sort of women." Pig-sticking and other forms of hunting, however invigorating, might leave more proper readers sitting on their hands. Earlier in the century, none other than Queen Victoria had written about hunting in a letter to her daughter, noting that "it was acceptable for a woman to be a spectator, but only fast women shot."

The times were changing, however. Women in England (and America) rebelled against their constrained lives, pushed back against the prevailing notion that they remain "an angel in the house," deprived of activity in the open air. Male physicians had begun to concede the benefits of *some* exercise, though few would have signed off on pig-sticking.

In the chapter "Chamba into Kashmir," Savory and her party set out and followed "mountain trails, our faces set towards the 'back of beyond.' There was no feeling like it! To be in your oldest of old clothes, to feel you are going out of the reach of letters, telegrams, and the faces of the civilised world; free to go and to do exactly as the spirit of the moment moves you; only yourself to answer to."

The ascent steepened, and Savory and others dismounted. The sun grew very hot. Finally, after twelve hours, the guide, Jemadar, "announced we were there, and the Kulel bungalow was before us." The party collapsed in exhaustion, and near the outbuildings "S. found the boy (one of the servants) weeping on account of the long march." Historians of India's later colonial period have noted that travelers saw themselves as representatives of the empire. And here Savory rose to that occasion—taking up the very gauntlet that Kipling had so famously thrown down. "A diet of rice and butter does not produce fine physique, and the ordinary servant is lazy, flabby, muscleless," she observed. "It thoroughly disgusts one to see men [in this case the weeping boy] behaving like children."

Savory embraced her Britishness in all its aspects. She stood shoulder to shoulder with S. to kill a bear and save a badly wounded servant—as if to reaffirm the beneficence of the British colonial system. Her English heart beat strongest in Kashmir, where in 1879–80, British forces suffered several humiliating defeats. If nothing else, Savory guarded against letting her femininity cloud the clear-eyed work of empire maintenance.

That night they prepared for bed with zinc baths and then slept the wonderful sleep of the just. They arose the next morning at 4 a.m. to squeeze in most of the hiking before the full heat of the day. With the elevation, the air cooled. Whenever the women asked their two *shikaris* where their camp would be, they "invariably pointed up at the snows far above our heads, and remarked, '*Ooper.*'" As Savory and her party began the last leg, they realized there would be "a good deal of *ooper* for the following morning."

The climb no longer had a path. The sun burned with "a universal glitter which I never saw till I came to India," and the scenery was exceptional, as "mountains rose like castellated and embattled walls round us . . . rising into the intense, unclouded blue sky. . . ." Savory was aware of her place in all this, "probably the first European woman who had ever penetrated as far into Chamba." The party reached the camping spot, the servants struck the tents, and they are kicking it.

Although Savory's tale unfolded in the tradition of military-hunting hero adventure, with an exotic setting, imperiled journey, and dramatic moments, she maintained her own voice and told her own story, one that seemed less about achieving and more about being. "It is the *only* life," as she exclaimed. She and M. discussed tea and mutton sandwiches, *while* they tracked goats fifteen thousand feet in the air. They less performed for an audience than embraced their freedom as two friends keeping an intermittent conversation going over days in the woods. Men of course did the same, but such conversations generally ended up on the cutting room floor, as if including them in the public narrative would have made the hunters seem less serious and, as a result, less manly. Savory had no dog in that fight; for her it was all about the joy of the hunt.

After breakfast, bathing in a sunrise over snowcapped mountains, "a light that never was on land or sea," the party hit the slopes for a bit of tahr hunting. The sheer ledges "afford scant foothold [as they] sank abruptly into rough, perpendicular precipices far below." The only way to negotiate was to hand the shikari their rifles and "hold on with our eyelids." They would inadvertently dislodge a loose bit of rock that would toll off the cliff. They would wait for the long silence before the sound of it striking more rock, "suggesting an unpleasant 'drop.'"

Then one of the shikaris spotted two male tahr, with their shaggy, gray-brown hair and short curled horns and "great, grey beards [that] almost reached their knees." Savory, M. and S. began their stalk, at points having to cut their own footholds. One shikari slipped and "came sliding—gliding—down the slope straight on to [Savory], in spite of all his efforts to stop himself with his finger-nails and stick." He took her legs out from under her, and the two would have "slid into eternity" but for the efforts of the first shikari, who managed to hold on to them. "But it was an uncomfortable moment," Savory admitted.

The stalk continued down to a valley below and then back up the cliffs on the other side. Working together, Savory and M. edged to within fifteen yards of the tahr, and M. missed the nearly point-blank shot. She fired again as the tahr bounded off out of sight. "M. looked more like suicide than anything," Savory noted, "and the *shikari*'s pity was so many coals of fire.

But not so fast. A blood trail showed that M. had hit the tahr on the second shot. It lay dead at the bottom of a steep drop. The hunt ended up glorious, and as Savory noted, "it is hard to imagine anything more grateful and comforting than reaching one's own little tent after a hard day's work." The "glorious" effort was "worth a caravan-load of doctor's stuff, and does give one an appetite!" The cold mountain air seemed to invigorate everyone, as they built a roaring fire and bundled up with "woollen gloves, caps, and flannel coats which went over everything."

The elemental nature of the experience certainly touched Savory, but she did remember where she was from. As she recalled, the party gathered around "a little rough camp-table," with no cloth, with only tin tableware and condiments that included "a cup with butter in it, a cup of sugar, a saucer of salt and another of mustard, and a whisky-bottle." Dinner was "recherché to a degree," and began with "mulligatawny soup; a capon and a hump followed—a really good Bengal hump is hard to beat; next the inevitable chicken cutlets; next curried mutton and rice, with (poppadums) thin wafers, only seen in the East, and excellent. A blancmange followed a savoury of sardines, and we wound up with biscuits and cheese." They lingered, luxuriant in their heavy clothes and fellowship of the hunt.

Before she drifted off to sleep, perhaps prompted by the day's adventure or conversation at the table, Savory thought "of how I have often wondered how one would define a real sportswoman." It should begin, she decided, with "an appreciation of the free camp life—such as ours." It should also include being "a fair shot, considering others, and never doing an unsportsmanlike action, preferring quality to quantity in a bag, a keen observer of all animals, and a real lover of nature."

From Chamba they descended, picking up their horses on the third day, Savory riding her beloved Sphai. They rode where they could, walked where they couldn't. "Many of the paths were barely three feet wide in places, with a cliff above on one side," Savory observed, "and a precipice below on the other. . . . It was very nervous work at first, but, as I said, we grew used to it."

At one particularly steep spot, "Sphai dug his willing toes into the rock and broke into a jog . . . [and] at the same time he turned a little across the path, inwards, which, of course, threw his quarters outwards. With one of his hind-feet he loosened a rock at the edge, and his foot went over with it."

Then came a moment she never forgot: "Instantly—there was no time to think—I felt him turn outwards still more, and both his hindlegs were over."

Somehow Savory was present enough to instinctively throw herself "off the saddle on to the path." As she wrote, "I do not know—I never shall know—how I did it. I kept hold of the reins, and for a second of time, kneeling on the path, clung to them, Sphai's head on a level with me, his two poor great fore-legs clattering hopelessly on the path, while with his strong hindquarters he fought for a minute for life, trying to dig his toes into some crevice in the precipice. It was only for a second. I was powerless to hold him up. There was not even time to call to S. Right over, backwards, he slowly went, with a long heave. I saw the expression in his poor, imploring eyes. . . ."

Savory wished it had been she. There was "a hideously long silence—such a *dead* silence—and then two sickening crashes, as he hit rock after rock." The scene became a recurrent nightmare. The life-saving detail: She was riding astride on a man's saddle. That permitted her instantaneous exit.

At such points, and there are several in the narrative, Savory performed as a British subject should. She mourns her horse with a poem, clears her head with a bit of Kipling, and straightens her narrative skirt. Then: Onward.

Savory, in short, lived for the gristle of hunting—and defined her own brand of femininity in the process. She had no interest in the role of the languid *meme-sahib*, even after the guns were greased and put away. She had the bloodlust typically seen as the confirmation of masculinity, though she claimed to kill "effectively and sparingly." No one ever knew what she would do in any given situation, though you can be sure that she would file a full and spirited report.

Did she inspire women to follow her lead? Legacies are difficult to measure, and Savory's should not be how many Surrey (or Scarsdale) housewives lit out for a spot of tiger hunting. Big game hunting, more than any other activity with the possible exception of waterfowling, remained a boy's tree house through the late nineteenth century, with "big game" nearly always involving considerable travel and expense that meant upper-middle class males.

A better question is how many girls and women found themselves more interested in trying any outdoor sport after reading adventures like Savory's. Women big game hunters and talented rifle shots, such as Annie Oakley and

Colorado huntress Martha Maxwell, assumed prominent places in the media and appeared before big audiences. There was little demure about them, at least in their public personas. Maxwell, a college-educated woman's rights advocate, hung the sign Woman's Work over her prize-winning display of big game heads at the 1876 Philadelphia Centennial. The buzz they created only sold more books like Savory's and clearly kept the issue of women's sporting involvement alive—in both countries.

"Once when I Was in Africa Lion Shooting"

JOHN McCUTCHEON

In Africa: Hunting Adventures in the Big Game Country, 1910

The globe-trotting thread of the big game hunting tradition gained serious ground as the colonial competition between Western nations heated up in the first decade of the twentieth century. The ideal hunt involved Edwardian opulence, immersion in native cultures, and personal indifference to the peril posed by dangerous game. For these features, India held the spot dearest to the English colonial heart. But for middle- and upper-class Americans, Africa remained the most exotic outdoors on Earth.

African adventure filled the air in 1909 America. One party set forth with scientist and taxidermist Carl Akeley, known for having killed a leopard with his bare hands, at its lead. Akeley intended to collect a group of elephants for display in the American Museum of National History. (He did so, and the Akeley Hall of African Mammals remains one of the museum's most popular exhibits.) The magnitude of this expedition—and others of the day—was substantial, even by Edwardian standards: By the time four white adventurers on his trip, Mrs. Akeley among them, reached the British East African bush, they had retained the service of 120 African servants—a reflection, in part, of lifestyle (supplies included, for instance, six large bottles of Pond's extract and twenty-four larger bottles of scotch), as well as the scope of the scientific investigation (darkroom equipment for developing photos afield).

And, Akeley's was far from the largest expedition on the continent. That distinction belonged to a second major African expedition of the day—Colonel Theodore Roosevelt's post-presidential, Smithsonian-backed magical mystery tour, which had begun months earlier and included some 260 servants and four tons of salt for hide preservation. Akeley and Roosevelt were friends—the two men hunted elephants together when the safaris met—but TR was never one to be outdone.

Americans took civic pride in such expeditions. The public saw them as important symbols of national power, hung on news from the adventures. Such was the interest that the *Chicago Tribune* sent popular cartoonist John McCutcheon along on Akeley's trip. McCutcheon began serializing his book *In Africa* even before he returned the next May. Certainly readers wanted adventure. But the fact that a cartoonist was the reporter also suggested something about the tone the paper thought would appeal to the Midwest audience.

McCutcheon's inclination to poke fun at himself made him the perfect male safari narrator, particularly since the public knew that TR was already over there and hardly the sort of individual that would ever be out-safaried. (You sensed that he had plenty of backup pith helmets.) McCutcheon was an inexperienced hunter with little to prove, but comfortable on adventures. (For all of his self-deprecation, he had cruised into Manila Bay with Dewey, corresponded from the Philippines, and later covered the Mexican Revolution and the Great War.) He was often credited with developing the "personal interest" cartoon, a departure from the political-attack drawings of the nineteenth century. McCutcheon gave a *Walk in the Woods* perspective, the perfect tonic for the incessant colonial chest-thumping on the eve of the Great War.

"Like everyone who goes to Africa with a gun and a return ticket, I had two absorbing ambitions," McCutcheon explained. "One was to kill a lion and the other to live to tell about it." He claimed that more than anything else, he dreamed of being able to, preferably offhandedly, start a conversation with, "Once, when I was in Africa lion shooting . . ."

On McCutcheon's African steamer, "the hunting talk was four-fifths lion and one-fifth about other game." In fact, "the cripple who had been badly mauled by a lion was a person of much distinction, even more so than a hunter" who'd shot some three hundred elephants. They passed famous lion spots—Tsavo and the man-eaters of legend and lore, a little cemetery "with many headstones that read 'Killed by lion.'" McCutcheon thought: Prior to this trip for rhinos and lions, he "had not shot at anything for three years, nor hit anything for ten."

And then they were hunting. Three days, no lions. The safari powers that be decided a drive was in order. Drives operated thusly, McCutcheon explained: "You take thirty or forty natives to the place where the lion was heard and then beat every bit of cover in hope of scaring out the beast." They did so. But no lions.

They camped in grasslands teeming with rhinos, zebras, kongoni, hippos, baboons, monkeys, and "nearly all of the eight hundred varieties of East African birds [that] gave us a morning serenade." Still, no lion.

To pass the time, "Mr. Akeley took out his moving picture machine, and edged to within a few yards of . . . unsuspecting rhinos, and then we tried to provoke a charge." They did this several times, "and if there is a more exciting diversion I don't know what it is." McCutcheon noted that he had "looped the loop and there is no comparison."

One day, however, matters apparently got out of hand and "it was necessary to shoot a big bull rhino." McCutcheon hit the creature twice, but it staggered off. The party caught up with the rhino that afternoon and found that it "didn't seem to be in the chastened mood of one who is about to die." McCutcheon was just about to shoot it again when "suddenly a sound struck my ear that acted upon me like an electric shock: Simba!"

The lion stood about one hundred yards away, partly hidden in the grass. Then he vanished, and they followed, or tried to, for the better part of several hours. McCutcheon observed that this particular individual animal was "apparently was not as brave as a lion." There was no "sign of the king of beasts. He had apparently abdicated."

The hunting party returned to chasing the wounded rhino, which Mr. McCutcheon likened to "going back to work after a pleasant two weeks' vacation." They finally spotted the rhino in the distance and reached him in another couple of hours. At one hundred yards McCutcheon shot him twice, and he "wheeled around and, stumbling occasionally, was off like a railway train." Again they followed over hills, before losing him entirely.

It was now two o'clock under a broiling sun, and they had not eaten since five o'clock that morning. They trudged home and on the way passed a dry creekbed, primo lion habitat. One of the gunbearers set fire to it, and "as the flames advanced they heard a deep growling." Simba II.

McCutcheon edged to within forty yards of the lion, and the beast "was glaring . . . with tail waving angrily and his mouth was opened in a savage snarl." Right away, McCutcheon realized, "I could see that he didn't like me."

McCutcheon raised his .256 Mannlicher, aimed, and fired. The lion somersaulted, then disappeared in the grass. A new fire was set. McCutcheon spotted the lion, and this time hit him twice with cordites.

The lion fell into his tracks. He did not move. Even then McCutcheon approached him carefully, as he'd heard stories of the dying lion that springs up "in a final charge, kills somebody and then dies happily."

But this lion was dead. One of his gunbearers took a picture, and "when it was developed there was only a part of the lion and part of the lion slayer visible. It was a good picture of the tree, however."

McCutcheon's humor was one representation of the African experience. Roosevelt's *African Game Trails*, which appeared the following year to critical acclaim, was another. As with the popularity of both Adirondack Murray's ebullience and Warner's satire, the two approaches to the danger of big game—it was both funny *and* scary—indicated the growing sophistication of the modern audience that saw thrills and comedy as two scenes in the same act. They remained important twin elements in the tradition of hunting dangerous game. Lion hunting was a different experience, as authors from Hemingway to Capstick reminded us, when stepping into the long grass yourself, .256 Mannlicher in hand. But the closest most Americans came to that was through the stories they read.

"I've Got Him by the Tail!"
Gifford Pinchot
CHARLES FREDERICK HOLDER

"Fighting a Swordfish at Night,"
Recreations of a Sportsman on the Pacific Coast, 1910

The formula of exotic surroundings and dangerous challenges pushed men and women to search around the globe for such sport. A few American sports searched in areas closer to home, at the edge of the continent, off the coast in California. The early whalers had taken on considerable risk. Herman Melville's *Moby Dick*, for example, was modeled after an actual sperm whale attack in the Pacific in the 1830s, as detailed in Nathaniel Philbrick's *In the Heart of the Sea: The Tragedy of the Whaleship Essex.*

Whale fishing was a bit much, even for sportsmen of the late nineteenth century, but a reconfiguration of the experience so that the risk came not from the creature itself but from the method employed out on the seas was another matter.

Enter Charles Frederick Holder, the man sometimes called the inventor of big game fishing. Whether or not he actually did, no one deserves the sobriquet more. Born to wealth in Lynn, Massachusetts, in 1851, Holder grew up with a brilliant naturalist father who once purchased a thousand-pound tuna from its harpooners and donated the magnificent creature to a local museum rather than watch it be sold for oil. The elder Holder conducted extensive marine research (with Charles in tow) and also helped found the American Museum of Natural History. As a young man, Charles married, and became assistant curator at the museum and a successful author. Then tragedy struck: the death of a five-month old-son, the Holders' only child as it turned out. Wracked with grief, Charles and his wife traveled to California—and in time found themselves at home. Holder became editor of the *Los Angeles Tribune* before founding his own publication—*California Illustrated History*—and continued his move west, literally as far as he could possibly go before falling off the shore shelf and into the oblivion of the Pacific. The fishing, it seemed, caught his eye.

If Holder "invented" big game fishing, he did so on June 1, 1898. On that day he hooked and landed a 183-pound bluefin tuna on rod and reel in the waters off Catalina Island. Other anglers had caught tuna on such gear, but none had Holder's instinct (or inclination) for promotion, as George Reiger explains in *Profiles in Saltwater Angling*. Holder contacted the press, describing his own success. An article in the *Pasadena Daily News* reported that he "played the big fellow with pertinacious skill" and that the "Professor eclipsed all previous achievements in the line of angling."

Holder was no professor, but the fight had been wild and woolly. Holder hooked the fish, and it steamed off, in time capsizing his boat. Holder and his guide, Englishman Jim Gardner, climbed back in; Gardner bailed and rowed, and Holder fought the tuna—for close to four hours and approximately twelve miles. Gardner eventually gaffed the tuna about one hundred feet from where Holder hooked it.

Holder probably believed that such fights warranted press coverage, and maybe an intensifying adjective or two. More to the point, he understood that such two-fisted stories had a ready audience, with Wild West shows drawing record crowds and TR's fame in Cuba, but a month in the future. In truth, Holder may have been less interested in self-glorification and more in the promotion of the sport's exhilaration. Along with a small group of anglers, he founded the Tuna Club of Santa Catalina (still in existence today) shortly after his catch, and until his death in 1915, he wrote numerous books and countless articles promoting sporting methods for big game fishing. A good example is a chapter titled "Fighting a Swordfish at Night," which appeared in his 1910 *Recreations of a Sportsman on the Pacific Coast*.

In this story, his guests on the island included Gifford Pinchot, current chief of the USDA Forest Service, who hooked a large swordfish that seemed intent on towing his skiff out into the middle of the Pacific in the middle of the night. Holder had been enjoying the afternoon with one of his other guests when he "sighted the launch coming in at full speed." At the helm was twelve-year-old Joaquin, who hollered "that Mr. Pinchot was fast to a big swordfish about three miles offshore, and would Mr. Holder not go out and stand by?"

Holder hopped aboard and, in the beautiful twilight, "took the helm and we turned out to sea" to search for Pinchot, his mate, Mexico Joe, and the giant sword. They were in a small open boat, difficult to see in the near darkness, so Holder did the only prudent thing: He sent Joaquin up the mast to scan the ocean ahead, and then put the hammer down. In a bit they "sighted it on a wave, a mere speck, about three miles to the southeast. I had Joaquin light the lantern so that the anglers could see us if we missed them, and headed directly for them at full speed."

Holder realized how quickly Pinchot and Mexico Joe were moving, as he constantly had to readjust, and Holder and Joaquin eventually caught up to the boat. Holder and Joaquin shouted hurrah, and Pinchot roared back "that the fish had leaped fifteen times immediately after it was hooked, and that he had brought it alongside several times, but could not hold it." Holder knew they had a big fish "due to the speed at which they were going. I had been towed once in an open boat ten or twelve miles by a large tuna, but not at such a continuous speed as this."

Moreover, "the sea was rising and the swordfish was constantly edging out into rougher water, holding the skiff down by the stern, and I fully expected the thing to happen to them, that did to me," which was ending up in the ocean—but that was in the day, not in the night. So being the safety nut that he was, Holder "had Joaquin break out two life preservers and had them ready to fling at the anglers as I thought they might need them if the sea picked up as it generally did."

Swordfish occasionally attacked boats, but "this did not worry Pinchot; what really worried him was Mexican Joe's eighteen-foot, snorting launch, under my guidance. I was a sort of a wild marine *toro*, coming at him from all directions out of the darkness; now nearly aboard on the top of a roller, now too much ahead, threatening the line, as the fish was constantly changing its direction several points, and I was always losing sight of them. Now I would stop twenty feet from the flying skiff, and in backing off get caught, broadside on to the sea, and nearly be thrown out of the boat as she rolled. Then losing them, I would slam back the lever, and put the launch ahead at full speed, until Joaquin in the bow would scream, 'There they are!' and heading around to port I would stop her, missing them by a few feet."

For more than four hours Holder followed the men. Then they heard Pinchot out in the darkness: "We've got him alongside!"

With the wind up, Holder couldn't see. "But Joaquin, my plucky lookout, and real engineer, as he knew how to start the engine if it should really refuse to go, rose to the occasion and let out a shout and cheer, and at them we went."

He was a little heavy on the throttle though. "Before I knew it, I saw Joe's back directly under the boy, and I nearly lifted that coughing, hiccoughing eight-horse-power engine out of the launch trying to back her away. But it was too late; a big sea tossed me over, and they seemed to suddenly come at me out of the night." Holder, it turned out, "sent the launch ahead instead of astern. He missed the skiff but freaked out Joe, "who thought I was aboard of them. . . . The gaff had slipped, or he had lost his hold, and there was a smashing, rolling, surging and bounding, choice talk in Spanish, I think, a medley of sounds with my own shouts to Joaquin, anxious to see the fish, and in my line of vision."

Then again out of the darkness came Pinchot: "'I've got him by the tail!' Joe got a rope around him, and he and the two men wrestled aboard 180 pounds of very unhappy swordfish." And so went another night of good clean fun out on the Pacific.

Holder's books and articles in the national press followed this wild adventure. With his fishing headquarters on an island in the Pacific Ocean and the nation's media center on the eastern side of the country, such promotion was essential to Holder's plan, which was basically the same as the approach of other leading conservationists of the day. Like George Bird Grinnell, he could downplay (in this story, anyway) his own technical skills; like Theodore Roosevelt, he told rip-roaring stories. Like both, he lauded the attributes of various game species and railed against unsporting methods for their capture—in

Holder's case, hand lining, harpooning, and netting. In what could have been an aquatic Boone and Crockett Club, Holder recruited wealthy, competent sports and organized the group into a conservation movement for big game fishing. The by-laws of the Santa Catalina Tuna Club stated that membership required the capture of a hundred-pound leaping (tuna from these waters frequently leapt when hooked) tuna on rod and reel with a line not greater than 24 thread, or sixty-six-pound test dry breaking strength.

By 1901 the club had become more conservation oriented, with a goal of "the protection of the game fishes of California," and in time became a model and inspiration for other organizations, including the International Game Fish Association (IGFA).

The club dispensed buttons to those who caught various gamefish of specified weights on specified tackle, and that became the signature of the Santa Catalina experience. Everyone from Theodore Roosevelt to George Patton Jr. (including the lucky angler in this story, Gifford Pinchot) had his buttons. Holder also did what he could to give the fishing an international flavor, cultivating relationships with anglers from Great Britain, in particular, many of whom came to Santa Catalina. They lauded the superiority of American ocean fishing and—predictably—found the Americans excessive in their self-referencing. As English sportsman Frederic Aflalo wrote in *Sunset Playgrounds* (1908), "it would be refreshing if a little of this button-hunger were to abate. . . . Dear old Ladies jostle their grandchildren on the quay, all on the warpath for buttons. Gentle females, so I am told, toss though sleepless nights on their pillows because they have failed to qualify. . . . Genial conversation on fishing round the comfortable fire in the hall is interlarded with such personalities as "By the way, when I won that gold button . . ."

Such complaints aside (Aflalo himself had missed qualifying with a yellowtail by just a pound and a half), the anglers out on the night waters in this story seem rather matter-of-fact in their insanity, enhanced by Holder's magical way of flattening his voice when the action becomes the most riotous and thereby making the extraordinary ordinary: "What, is that you again? Twenty feet over our heads on top of a wave?" Or thinking about flinging Pinchot and Mexican Joe the life jackets if "the sea picked up." Or remembering the twelve-year-old mate somewhere on top of the mast, when he's not roaring into shore at the "seat of war," or restarting Mexican Joe's engine, an important skill given that Mexican Joe is the gaffer/oarsman aboard the good ship Pinchot, which is currently riding the twenty-footers some three miles off shore, with a big swordfish on the other end, though it's hard to tell where they are in the dark.

Small wonder that Holder later observed that one of his favorite photos showed him floating free and treading water, holding his rod overhead, playing a tuna that was leaping thirty to forty feet in the air. Relaxing, apparently, after a long night on the boat.

"Deliver Us a Moose"
Jim, the guide
WILLIAM BARBER HAYNES

"A Moose Hunter's Letters," *Outers' Recreation*, December 1918

Back on continental land, the moose stood alongside the grizzly as the most important game animal in the American pantheon of lordly creatures. Outdoor magazines and promotional material of the day gave the moose hunt an actual shape, with stories of plaid-shirted hunters calling lovelorn behemoths from birch-bark canoes, and cover pictures of charging bulls and hunters reaching for the rifle. Many suburban hunters, delighted with a pair of mallards, found themselves dreaming of a big trip north.

In "A Moose Hunter's Letters," Haynes found himself livin' the dream, using a template similar to the one employed by Ring Lardner in *You Know Me Al*, stories about the experiences of a young baseball player who shows his ignorance in letters home. (On Walter Johnson, the best pitcher of the day: "Honest Al, he ain't as fast as me. He shut them out, but they never was much of a hitting club.") In this moose hunting version, Haynes kept his duck-hunting buddy, Fred posted on the progress of his north woods quest.

Haynes (Bill in the story) wrote: "This letter keeps my promise to tell you about this moose proposition, in case you decide to come up. We are about fourteen miles from Kipawa station, Quebec, on the Canadian Pacific Railway, in a comfortable log cabin, which I am glad to say, is rainproof, as it has rained every day since I left." Bill added that it was good to get along with your guide on these trips, as you spent a lot of time together—trying to stay dry and warm.

Each day the possibility of moose seemed more remote, the likelihood of unceasing rain only greater. Bill hit a low point when he realized he was swinging on a flock of black ducks with his rifle. Jim stopped him from shooting, however. Before long, Bill wished he were back home duck hunting with

Fred. In his letter he bravely promised that if the rain stopped, he would get a moose, or "Jim is one of the sincerest liars in all of Canada."

His next letter described the (brief) sighting of a large black bear near the lakeshore. Just as the bear had lumbered into the water (where Bill would have had a shot at it), Jim's two dogs, which he'd forgotten to chain, spooked it. No bear. But Bill did see two big yellowlegs (plover). "They should be coming in to the mudflats on our lake, and I suppose you are getting them."

It rained the next day too. Bill realized what a good deal Jim had. "Just think of it," he wrote Fred. "Here's Jim up here having a good time getting by in fine shape and living on the fat of the land, while you and I must work as hard and then pay to come up here and listen to him tell about it."

The next day's letter was written on birch bark, Bill's way of communicating that "we are seven miles from the camp, in a tent." Oh, and "it has been raining like hell almost every minute we have been here." They were about a mile from a lake that "stands ready to deliver us a moose, according to Jim." Bill saw a flock of black ducks and another of yellowlegs. But to have shot at them "would [have] queer[ed] our moose chances." Bill advised Fred to stay home.

Then the moose gods smiled. The next day the men saw a cow wading into the lake. They waited, hoping a bull might follow. "Then as never before did the similarity of moose hunting to duck hunting impress itself on me," Bill wrote. "Not only were we awaiting on a lake, blinded down, but it suddenly dawned on me that we were shooting moose over decoys, and live decoys at that."

Sure enough, mark right. A huge bull moose strutted out of the brush and toward the cow. Jim paddled, maneuvering the canoe, using a bog for a screen. Bill got the classic shot from the bow, as the bull pounded along the shore. His aim was true—and the bull collapsed dead.

Bill watched Jim skin the moose, and "it awed me to see so much fresh meat all at once, Freddy, and me the cause of it being so, although in the present condition of a hungry world, perhaps men such as Jim and I are of use." Fred never did make it north that year, nor any other, we suspect.

No doubt about it, a moose is a lot of meat on the hoof. For the rest of the century, they stomped about our national imagination, as reflected in the various lakes, lodges, first basemen, and political parties bearing their name. As Bill noted, they are even bigger up close. Generations of brook trout fishermen will testify that they can certainly fill up a streamside trail.

Where you hunted largely dictated the challenge of the experience. Sportsmen in Alaska and the Western mountains (where the moose population remained strong) still-hunted moose, and their stories emphasized the difficulty of negotiating the moose's exceptional senses of smell and hearing. Hunters in the bogs of eastern Canada faced challenges of a different sort—in Haynes's case keeping a sense of humor when bound to a cheerful guide in a soggy northeastern wilderness that had French missionaries praying for a tomahawk to the skull.

Were moose dangerous game? The magazine ads typically portrayed the hunter on one knee yards away from a bull moose interested in rendering him into compost, and on rare occasions, with their ton of weight, antlers, and hooves, moose did just that. But their poor eyesight and undifferentiated anger left them charging trains too. And for every ornery moose that upset a canoe, a hundred more fit Thoreau's description as ". . . great frightened rabbits, with their long ears and half inquisitive half frightened looks." Even in the nineteenth century, there was a bit of Bullwinkle in the majesty.

And that side to moose hunting certainly gained appeal in the months after Armistice. One of the outcomes of the unspeakable horror of the Great War was to destroy the nobility of lofty purpose and replace it with irony at every turn. So it was that the turn-of-the-twentieth-century grand exploration big game hunting trips came to be seen as pre-war relics of the grandiose Edwardians. Before the "lights went out in Europe," adventure tales from London, Peary, and Roosevelt had thrilled audiences and stood as reminders of the fame awaiting the stout-hearted.

But such experiences only seemed like orchestrated affectations of a bygone age after death tolls of millions of men. The Great War bleached at least some of the romance from the outdoor experience, as surely as it did every other element of daily life. The great exploring hunter was one of the first casualties, with even lower points such as scandal in the national pastime to follow—before heroism in other sports, the miracle of trans-Atlantic flight, and avenues to mass culture such as the radio emerged in the 1920s and washed the slate clean.

"An Old Curmudgeon of a Hunter or Moonshiner"

A Railroad Executive

CHARLES D. LANIER

"Sawney's Deer Lick," *Scribner's Magazine*, January 1895

If the story of the most dangerous big game is about leaving home, the story about the most treasured big game, the white-tailed deer, is about finding it.

The remote woods of the northern Midwest, Maine, the central Adirondacks, western Pennsylvania, and West Virginia were the only regions in the country capable of hosting a deer season in the late nineteenth and early twentieth centuries. Not surprisingly, most of the white-tailed deer stories from the 1890s came from those regions. City hunters relied on guides or locals with inside information to assist them in the hunting, as is the case in "Sawney's Deer Lick."

The narrator and his longtime guide were on one of their Allegheny big game hunts when they stopped for a break. "I've killed some 37 deer from this spring," said Sawney Moore, the lanky mountaineer guide, standing "with hands clasped over the muzzle of the old mountain rifle, which was long enough to act as a comfortable support for his chin."

The narrator tried a drink of the water, and instead of a sweet spring he tasted sulfur.

"Bucks will have sulphur," Sawney allowed, "when they git ready for it if they *know'd* hunters was waiting for 'em." He paused for effect. "It's *my* lick," he continued. "An' this piece o' the Beard Mount'n we're standin' on, is my land, my reel *e*state."

The narrator knew Sawney's reputation: a widower, "a shiftless Nick o' the Woods, who had no business to be the father of such a pretty, capable daughter as Linda Moore."

"Where are you going to put up your furnace, Sawney?" he joked, and then immediately felt bad because he "knew the old man had become unhappy over his poverty and low estate, because of his daughter." But Sawney didn't appear to take offense.

Sawney explained that some time ago, a former client, one Colonel Bob, the head of the syndicate that owned the mountain land, gave him this tiny slice of heaven before he died, a repayment for years of excellent deer hunting. Sawney tried to sell it to help finance Linda's education, but the most he could get was about a dollar per acre. So he kept it and . . . Just then Sawney's concentration was broken by the appearance of a big buck. Break was over.

Some time later, back in the city, the narrator received a letter from a railroad executive who wanted to—needed to, actually—buy the land around the spring to complete the building of a resort and had learned that the land "belongs to an old curmudgeon of a hunter or moonshiner, whom I understand you have at times employed as a guide." Sawney had directed the buyer to the narrator.

The narrator, for his part, enjoyed the thought of showing Sawney something for once, in this case the fine art of financial horse trading. In the end Sawney made a tidy sum, which could put Linda through school, even send her to Europe. He could build a big house in town too, but he told the narrator he wanted to move to New York City, where he could learn to be the sort of father that would make Linda proud. Sawney "thought he could get used to city clothes and their fine ways against the time they [Linda and her party] came back." The narrator "took mental note that the poison was getting in its work."

The narrator surmised that he knew Sawney better than Sawney knew himself, in part because of their time deer hunting. That partnership was "unlike other comradeship—that of the woods and streams and mountains—and it respecteth neither birth nor fortune nor temperament." To the narrator's way of thinking, "the days and nights of a still-hunt were the best of a man's life . . . [and] it is a true and sweet bond between two men to love the same things—all the more so when few people love them, or even see them. The hunter speaks but little of them, and that awkwardly . . . but either understands, and is content and remembers." Sawney brought him to deer, bear, and turkey, carried him across icy streams, inconvenienced himself to make his hunt better. Now it was the narrator's turn to repay him. Seems like sports are always trying to repay old Sawney. He must have been a pretty good guide.

Sawney didn't know quite what to make of city life—at first. He found it challenging to refuse street beggars, in spite of the narrator's admonition that they would only "spend it on drink." Plays were exciting, but it took him some time to realize the drama was not "real." And newspapers presented yet another challenge: "When there's a good piece in one of 'em," he told the narrator, "I start to read it, an' I hang to her pretty steady now, an' I believe I'd finish some of 'em all right if there wa'n't a new paper comin' out again befo' I've had half a chance." He ran afoul of the law in trying to protect a young boy whose pet fell victim to the city dog catcher. But in time he adjusted, and the narrator saw less and less of him.

A year or so later, the Allegheny Mountains called the narrator once again. It had been a while. He took a train down and hiked the hills to the area of the lick. Out of the beautiful silence of the wood echoed the *Kyouck, Kyouck, Kyouck* of a turkey. Winchester cocked, he eased toward the sound. Then he heard a shrill whistle, given twice, the signal of a still hunter to his partner. Out of a laurel stepped Sawney, who had seen him and decided to "call him in."

Sawney Moore stood there. The city life wasn't for Sawney, the narrator realized. He could just tell. Sawney really said nothing, other than that, no, there was no activity on his land. He still had his cabin, though, where that night the narrator fell asleep to the soft chuckles of Sawney recalling how he'd called in the narrator like a turkey.

In the end, the terms of exchange (aside from profit Sawney made on his land) in this piece were emotional; no money changed hands between Sawney and the narrator. Otherwise, a big-game hunter like the narrator, who imagined himself as "going native" in the tradition of Boone and Crockett, would have to answer the question: Could you hire a guide in order to become independent? (Maybe a life coach?) Probably, but only if the hunter "demoted" the guide, perhaps by constructing him as Lanier does, with a "simplicity of character, or limitation of intellect." In this way, and by helping Sawney out in the social world, they could do each other a favor.

In many ways, author Lanier imagined the world that had been, not the world of 1895. Any informal arrangement based on an exchange of favors was increasingly becoming a business transaction with a bottom line. As the popularity of sport hunting grew, city hunters insisted on defining its terms with self-imposed challenge and restraint. This attitude saved American wildlife but in the short run encouraged dismissive attitudes towards an "old curmudgeon of a hunter or moonshiner" like Sawney.

With increasing frequency, one driven by the growing anonymity of modern life, this antipathy emerged in the relations between "sports" and guides. As historian Daniel Herman notes, some guides contracted with hotels or inns, and—in the Adirondacks, for instance—even began establishing standard rates and trade unions. The tension became so great that in 1907, *Outdoor Life* devoted a series of articles to it. It sounded a lot like the famous (contemporary) series of *Ladies' Home Journal* articles titled "Can This Marriage Be Saved?"

Sawney and the narrator were comrades who "love the same things." (One wonders how Sawney might have described the relationship.) The men, in Lanier's rendition, are bound by their yearning for the transformative power of the still-hunting experience. It is less that they are friends than fellow devotees. They don't have to go to church *together;* they just have to go.

In all likelihood, *Scribner's* readers read the stillness and purity of nature and the mountain's tabernacle woodland with a religious frame of mind. In many ways, this was a story author Lanier was born to tell. He was the eldest son of Sidney Lanier, the martyred poet of Georgia and champion of a New South, felled at age forty by consumption contracted in a Yankee prison camp. The younger Lanier spent considerable time in the uplands of the Alleghenies and witnessed his father's effort at healing through love of the land. By seventeen, Charles was a skilled outdoorsman. After college he moved to New York, where he worked on Wall Street and at the *American Review of Reviews* and also wrote stories for *Scribner's.*

This story of a kind, gentle woodsman fleeing the city, told through the eyes of a narrator who does the same as often as he can, probably came as little surprise to those who knew the family. Edward Mims, in his 1905 biography of the elder Lanier, wrote that three of his four surviving sons "through their magazines are doing their best to foster among Americans a taste for country life."

In doing so, Lanier laid out a ritual that would become very familiar to American still hunters of the twentieth century. That is, there is only so much city life an outdoorsman can take; he can feel it "backing up in [his] heart." When the deer hunter eases through the woods and over the ridges, he feels himself entering what can only be called a state of grace. The story confirms as much when, Christ-like, the old mountaineer emerges from the animal world, rises from the American land, and welcomes the narrator on his hunt. The idea of the whitetail is present, interestingly, even when they are not. Like Sawney, they will be back.

"Glad Y'are on Time"
Elijah, Philip, and David
B. W. MITCHELL

"A Thanksgiving Deer Hunt in West Virginia,"
Outing, November 1898

If the spiritual journey in search of the whitetail is one part of the modern deer hunting tradition, linking perhaps with Native Americans, the other part emerges from the place of the deer in American society. Unlike the white goats that live on a mountain, whitetails can belong to a community. To this day, there is nothing that will fill a high-school gym quicker than a forum on the state deer herd. In part this attachment has to do with the land whitetails inhabit; in the late nineteenth century, their scarcity only intensified such an attitude.

"A Thanksgiving Deer Hunt in West Virginia" is a good example of how the local hunting culture organized around "their" deer. In West Virginia, as elsewhere, the whitetail population struggled—and fell to a thousand animals over the next decade. In such scarcity, you needed either Sawney Moore or local friendships to have a prayer at even seeing horns.

As prearranged, on Thanksgiving morning author Mitchell arrived at the home of friend who lived on the border of agricultural areas and woodlands, "not the 'backwoods' counties with their virgin forests and untrailed ranges." Mitchell brought a buddy with him.

"Here y'are at last," came the shout to Mitchell and his friend. "Glad y'are on time."

"Three brothers—Elijah, Philip, and David—lead the hunt," explained Mitchell. "And no more skilled woodsmen, more unerring shots, more noble, steadfast friends" could one ask for.

The men gathered and planned the deer drive. They had dogs as well, though they would be used just "to start the deer," for this was an honest expedition, not one of those hunts where "all you have to do is to go out into the forest with your guide and wait till one walks leisurely past you;

nor . . . where dogs drive the creature to water" and you canoed out and killed it. Here the owning of local land and subsequent membership in the community conferred a certain "ownership" of the deer—and a say in how the hunt would transpire.

Moving down the road, the group ran into a pair of ne'er-do-wells huddled around a fire, swilling moonshine. They were "thin-weather beaten" men with "long tangled beards that reach to their waists." They looked up to Mitchell and the rest, handed them some drink. Mitchell ID'd them as "typical natives," with rusted old flintlocks, quite different, he noted, from his industrious hosts who'd moved here. But the hillbillies were invited to join the drive anyway, for they were members of the community, and numbers mattered in a deer drive. The men immediately agreed, knowing that any game would be split up "communally."

Mitchell explained to his friend what to expect, how not to move when the deer were coming, how not to leave your post, which could let the deer slip through—and then everyone would be out venison. The idea of individual sport, as in still hunting, was notably absent.

Mitchell's friend actually shot a deer, and he was beyond ecstatic. The real story was just starting, however. A local farmer told the men that he'd seen several deer in among his sheep, so the boys put on another drive. But a couple of fellers from across the line in Maryland sneaked in and killed a deer the boys were driving. Then, in the ultimate act of deceit and cowardice, they scurried back to Maryland with the venison.

That night, after a proper Thanksgiving feast, the three brothers rounded up a small party, Mitchell among them, and headed across the Maryland line to Cresaptown, where the deer thieves reportedly lived. "It was a sight to see all those broad-backed mountaineers galloping off to right their wrongs in the swift, direct style of the mountains," Mitchell wrote. He was even more moved by the confrontation with the thieves, for "never was the statement clearer, and the logic was convincing." The ride back was heavenly beneath "the silver light of the fullest moon that ever shone. Jests and merry tales rang on the still night air, and the deer was slung across the horse of the writer."

Like other writers of the day, Mitchell spun the deer's scarcity as positive. What had once been a mark of the nation's bounty, in this story anyway, served as a mark of a community's character. Missing a shot was less about personal embarrassment and more about letting down the team. In the end, the honor, industry, and forthright nature of the middle-class center of the community triumphed; how different that was from the way individuals outside the community were represented (i.e., morning drinking around a fire or sneaking into deer drives).

Mitchell took pains to note that his hosts "have come in from other States" but had been sanctified by mountain farming, rendering them, somehow, "mountaineers." They had "broad backs," unlike the moonshine drinkers, who had "thin-weathered" looks. In the end the communal hunt took its place as a legitimate deer hunting tradition, stretching back to the days of Crockett and Boone. The hunt was a different enactment of the Grinnell-Roosevelt strategy of enshrining the past to provide for the future. In this case, the deer hunting became not simply an activity to confirm a single man's worth but also a way of working together to strengthen a community. Today when a hunter is asked, "Did you get your deer yet?" the phrasing is no accident. As a member of the community, he or she deserves one.

"Like a Flash I Cocked My Gun"
GEORGIA ROBERTS

"An Adirondack Buck," *Outing*, October 1897

Community whitetail hunting assumed a different form in one of hunting's beloved traditions: the deer camp. And whether the hunters worked as a team—as in Mitchell's story—or as a loose group of still hunters or stand watchers, deer hunting increasingly developed a social meaning. Young men who killed their first deer could expect some sort of ritual. The camp "worked" together in the place of a single guide. People went to the woods to get away from society and be different persons—all of which was not possible of course, but trying to do so was great fun. In the end it made little difference whether people were shedding their label of nimrod or klutz, maintaining a Leatherstocking reputation, or breaking through a gender barrier, as did Georgia Roberts. It was all about the trying.

Roberts was the woman in deer camp doing her best to keep up with the boys. A well-educated nature writer, she wrote many stories and poems (the most famous of which was "The Wolf") under a number of pen names. This particular story, like Savory's travels, debunks the myth that women hunted to be fashionable or because they only wanted to copy men. Roberts had an elemental desire to kill a deer. Period.

Roberts, her husband, and a couple of other men hiked some fifteen miles into their cabin in the Oswegatchie River country of the western Adirondacks. After a slow first week, the hunting picked up, with nearly everyone seeing deer and "getting several shots." There was no mention of deer killed, other than one "rabbit," a reference to a small deer brought back to camp. The hunting was not easy, and "the lucky hunter . . . could not expect to have his game led leisurely up for execution. He must have a steady hand, a true eye, and a good gun. In nearly all cases, the only chance is to shoot while the deer is in motion; unless one is fortunate enough to catch him as he strikes the crossing and pauses to listen to the distant hounds."

This deer camp, like most others, featured good-natured ribbing. One man, Pender, always fell asleep on watch, and then missed any deer that woke him up. When he missed one at twenty yards, others advised him to bring a shotgun loaded with buckshot, which he began doing. It didn't help much.

Inside the camp, Roberts was one of the hunters. The expectations for a woman's role did not follow her, or if they did, she ignored them (in print, anyway). Roberts had little to say about evening camp life. In her head she remained self-conscious about her own hunting performance, however. With no deer to her credit, she grew discouraged, though not whiny. More just quietly bummed. Her husband, Sydney, gave her a pep talk and encouraged her to head out for the last day of the trip. She didn't see anything on her stand, from dawn through till five o'clock or so. At one point she heard a couple of shots—must be Pender and his shotgun, she thought—then returned to her daydream in the beautiful October woods.

Suddenly, on the far side of the river, across some shallows, a majestic buck strode out of the alders. "Like a flash I cocked my gun," she wrote, "and with a movement that would have done credit to an India-rubber woman, shifted my position and took aim just where the generous curve of the throat sprang from the chest." Roberts fired. The buck leapt back in the brush, and she feared that she missed her chance.

But when she waded across the shallows of the river, she noticed blood on the flat rocks. The two dogs, Major and Sport, showed up, as did a couple of the other hunters. And, just at dark, Roberts found her deer.

Pender came running up, breathless, and pointed to the small hole in the buck's ear. "See," he shouted, "I got it." But the .38 left a clear (and bigger) hole in the chest of the beautiful buck. And everyone agreed that it was Roberts who'd made the kill.

Roberts and her husband had good hearts. When Pender came to the Roberts household, he was allowed to brag about the deer he shot: They never closed the hole in the ear of the mounted head, which looked down on their table. Hunters from the same camp look out for one another.

"The Hole He Faded Into"
The boys back at camp
LEONARD DEWITT SHERMAN

"That Ten-Point Buck," *The Illustrated
Outdoor World and Recreation*, November 1912

Manliness, strength, and stamina, in general, were all part of being a good deer hunter, but as Roberts's success suggested, deer hunting's skill was tapping into different abilities. Roberts was persistent—and kept cool when a shot came her way. But, as she conceded, she was also in the right spot at the right time. Increasingly, the complexity of hunting strategy became part of deer hunting's appeal. The modern deer slayer saw hunting as a challenge to his personality. Stories celebrated the cerebral dimension of the hunt, which began with a veneration of the trophy buck's elusive nature. There was nothing like a camp in the woods to keep these stories alive forever.

The country around the Rangeley Lakes area of Maine had some of the biggest deer in turn-of-the-twentieth-century America. That was where Leonard DeWitt Sherman headed at the tag end of the season.

It had been snowing for some time when Sherman and his buddy, known only as "The Other Fellow," reached the shelter, an old logging works refurbished into a sporting camp. Johnny, the cook, was one of the mainstays, as was Ross, who had earlier hitched up the team and met Sherman and his pal at the rail station. The first night in camp made Sherman wish he'd been there earlier. Johnny cooked a meal of venison pie and baked potatoes and maple syrup and biscuits and coffee, and the members of camp "all put . . . [it] where [it] would do some good." After supper the guys cleaned guns, shuffled cards without playing, smoked—anything that could be done while discussing modern life, including "the subjects of war, the high cost of living, love and the best accepted methods of handling skunks."

The next day, Sherman stayed out in the snow till after dark, crossing a cedar swamp through which a straight line was virtually impossible "with or without a compass." The storm picked up. Eventually he hit the trail and suddenly, "a point of light pricked out of the gloom." Camp! He relaxed, joyous. And just then he jumped a big deer that blotted out the light, and he fired "away at the noise the buck was making as he sailed through the woods. . . ."

Well? Well? They wanted to know as he stamped off the snow, removed his boots, and sat down. That you shootin'?

For the next two days, Sherman had in mind a ten-point buck. But dreams were one thing, actual deer another. As he wrote," I am an authority on hunting, but not on shooting." He knew, he sighed, "what a deer does when you step on a dry stick, or sneeze, or stumble over your own feet, or try to hunt down wind—it breathes you into the next county."

The snow fell every night, driven by a sharp wind, leaving a crust beneath the powder that made still hunting difficult. Sherman poked through a cedar swamp the second day, following a trail that at points "fairly steamed." Suddenly he heard *Whang! Whang!* He hustled over a hill to see The Other Fellow looking at a blood trail that would end in two hundred yards with a beautiful spike horn.

Still, Sherman pined for the ten-pointer. The dreaminess reminded him of the fellow who saw a giraffe at the circus, stared at it up and down, and finally declared, "by gum, they hain't no such critter."

The next morning they slipped through some hardwoods—Ross on the left, Sherman in the middle, The Other Fellow on the right flank. Before long, Ross's gun sounded five times. The other two hustled over to see Ross standing over a spike horn of his own.

By the final day everyone else had shot a deer (The Other Fellow, two), and Sherman's ten-point mission had become a cause célèbre—but it was not to be. He saw one tail, and that was it. "Yes, I know! I should have shot at the hole he faded into. That's what they all said."

The ten pointer?

"They hain't no such critter."

Whereas Roberts's Adirondack story emphasized her good luck and her beautiful days in the wilderness, Sherman's focused more on the skill involved and the domesticity of the deer camp. Another home to manage was probably the last thing Roberts needed. But oddly, that's just what Sherman wanted, along with the ten-pointer of course. Roberts's story was about the world she found, Sherman's about the world he and his friends were creating.

Writing fifteen years after Roberts, Sherman also laid out the template that enacts Grinnell's philosophy—a devotion to the process of hunting. The ultimate one-on-one deer hunt, as celebrated in *The Still Hunter* by T. S. Van Dyke, enjoyed a new currency. The modern deer hunt began to take shape: Travel to rural areas, hunt all day in tough conditions for a chance at a big buck, lounge in the modest comfort of a deer camp. You can see the light through the woods. Home.

The idea of deer camp—something that might possibly have been of interest to a buffalo hunter or mule skinner fifty years earlier but certainly to no one who would call himself middle class—took on an almost mythic quality for the fellows in this piece. Like cowboys, soldiers, and other heroes of the late nineteenth century, the participants worked outside, but their efforts attained worth only when replayed inside in front of the others.

Deer camp recapitulated the previous three centuries. It became an outpost with a leave-a-light-on-for-you welcome. Enhanced by the wilderness surroundings, the camp imitated the suburban homes the hunters couldn't wait to leave.. There is clearly sport here, but it is less about the shooting and more about the hunting, less about the accomplishing and more about the being. As if to parallel another world, the daily arc of the experience seems quite familiar. It is each man for himself by day, the hearth and community by night. There is cooperation, teasing ("How could you miss that one?"), and fellowship—but the bond is not one of family, which comes with expectation, but of individual hunting, which bespeaks freedom. "The days and nights of a still-hunt," in Charles Lanier's words, are "the best of a man's life . . . [and] it is a true and sweet bond between two men to love the same things—all the more so when few people love them, or even see them." Except for the guys back at camp.

CHAPTER 6

"Deluding That Old Trout"

FLY FISHING FOR TROUT, 1865–1912

A ngling author Thaddeus Norris was standing with a companion beside the fish tanks at the 1876 Philadelphia Centennial when a "brother of the angle" approached and launched into an account of his fishing prowess. Fish culturist, consultant to the Centennial, and the most famous angler in America, Norris braced himself. In his 1864 *American Angling Book*, he had outlined the angling "types": the Fussy Angler; the Snob Angler; the Greedy, Pushing Angler; the Spick-and-Span Angler; the Rough-and-Ready Angler; the Literary Angler; the Pretentious Angler. Norris knew what he was in for.

He nodded as the man claimed to be the best fisherman in western Pennsylvania.

"I am pleased to meet a thorough angler," Norris said, finding an opening. "I suppose you fish with a fly?"

"Always, Mr. Norris. Always."

"Always rig the line properly with a float and a sinker?"

"Oh, yes, always use the float and sinker."

"I see that you are really an expert angler," said Norris, "and I am glad to know you." After the man left, Norris explained to his companion, Fred Mather, that he often met such men. Like the others, this fellow probably would "need a float and sinker if he tried to cast a fly." The anecdote, reported in Mather's *My Angling Friends*, indicated Norris's stature, to say nothing of the increasing status of sportfishing and fly fishing in general.

This particular individual may not have been a fly fisherman, but he understood that posing as one brought him into a certain social sphere, even if he didn't know the rules. (Contemporary anglers will note that Thingamabobbers and ecologically safe weights do not constitute floats and sinkers, respectively). But what might be most telling is the polite way in which Norris responded to the guy's fronting. From the start, fly fishing was a genteel undertaking.

As more Americans fly fished, they joined clubs and formed associations and built lodges; as they read the same books and magazines, they embraced this philosophy, adopted from England. In time a fly-fishing culture developed in the United States. And while fly fishing wasn't a book club or a philosophy group, the expectation for decorum came with the territory. The first fly fishermen in North America knew, if they knew anything at all, that they owed a good deal of their orientation to the gentlemanly traditions of England's streams. Early North American sport hunters? David Crockett would have thanked the bears and voters of Tennessee.

Fly fishing's gentility and canon encouraged a tradition of debate and, perhaps not coincidentally, inspired a forward-looking vision. Norris and Robert Barnwell Roosevelt, the other famous American fisherman, were rivals of sorts. Their main dispute involved imitation theory. Norris preferred a ladder of flies, usually three. Roosevelt, fishing in the waters of Long Island, where there was actually some fishing pressure, stressed the importance of imitation and careful presentation, explaining that Norris was used to fishing unsophisticated wilderness trout. Norris responded that Roosevelt was basically full of hot air.

To be certain, the disagreement was fueled by personality, but it is interesting that a debate would even exist at such a point in the development of fly fishing—and on what can only be called an esoteric point, given the general state of fishing in 1860s North America. The disagreement between Norris and Roosevelt started a fault line in American fly fishing that has continued to this day: the importance of presentation versus pattern, the generalist versus the imitator.

Their disagreement aside, Norris and Roosevelt read British authors of the nineteenth century such as Alfred Ronalds, Francis Francis, William Senior, and F. M. Halford. American writers saw themselves as trying to improve the same practices as their British cohorts, although differences stood out from the start. North American waters were tumbling, brush-choked streams filled with brook trout, whereas British waters, particularly those favored by fly fishers, were often open and silky and home to brown trout—as visitor George Tattersall observed in the 1830s. The two nations had different approaches to ownership of the waters, with American waters, starting anyway, as public. Brook trout fared poorly around civilization, which meant that the best fishing existed in areas where people weren't—i.e., wilderness, where gentility doesn't always fair so well (see again, George Tattersall).

Some adjustments came with the growing interest in fly fishing. In order to Americanize it, some new fish and new thinking would be necessary. In short, American fly fishing's past might have existed in England, but its future, to paraphrase Emmett "Doc" Brown in *Back to the Future*, had yet to be written. This is the story of how that happened. But first, the English should have a few words.

"We Both Enjoyed Ourselves Very Thoroughly"
FRANCIS FRANCIS

"Squaring the Keeper," *Hot Pot*, 1880

As in America, sporting participation soared in nineteenth-century England, and, more than any other activity, fishing accommodated the recreational and cultural demands of a growing middle class. Unlike shooting, which came with a prohibitive cost, or bowls (bowling), which carried the taint of commonness, fishing beckoned one and all, seemed to transform the participant. Business and professional men, barristers, merchants, ministers—even those inclined to socialism, such as artist William Morris—claimed to find meaning, if not lessons, in a day astream.

While visiting the Cobden family in 1889, Morris landed more than thirty fish, only to have the best of them pilfered. His hosts responded "that as a Socialist, he should have rejoiced that others had enjoyed his fish at their evening repast." He apparently missed the irony, according to historian John Lowerson, and promptly "lost his temper." But the point remained that in most instances, fly fishing for trout and salmon offered a class marker and an antidote to the pressures of the new age. You just had to keep an eye out for any wood urchins with designs on your basket of fish.

The matter of who owned the trout vexed anglers in both countries. In England fly fishermen maintained private waters. In America most waters have remained at least partially public, though by the 1880s, clubs were buying up land on the Beaverkill and other Catskill rivers. Posting land for fishing (and hunting) generated considerable venom among the local residents and invariably stirred the class antagonism that lurked just beneath the surface of nineteenth-century American life. In hunting, the warring sides often fell into ignorant rural landowner versus entitled snobbish city sport; fly fishing sometimes reversed the roles, with city snobs buying the river because they could afford it and keeping locals from fishing waters they always had. This initiative didn't make city anglers a lot of friends in small towns, particularly as stocking waters became more common. If the state of New York was doing the stocking, didn't the trout belong to everyone? What about hotel owners who were trying to attract tourists? Who would want to come if they had no place to fish? In England, with its more rigid class boundaries, these questions seemed resolved; in America, they most certainly did not.

Fishing was supposed to be an escape, fun, an elixir of adult curiosity and childish oblivion. But stuff happens—be it an annoying fellow angler or inadvertent trespassing. Having been fly fishing for centuries, the English had some words of wisdom on how to handle such situations. The inestimable Francis Francis, fishing editor of *The Field*, the most influential sporting publication on either side of the Atlantic and one read carefully by American fly fishermen, was the voice of authority on these matters of social sensibilities. Fishing tempered Francis, leaving him laughing at his own foibles, generous, optimistic—". . . always hopeful for tomorrow no matter how hopeless today had been," was how fly-fishing authority F. M. Halford put it. That was the attitude Francis, in turn, gave back to his readers.

Francis became fishing's nineteenth-century ambassador and codifier, writing hundreds of articles and a score of books on all aspects of fish—raising them, protecting them, catching them. He posted a half dozen letters a day to people he didn't know, other than they'd sent him letters requesting information on fishing. Francis certainly promoted technical advances, such as upstream fly fishing, but as Jim Babb, *Gray's Sporting Journal* editor, has observed, he remained more a connoisseur than an innovator. At a time when fishing was beginning to organize itself, he became its great generalist. Everything from salmon to perch kindled his spirit, and he wrote about them with a sly humor and a welcoming voice. His beneficence inspired anglers around the world. In a fit of Victorian gratitude (for introducing brown trout eggs to New Zealand), some Australians sent him an opossum rug. Twelve thousand miles away a young Philadelphian named Theodore Gordon, in time American fly fishing's deity, couldn't put down Francis's treatise, *A Book on Angling*.

"Squaring the Keeper," a story in *Hot Pot*, an 1880 collection, tells the story of Francis as a young man on business, the butt of a tavern joke: He believed he has a hot trout-fishing tip from some locals, namely about "the stream down agin th' steation."

He didn't have his fly gear with him but decided he'd have a try at it anyway. He did think it strange that a stream flowing through the center of town had an unmolested population of trout, but the next morning, as he stepped over "a stile opposite the public house," he could see that the stream was seldom fished perhaps because it didn't look inviting.

His first cast barely touched the surface when *Spang!* went the line, cutting the water, out toward the opposite bank—the fish was a good one, and Francis landed "some three or four brace of them pretty quickly." At a railway embankment he ended up in a tussle with a beauty and "a train rattled by, and a row of heads popped out to note my battle." Before long he was stuffing trout in his pockets and returning to the inn for a bite to eat.

"What! Bin a-fishin', sir?" inquired the hotel manager.

"Yes, and had some very nice sport—eighteen brace and a half, and one two-pounder."

"Why, where *have* you been then?"

"Oh, up the ditch in the thicket yonder."

"Ditch! Why that's the head of the Mole! Don't you know that I'm the keeper to it? And master's so dreadful particular that he won't give leave to no one, and there hain't been a single rod in there two years (Francis thought to himself that he could well believe it) and, by jingo, here he comes! Here, bring them fish in out of sight."

From behind the door the two observed the master and the "see-you-hanged-before-I-give-you-leave" look on his face. The keeper explained that he must return to the office to see what should be done. "Ye ought to be summoned, that you did!"

But Francis wondered if they might talk about it first. "If you've got to do anything professional, why we shan't either of us be the worse of it for a pipe and a glass of brandy and water. 'You can always take up a quarrel at any time; but a limited portion of spirits and water you cannot,' quoth I, quoting Dickens."

The keeper shook his head "no," "but . . . it was like the shake of a pointer's tail when he is not certain whether he has game before him or no." So Francis "filled up the two big rummers with a stiff dose of mahogany," and got out his pipe and filled "it with the finest of birdseye, with which my pouch was well stocked."

"Well, I be dashed if I knows what I ought to do! 'Tis clear to me as ye did'n knaw ye was doin' wrong," the keeper said. "The pointer's tail was wagging," Francis observed. The keeper picked up the "big rummer, and a third of the mahogany vanished at a swig." The narrator "pushed the big pouch across to him" and "his eyes lightened at the sight of the birdseye."

"'That be true,' he continued, filling his churchwarden in an absent kind of way, as if the question was still one of uncertainty; and he repeated, slowly, "That be ver-ry"—puff, puff—pause—"mazin' foine backer this"—puff— "Lor!"—puff, puff—"it dooes one good, sich a bit o' backer as this."

The conversation picked up, moved off the topic of poaching, and "branched off into general sport. Mine host was a real enthusiastic sportsman [who] loved a crack about it like the present. We went the whole round of hunting, shooting, coursing, fishing, with a touch of ratting and badger 'droring,' and we both enjoyed ourselves very thoroughly."

After a number of rounds, "mine host and myself grew more and more . . . pleased with our company." When he made ready to go, Francis left his tobacco—and the keeper allowed that if anybody "a seed you," he would have been removed. "Now, mind, you must promise me you woan't never goo there no more. . . . But, lookee here" (catching hold of Francis's arm just as he left the door, and whispering in his ear), the next time as you cooms, goo up droo my garden, and out at the little gate at the back; there ben't no footpath at all there, and the vishin's a sight better nor 'tis down thik way."

Ah, the coveted inside track. A bit of generosity (the preferred currency leaning toward smoke and drink, with food running a weak third) could certainly pay off. Short of that, resolving a dispute called for civility, appropriate for a sport that confirmed a certain social standing. Back at the Centennial, Norris had to duck the verbal social climbing; on the Mole, Francis had to condescend (in the best sense of the word) to his host. But in either case, cordiality remained an essential ingredient in fly fishing's social patina.

Two years after *Hot Pot* appeared, Francis suffered a crippling stroke, followed by three operations for tongue cancer. His speaking and movement were impaired, but he continued to fish with his friends and other members of The Angling Club until, in the words of his memoirist, he finished out ". . . a gusty showery afternoon in autumn to the chill end, and reeled up his last line on the Old Sheep Bridge at Houghton." After that he worked on angling from his room, painting river scenes and correcting proofs, eventually dying in the morning while getting dressed, the day's work waiting at his bedside. Some might think it odd that an activity premised on indulgence could produce heroes, but here, in fact, we may have had one.

"D'ye Call That a Fush?"
Jock, the understrapper
WILLIAM SENIOR

"A Lovely June Day," *Near and Far: An Angler's Sketches of Home Sport and Colonial Life*, 1890

As good trout fishing increasingly required some travel, many fishing stories became what we might call "travel pieces." Such narration, with anglers themselves at the literary helm, presented problems, truth-telling among them, particularly since readers came to depend on outdoor publications for information. Writers always tried to capture the essence of an area, though, as Adirondack Murray discovered, you want to keep your wits about you when tossing around those word pictures. Not unlike earlier transcendentalists, fly fishermen in effect traveled to find the heavenly spot and once there strived for an induced state, in their case usually brought on by hungry trout. In the words of English clergyman and author Charles Kingsley, the angler sought a "dreamy contemplative repose, broken by just enough amusement to keep his body active, while his mind is quickly taking in every sight and sound of nature." I suppose I like a little more of the fish catching, but Kingsley has a point: There was the genteel tradition to uphold, after all.

None portrayed the alchemy better than William Senior, who followed Francis at *The Field* and wrote a memorable travel piece, "A Lovely June Day," which appeared in *Near and Far: An Angler's Sketches of Home Sport and Colonial Life*, published in 1890. If Francis's piece told an intimate story of two men coming to a meeting of the minds, Senior's opened up an entire vista on a fishing trip to Scotland—the ultimate destination for English anglers at the time, thanks to the spike in fishing pressure and the northern extension of the rails—the "permanent way," as it was called. By 1872, as historian Andrew Herd notes, railroads had begun offering "angler's concession tickets" to fishing clubs (whose memberships exploded in this period), further easing the financial burdens of travel. Articles such this one drew throngs of anglers to Scotland's wild waters.

This particular June day started early, in the half-light of 2 a.m., when Senior heard the "little burn tinkling" by his window. He knew it had plenty of that particular kind of burn trout "which few but worm-fancying boys angle for; yet which make a most toothsome breakfast-dish." Senior hurried out to have at them, accompanied by "Jock, the understrapper about Glenalken," who decided to watch the angling, "there being no 'whusky' or handy tap at that preternaturally early hour."

Senior derricked out one trout after another. "That makes twelve fish," he exclaimed, making the rookie error of calling anything other than an Atlantic salmon a fish. Jock corrected him. "Fush! D'ye call that a fush? I call it a fengerlin'."

Set straight, Senior took a moment to bask in the "exotic" world around him. "The sun rose boldly. . . . How clear and champagny in its exhilarating effects was that atmosphere! Away from the world, determined to throw care to the winds, with at least sixteen hours of a superb June day before us. . . ." Fly fishermen liked to see themselves as interested not only in the genteel but in the pastoral as well. The romance of outdoor beauty dominated the outdoor paintings of the time on the American side of the Atlantic too—in the Hudson River School but also on the canvasses of artists such as Winslow Homer. Senior noted the "pulsation behind the unfolding curtains of Heaven, and lines of light, that had been just touched by the sun in their hasty darting, spread out fanwise . . . goldened by the god of day stretching forth his hands upon the glad world."

The combination of pastoral lushness and social irony served as the story's guideline, and continues as a cornerstone of fly-fishing sensibility on both sides of the Atlantic. Senior's nonplussed companions helped him temper the hyperbole: "The ponies had enough to do to pick their way over the rocks, and Jock seemed to surlily ignore everything. . . . The way in which Parker [his day's companion] and I passed off our sensations was characteristic of an affectation cultivated by Englishmen who want to be thought knowing and self-contained. We did not burst into raptures. . . . In point of fact, we never uttered a word."

But Senior struggled to stifle himself. "Two dozen trouts caught with a fly, a sensational sunrise, and a mile and a half of hillside, jogging on a pony not much bigger than a sewer rat," he remarked at length. "Not bad for half-past four in the morning." Jock, who trudged stolidly along near [him], grunted, "Call 'em fengerlens, call 'em fengerlens!"

They stopped at a loch, where rises dotted the surface. The first order of business was to get Jock settled down, and they "conciliated him with a dram, which operated upon his temper like magic, and sweetened his sour old face and voice on the spot." Senior followed that with an offering of Cavendish from his tobacco pouch, "which made him more genially disposed," to the point that "he was so good as to refer to my favourite eleven-foot trout-rod as "'that thing.'" Senior hooked a trout "at every throw, and occasionally a brace at a time."

For lunch there was cold chicken and loch water, the latter "rendered harmless by an infusion of Glenlivet." Parker and Senior wrestled in nearly forty trout, "yellow, darkly spotted, burly fish, of herring size, and as like in size, shape, and characteristics as peas. Merrier fish never came at a fly."

At the next loch the three men boarded a "small and rickety" boat. Senior "elected to sit in the stern, and trail behind with a hand-line for pike," which in this water were considered vermin. He ended up leaving seven of them on the bank. While Jock handled the boat "upon this lovely June day . . . Parker landed two brace of brown-backed, coarse-headed trout, marked like a plum pudding, and magnificently fierce when hooked."

At six o'clock, after Jock had been packed off with the fish, Glenlivet, and pony, Parker and Senior arrived at the village of Stomally to fish along the shoreline of "the narrow salt-water loch." Waiting was a "stiff jolly-boat" and a couple of men to row, "one of whom could not speak a word of English, and who gruffly swore that he hoped he would never be guilty of doing so." Saithe and lythe (pollack-like fish) were the targets, with Senior trolling a pair of flies made of "dirty white wool" attached to a sapling and "Parker still wield[ing] his double-hander, and us[ing] a monstrous white and red fly." Both fly patterns and rigs "fulfilled the beneficent purposes for which they were rudely designed."

The men had indeed enjoyed their sixteen hours of fishing and were treated to a beautiful sunset of "fiery red mountains in the sky, orange-tipped pinnacles, prairies of copper-hued strata, lakes of pure pale gold, and finally a succession of fairy-like purples and violets." And in this beautiful scene fellow brothers of the angle, in "a dozen boats like [theirs], only with sapling-rods stuck out in all directions, moved at measured speed to and fro. The laughter, song, and converse of the fishermen sounded clear."

Senior was at the midpoint of a writing career that stretched across six decades when he penned this ode to Scotland. He'd knocked about at various papers, beginning in 1858, eventually caught a trout on fly, and before long was writing for magazines under the pseudonym of "Red Spinner." Like Francis, Senior became one of angling literature's great generalists, as content in the stern of a leaky rowboat dragging a phantom gudgeon on hand line for pike, as he was casting a fly to a "fush" on the Tweed.

American anglers read his books (notice of their publication appeared in library circulars and *The New York Times*, for instance), and his conception of the ideal June day certainly spoke to all fishermen. The Arcadian frame—particularly the idea that anglers saw the heavens in a way that others could not—beckoned to sportsmen on either side of the Atlantic. Wilderness destinations such as the Adirondacks, Maine, Canada, and the West had already entered the American imagination by 1890, and the city angler with boyish enthusiasm paired with a rural guide filled with gravelly retorts had become as much of a stereotype in America as in England and Scotland. The upper crust of England's angling fraternity often chastised the lower classes for their penchant for drink, but it is worth noting that in this tale, the expedition definitely hits all cylinders only after the Glenlivet made an appearance. American anglers would have no doubt added a nineteenth-century version of "Party on, Wayne!"

The pan-Atlantic appeal most clearly appears in Senior's own position, his comfort in angling's big tent, his sharp-eyed humility, his crafting of the ideal fishing day so that it draws the arc of an ideal angling life, beginning with small fish and many of them, fending off the villainous at midlife, and ending in the embrace of the angling community beneath a blazing sunset. If that is the promise, most anglers would surely sign on, regardless of country—or century.

"I Allers Sells 'Em My Trout"

Shorty, a local entrepreneur

THAD S. UP DE GRAFF, MD

"Shorty: A Native Fishermen Who Takes 'Em on a Fly,"
Camping in the Alleghenies or, Bodines, 1883

American fly fishermen traveled more in the late nineteenth century in part because of fishing pressure near towns and cities. But the traveling also reflected the blossoming romantic appeal of the natural continental beauty and bounty. The first loves were the streams and rivers and areas closest to the eastern cities, the Catskills being one, along with the Adirondacks and Maine. Later other areas in the West and in Canada would join them. Charles Hallock titled his 1873 book *The Fishing Tourist* for good reason.

The tensions that Francis and Senior effortlessly deflected often proved stickier in America. If anything these tensions grew with the century, typically over posted land or some other aspect of contested river space. Other conflicts between landowners and sports, guides and clients, fly fishers and bait fishermen, conservationists and limit keepers, lawbreakers and game wardens, have characterized different streams and locations. The polarities might change form, but disagreements over partitioning of resources have remained a part of the American fly-fishing tradition.

In the late nineteenth century, relations grew particularly fractious between fly fishers, generally city people, and their rural hosts, even though both benefitted from the presence of the other. Farmers and "natives" (such as Sawney Moore) provided lodging and guiding, while visiting fly fishermen paid for the services. Many city people saw farmers and "natives" as ignorant and lazy; rural folks considered fly fishers intrusive, condescending "fancy Dans." The more fluid class boundaries in America made the issue more volatile than in England, where class status was fixed rather than sought. The Beaverkill angler appalled at the "harvest" of brook trout (p.69), it should be noted, never disputed the men's right to do as they had—which is why he posted the stream.

As early as 1864, Thaddeus Norris had alerted readers to the possibility that a landowner might appear singularly unimpressed with a party of anglers wading down the middle of his stream. Perhaps Norris's move from the rural South to Philadelphia left him with an understanding of both points of view. In any case, Norris wrote, "a chew or a pipeful, and a swig at your flask, will make him [the native] communicative." Some roasted trout might encourage him to "post you as to all the trout streams within ten miles. It is therefore a matter of policy to cultivate the good feeling of the natives, the boys especially, as stones are of very convenient size along a creek to throw at a surly fisherman." It was certainly not befitting of exemplars of the genteel tradition to engage in a rock fight with the local youth.

As more and more anglers took to the streams, relations between locals and visitors only deteriorated. "Shorty: A Native Fishermen Who Takes 'Em on a Fly," a story by Thad S. Up De Graff, MD, explores the city mouse–country mouse aspect of trout fishing in some detail.

De Graff and his companion, Hamlin, were fishing Lycoming Creek in Pennsylvania, near Ralston, and planned a stay of several weeks, bunking part of the time with a prosperous farmer, Squire Bodines, and camping the rest of the time on his land. The latter setup included a cook, a parade of fishing buddies, and extended visits from families—babies and all (Ralston was on a rail line). The men named their headquarters "Camp-Don't-Care-a-Darn" and put up tents, but on balance the operation felt closer to an Elks Club picnic than a wilderness adventure.

De Graff made a good narrator. He had no compunctions about laughing at his own ineptness, nor any interest in establishing himself as the expert fishermen (a title he gladly ceded to Hamlin.). Accounts from contemporaries characterized De Graff as driven and big-hearted in his professional life (a surgeon and researcher), as well as in writing, photography, and fishing. He died at age forty-six, just six years after publishing this book. The Lycoming was apparently an annual trip.

This particular chapter portrayed Shorty, a local fellow who made his living off the land. Others called him the "Shark of the Stream." He was a local fishing legend, though Shorty's "depredations upon Pleasant Stream" typically employed "nets, set poles, outlines, and other abominable contrivances for slaughtering the fish of this most delightful of all trout streams."

At one point, De Graff had a big fish on. He and Hamlin swatted at it with their nets as the trout darted "hither and thither, between Hamlin's legs" before escaping. That brought Shorty out of the bushes and into the scene.

"I knowed you'd lose 'im," he said, "I caught one bigger'n him, over on Pine Creek, once, and he mixed three of us up just as this 'un did you fellers, and jumped clean over my head and knocked my boy down."

De Graff described Shorty as around fifty, "short of stature, with a small . . . head, densely covered with long, shaggy, unkempt hair [and] whiskers of the same bountiful supply." He had bright eyes, and his broad grinning mouth was "well filled with tobacco-stained teeth." His "threadbare" formal dress included an "abundantly patched black coat [and] a once white shirt." Topping it was "a black slouch hat, profusely ornamented with artificial flies." He clutched a cut pole and "an old, six-quart tin pail, covered with a dirty rag, a hole cut in the center, through which to thrust his trout." One of his sons tagged behind, carrying a net in a black bag.

Overhearing the lunch menu of roasted trout on buttered paper, Shorty extended the use of his fire back in the woods, and hinted that he and his son could use some sustenance too. De Graff responded, "Yes; trout are very delicious when prepared in this manner, Shorty." And while they dined, he intended to find out more about this woodland trout predator.

"Do you fish upon this stream much?" De Graff asked. With a wink not only at Hamlin but at the audience of city folks, he added: "You catch many fine fish, no doubt; take them all on a fly, I suppose?"

"Indeed I does. . . . Why, ye only jest oughter a-bin up here this mornin', afore the wind got to blowin'; why, I ketched—well, ye kin see"—(uncovering the six-quart pail for [Hamlin's and De Graff's] inspection, revealing it more than two-thirds full of trout, from one inch to twelve in length)—"I ketched every blessed one of 'em in less'n a hour. I never seed 'em jump so; why, I took 'em four and five at a time."

"Four and five at a time!" . . . Hail Columbia! Why, you must throw a whole out-line," Hamlin replied. "Of whom do you purchase your flies? I see you have quite a collection," a reference to the tangle of flies festooning Shorty's hat.

"Oh, my 'oman makes all *my* flies," said Shorty.

"Indeed; let us look at them," said De Graff and Hamlin in unison.

Shorty handed over his hat. "'That 'un there,' he said, pointing to one of McBride's grizzly kings, 'that 'un she made yesterday, and I reckon on its bein' first-class, cause I took a whopper with it this mornin' already.'"

With more winks at the audience, the interview continued. "Shorty, where do you live?"

"Well, right there's a bridge that goes acrost the creek; my shanty's there, in the clearin'."

"What do you do for a living?"

"In summer I raises pertaters and corn; fishes, and sells my fish to city chaps what comes here a-fishin' and ketches notftin', and shoemakes in the winter."

"You make enough to support yourself and family, do you?"

"Oh, yes; easy. Why, I makes as high as twelve dollars a day sum days, a-fishin'. I keeps all the fish me and the boys ketches, and when I can't sell 'em to the city fellers, I jest runs down to Williamsport, and gets fifty cents a pound for 'em."

"What, such little ones as you have there in your bucket?"

"Yis, sir; they all counts in a pound."

"It's a shame. Shorty, to take those little fish from the stream; you will soon ruin the fishing."

"Yes, you city fellers all says that; but I allers notices that you never throws 'em in yourselves. They all says them little uns is so sweet to eat, you know."

"But no *true* sportsman will do that, Shorty."

"Well, I dunno: it 'pears to me what you calls yer true uns never comes this way, then. . . ."

With that the two men stood up from their lunches, lighted their pipes, and headed back to the stream for the afternoon's fishing. Now it was Shorty's turn to ask the questions:

"Say, you uns, I forgot to ax ye, doesn't ye wanter buy my trout?"

"Buy your trout! You whimpering, shivering scoundrel, what do you take us for?" Hamlin protested. "We are not pot-hunters, you miserable shark; get out!"

"Well, ye needn't git mad about it; I didn't know but what ye *might* buy 'em; but I didn't see no flask a-hangin' over yer shoulder, I must say, but thought, maybe, ye carried it in yer basket."

"Flask! flask! What's that got to do with it?" Hamlin asked.

"Oh, a heap. I allers notices that them fellers whot carries their basket under one arm and a, flask a-hangin' under t'other have more luck a-drinkin' than they do a-ketchin' ov fish, so I allers sells 'em my trout, and gets a good price for 'em, too."

"That's all right, Shorty; but we have no use for your fish; we are out for sport only, not to see how many trout we can destroy. By-by."

"Good-by, surs. When ye cum this way agin ye will most allers find me here on this stream, sumwheres about, a-ready to build fires or do any other work ye may stand in want of." Shorty tipped his hat, made "an attempt at what resembled a bow," and slipped into the brush in search of some trout-fishing customers who did have a flask.

Even in the 1880s apparently, destination streams had a social dimension that belied the pastoral essence of fly fishing's promise. The Lycoming Valley developed such a "name" that Shorty built his fire away from the stream, so as to avoid the crowds. De Graff hinted at other social elements of the burgeoning American angling community. McBride's Grizzly King, for instance, referred to the flies of Sara McBride, an elegant, imitative tyer and author. De Graff counted on his audience knowing as much, the joke being that someone as uncultured as Shorty's old 'oman couldn't possibly have tied that fly.

The same excesses of industrialism that opened the door for fishing vacations also led writers to look more closely at rural life in general, and Shorty clearly merited an "interview," as De Graff termed it, as though he and Hamlin were anthropologists on a field expedition. Like Fishin' Jimmy, Shorty belonged to a sentimental literary world of women, children, and avuncular, harmless men who are part of the natural surroundings. But Shorty also had a salesman's foot in the door of the growing market economy, say nothing of a jaunty sanguinity about his business plan: If you were going to make your living selling trout, the last thing you needed was a river lined with sober fisherman. (Maybe he should consider opening a streamside tavern.)

Like De Graff, Shorty worked hard. He had a house of sorts and his teeth, or most of them anyway—impressive for any nineteenth-century man of fifty. In these earliest days of tourism, he had, in fact, figured out how to provide services city folks might desire. And he certainly played through the whistle, as when he tried to sell Hamlin some trout as the latter waded out of sight. No two ways about it. Shorty was a pretty fair country businessman.

Hamlin's peevishness at the offer of trout, along with Shorty's disparaging introduction as the "target of ridicule," suggested how sportsmen of the day drew distinctions between themselves and "pothunters." De Graff described Shorty as clearly uncouth, but he proved to have more on the ball than his appearance indicated. At the same time, without the "protection" of the class boundaries that existed in England, the lunchtime interaction had little camaraderie and more posturing. Shorty's angling, predatory and instinctive, showed no evidence of restraint or civility, and he didn't actually join Hamlin and De Graff for lunch, so much as he failed to leave—a reminder that the class tensions between city folks and country folks would only grow more pronounced.

The characterizations also remind us that the fly fisher is telling the story. Part of De Graff's challenge was to unite the two opposing worlds in a single narrative. Not every part is going to fit, given the sensibilities of the upper-middle-class fly fishers and he of small, shaggy head. There was some obvious condescension (and not in the more benevolent English sense of the word, either.) The writers of such "class" stories advanced a world they believed existed. Their exaggerations, which we read as stereotypical and unfortunate today, had middle-class heads nodding in agreement then.

But fly fishers were and are optimists. And what lifts this story is the rule of democracy on the American streamside: Everyone has a right to be there and to expect a certain cordiality. Encounters enjoy an equanimity not always possible elsewhere in society. And Shorty seems to grow in stature as the story evolves. He always manages to answer questions with a story—so that his audience never really has to worry about slippery matters of truth.

In the end, Shorty's unassuming demeanor and deep knowledge of the stream offer evidence for fly-fishing historian Paul Schullery's suggestion that he may be an early "trout bum." Shorty makes no pretense at being a sportsman, but he does like his work, which muddies the waters when it comes to deciding who the real fisherman is. He's oblivious to the sporting code, escapes its assumption that methods of harvest matter, and in the end, ironically enough, embodies the very freedom that Hamlin and De Graff go on vacation to find.

"It Depends upon His Heart"
BLISS PERRY

"Fishing with a Worm," *The Atlantic Monthly*, 1904

When Shorty prowled the banks of the 1880s Pleasant Stream, the brook trout was the only trout. Tales of five- and six-pounders from Maine lakes drew trains of sportsmen north. In rivers closer to civilization, brook trout continued to decline in numbers and size through the period. In the mid-1880s, brown trout were introduced to Eastern rivers, most notably in the Catskills, and fly fishing would never again be the same.

Still, for many American anglers, brook trout fishing with worms continued to anchor their daily lives, which by all reports increasingly felt adrift as the pace of living accelerated with the new century. Even today, a good day of fly fishing for rainbows and browns can make you feel skillful or accomplished, but a good day with brookies leaves you feeling like you are where you belong.

Worm fishing was a way of life for generations of Eastern brook trout anglers, in large part because of the environs that sustained the native trout. Brush-thatched trout trickles accommodated whatever equipment a nineteenth-century boy could whittle or steal, and the hidden worlds and fontinalis treasures worked their magic on the imaginations of young and old. Authors might have written of fly fishing's grace, but most nineteenth- and early twentieth-century anglers remained intent on a full creel, or "fishing for count," as it was sometimes called.

By the turn of the twentieth century, the steady harvest and vanishing forest had further reduced the brook trout's range, as well as limited the size of the fish within that range. The allure of small streams lingered, however, and, if anything, grew as the industrializing nation left the native trout behind in the countryside of its youth. Brook trout remained the connection to pre-contact America, to wilderness. North America was the brook trout's home.

Fly fishing for brown and rainbow trout came into such vogue in the early twentieth century, and with it the criticism of worm fishing that it was too easy, that none other than *The Atlantic Monthly* published a 1904 feature article titled "Fishing with a Worm." In some ways this story responded to the ever-present gap between what goes on in print and what goes on astream. In this case the author was the magazine's editor, an eminent scholar named Bliss Perry. He rose to defend the worm, arguing for its facility in catching trout in brushed-over streams, celebrating the skill and sport that such a venture entailed. "There are some fishermen," Perry noted, "who always fish as if they were being photographed." His article, he explained, was not for them.

Perry set the story on a thread of black water that wound through the tangles of northern Vermont, a stream so small and wooded that you sometimes had to fish by sound. "The trick," Perry explained, "is to shorten your line to two feet or even less" and then ease the worm-baited hook "into that gurgling crevice of water." Chances are "before it has sunk six inches" you'll have one of those "black-backed, orange-bellied, Taylor Brook trout fighting with it."

Perry's friend, an expert fly fisherman and former baseball pitcher, was also an excellent small creek worm fisherman. One day the two fished Taylor Brook during a rainstorm. Perry went off downstream with flies (certain stretches of the stream opened up) without catching much and returned upstream, soggy, only to find his friend with a basket full of trout, including two that were each three-quarters of a pound. Turns out he had found an old sawmill, got in out of the rain, and dropped his worm through a floating mat of sawdust, and . . . well the rest of the story was in his basket.

"I'm afraid you got pretty wet," said his friend.

"I didn't mind that," Perry recalled. "What I minded was the thought of an hour's vain wading in that roaring stream, whipping it with fly after fly, while R (his friend), the foreordained fisherman was sitting comfortably in a sawmill and derricking that pair of three-quarter pounders in through the Window! . . . There is much to be said in a world like ours for taking the world as you find it and for fishing with a worm."

Perry conceded that when possible, "the fly is the more pleasurable weapon." But he insisted that there was nothing quite like feeling a trout taking a worm "with a straight downward tug" as it headed for a tangle. Perry explained that this was not "a disguised defense of pot-hunting." Some of the most "skillful fly-fishermen I have known were pot-hunters at heart." He quoted former President Cleveland, himself an avid sportsman, who wrote, "A true fisherman's happiness is not dependent upon his luck." No, Mr. Perry concluded, "It depends upon his heart."

A challenge needed to be present for the activity to qualify as sport, and for brook trout, that meant squirming into their world of comfort and leaving yours. Get dirty. That was step 1. Step 2 called for secrecy. Brook trout were not difficult to catch. Fishing pressure killed every pond or stream it reached. The challenge was social, less about outfoxing fish than other anglers—like catching fat brookies beneath a floating mat. The best anglers were trickster smart.

As "Fishing with a Worm" suggests, Bliss Perry embodied the tensions inherent in the transition from brookie fishing with a worm to dry fly fishing for brown trout. Dismayed at the increasing number of anglers, he nevertheless "basketed" as many trout as he could. As a youth he fished, hunted, and trapped in rural Massachusetts; as an adult he taught at Williams and Princeton and wrote stories, essays, and books of criticism. After editing *The Atlantic Monthly* for ten years, he was called to Harvard and named Professor of Literature, a position of such prestige that it had been unfilled for forty years. Students responded in kind. His course on English Literature drew so many pupils, he was forced to limit enrollment—by moving to a lecture hall seating three hundred. On occasion Perry's worlds collided, such as the time he remembered he was scheduled to deliver some remarks to the local congregation—the only complication being that his recollection came while he was sitting in a rowboat in the middle of a Vermont pond during a nighttime hornpout expedition.

Perry waded trout streams till his eightieth year, and as a fly fisherman he later admitted some embarrassment at having written so proudly of worm fishing. But the concession, if anything, seems a function of his natural modesty. He appears comfortable in his own skin, a trout predator, celebrating the elemental nature of stream fishing as he stalks, snatches, pounces his way along Taylor Brook, fighting the briars and alders as much as the fish. One senses that there were a good many fly fishermen who had to wash the dirt from their hands before communing with others of their kind. (It is still remarkable how many worms get hooked on backcasts!) Perry's article may have led them to a certain acceptance of the deed and earned them some humility in the process. But, please, no pictures.

"Skitter 'Em"

A fish-hungry neighbor

LEWIS B. FRANCE

With Rod and Line in Colorado Waters, 1884

It was not without some wistfulness that American fly fishers moved into the modern era. But inevitably they did so, for fly fishing had a forward vision, with new places, new tactics, new anglers, new fish. Brook trout purists who fished the private waters of the upper Beaverkill worried that the immigrant brown would ruin the fly fishing, but in fact the immigrant brought it back to life, better than ever. As legendary dry fly innovator and angler Theodore Gordon wrote in the June 29, 1907, issue of *Forest and Stream*, the fishing was now much better. "The first time I fished the Willowemoc, thirty years ago, one could take many trout, but a large proportion were smaller than I would now care to basket. It was the same on the Beaverkill and Neversink. We did not have nearly as many battles with sizable trout as we do nowadays. We never killed any two or three pound fish or had occasional sight or touch of monsters that thrilled our nerves with wild excitement."

The story of the British heritage meeting the American wilderness found one of its clearest articulations in Lewis B. France's *With Rod and Line in Colorado Waters*, the first book solely devoted to fly fishing in the American West, and also one of the earliest American books solely devoted to fly fishing, period. (George Dawson's *Pleasures of Angling with Rod and Reel for Trout and Salmon*, 1876, was the first.) The injection of the genteel tradition with tumbling waters led eventually to an American fly-fishing tradition.

France's book tells the tale of Western rivers—where American fly fishing ultimately built a beautiful vacation home. A fly-fishing pioneer in every sense of the word, France was born in Baltimore in 1833 and grew up in a well-to-do family, attending Georgetown University and becoming a lawyer. He "drifted with the tide," and in the winter of 1861, as the nation teetered on the brink of war, newly married France and his wife, Rowena, lit out for Colorado, joining the rush for gold, which ended before they arrived. The newlyweds stayed on, however, moving into "an unchinked log cabin in tiny Denver City," in the words of Colorado historian John Monnett.

Not long after, a "fish hungry" neighbor came by, inquired of Mrs. France whether she might briefly excuse her husband from his duties as *paterfamilias*. "Of course I could," France recalled her saying, "was glad to be rid of him." (What else would we expect of a young woman who'd traipsed across the 1860s prairies in search of bonanza gold?) With "old Charlie" hitched to the buckboard, the two adventurers headed off. Fishing tackle was rare in Colorado in the 1860s, so France cut a plum bush sapling and his older companion gave him a packet of flies.

"How do you fish these?" France inquired.

"Skitter 'em," his companion said.

Unfortunately, he never got a chance, for no sooner had he given "that plum sapling a swing and landed the fly . . . than [he] saw a salmon-colored mouth, felt a tug and the following second [his] first trout was flying over my head." And with that, France "struck it rich"—not as gold prospector, but as a fly fisherman. He waded in the boot steps of other earlier pioneers who, to the consternation of Englishman George Tattersall, had also cut "fishing poles" from "their adjoining woods."

France seemed possessed of that spirit of movement, what visiting Frenchman Alexis de Tocqueville may have meant when he called nineteenth-century America "a land of wonders, in which everything is in constant motion and every change seems an improvement." That winter, the plum sapling's limitations apparent, France roughed out a rod from lengths of pine, cedar, and hickory. For $7 in gold dust, the local watchmaker fitted "the blank" with ferrules, and since "Drug stores and whiskey shops get to the frontier with equal facility," France managed to locate some shellac, with which he coated the finished product before presenting it for inspection to Rowena, who pronounced it "just perfect."

As time passed, fishing became a larger part of France's life. A good example was a trip that probably occurred in the late 1870s or early 1880s. He and his companion camped near the Grand (now Colorado) River. They rode horses along narrow cliffs to reach a secret spot. (I know, right; a secret spot in the Custer-era West.) And you know what? The trout were not impressed. The two men hooked one six-incher. They returned to camp in silence.

But the next day they returned to the pool and found the trout ready to rumble. France cast "a brown-bodied gray hackle gently upon the placid water." This time "the fly had hardly touched the surface, when suddenly from out the depths there flashed an open-mouthed beauty, and that hackle disappeared as, turning head down and revealing his glittering side, its captor plunged again into the till-then silent pool." France tussled with that trout, and with writerly ambition, as well. Fortunately he remembered old Adirondack Murray, "wherein he described his "happiness" under like circumstances; cracking bamboo and spinning silk, with a half dozen Johns with landing nets." France thankfully dialed in some restraint and demurred. In the end, he had an excellent day with his Gray and Brown Hackles, while his companion, a man of practicality not letters, did equally well—on live grasshoppers.

Unlike Murray, for whom irony remained a mystery, France wrote with self-effacement, perhaps to insure that the scene in print would come as close as he could make to the actual scene on the ground, perhaps as an early incarnation of the droll western voice, or perhaps as both. A good example came in his comments on that day's success astream:"The rapidity with which news of success in trouting will travel through the various camps in one's vicinity is somewhat singular, and is only equaled by the celerity with which the reports of the quantity captured is multiplied. . . . We learned the next day that we had caught anywhere from twenty-five pounds to a hundred, and I am unable to say how many went exploring for trout on the day following." Travel writers were among the biggest offenders of course, and they sold the entrancing Western bounty like it was the last Gray Hackle in camp. But France wasn't a tourist writing for other tourists. He lived there. He seemed to have no interest in fashioning an authenticity through florid descriptions of hyped fishing.

That evening France met a younger brother of the angler who was having a tough time of it. The young man looked the part of a fisherman, with "light drab pants, cheviot shirt, and a broad-brimmed felt hat, the band of which was stuck full of flies of all sizes and a multitude of colors. He had a fifty-dollar rod and a fifteen-dollar reel of wonderful combination. . . ." But luck was not with him, and with "his eyes, emphatic with disgust . . . he avowed there were no fish in the Park." France noted the bright red fly he had on his rod. The young man explained that "he had whipped five miles of water with that fly and could not get a rise."

Small wonder, France said, joking that a blue rag torn from his shirt would make a better fly than the bright red monstrosity fixed to the guide of his rod. When the young man took offense, France calmed him down and suggested either a Gray Hackle or a live grasshopper. The next evening the nimrod reported in, rather excited, explaining that he'd tied into a behemoth trout that had broken his tackle, pulled him through the sage brush, and tore up his clothes. A passing angler had fished him out of the river. The man had the fever now, and the next day France "saw him following a trail down the Grand" in possession of "some hackles and . . . a pole cut from a plum bush."

France enjoyed a laugh with the audience, but he also remembered his manners in his treatment of the newcomer, offering free advice and free flies. Even across the century, his voice reveals a certain courtliness, perhaps the remnants of his upbringing in the antebellum South, perhaps the gentility that comes with fly fishing, albeit Western style. Even more interesting is the fact that as early as the 1880s, there was a fishing "encampment" and an accompanying general traffic of fishermen, with both beginning and experienced anglers, who kept one another educated and entertained.

Moreover, the homegrown fly-fishing *techniques* in practice on Bear Creek and the Williams Fork seem strikingly modern, particularly with regard to "dry-fly" fishing. Experienced anglers used natural colors not bright red. France "skittered" his dry flies sometimes. Other times he "gently" cast so that "the fly had hardly touched the surface." Even the tenderfoot knew the lingo, if not the technique: He'd fished five miles of river and "could not get a rise." Somewhere on the Test, Frederic M. Halford was completing *Floating*

Flies and How to Dress Them, and upon reading his book in the late 1880s and 1890s, many Eastern and British anglers would feel as though the front entrance to dry-fly fishing had finally been opened. France and his buddies, more drawn to coulds than shoulds, had been using the side door for years.

This was the West, the frontier, where possibility drifted beneath an endless sky. For trout fishermen, the West was American wildness, with virgin fishing so compelling that just a decade earlier in Montana, it had kept General Crook and his men deliciously diverted on Goose Creek. Meanwhile, not far away, General George Custer and the Seventh Cavalry could have definitely used some backup.

"What Kind of Animal Woman Is"
Cornelia Cochraine DePeyster
HENRY VAN DYKE

"A Fatal Success," *A Fisherman's Luck*, 1899

The defining element of fly fishing lay in its forward gaze, be it exploring the wilderness, as with France, or in protecting waters, as with Roosevelt.

Fly fishing has always been a gateway into the sporting world for those not invited initially—as in the anecdote of France and his young friend or, for that matter, France and his old friend, who took him on his first trip. In terms of its craft, fly fishing has always been propelled by possible improvements, as reflected in the presentation versus imitation debates between Norris and Roosevelt early on, and the dry fly interest that intensified with the century's turn.

Such a result-based meritocracy offered a real opportunity to newcomers, and fly-fishing history is full of those who made great use of it—none more notably than late nineteenth-century women, who played a prominent role in fly tying and fishing innovations, a trend that continued into the twentieth century. One of the earliest examples occurred on Lycoming Creek, some twenty years before Hamlin, De Graff, and Shorty cooked lunch on the banks of Pleasant Stream. The innovation in question marked one of the earliest attempts in America to place entomology in the service of fly pattern.

Apparently the Lycoming trout had a reputation for being difficult to catch, even in those early years. But a summer resident named Elizabeth Benjamin noticed that one angler, the local tavern owner, never seemed to have much difficulty filling his basket. She began a bit of streamside spying, "wading out in the Creek unnoticed by Conley (the tavern owner)." She noticed "that the largest trout would always jump for certain kinds of flys (sic)." Benjamin and her husband fashioned some nets to catch the bugs, which she then imitated with thread and feathers from some chickens. Before long the word was out, and visiting anglers paid her "fabulous prices for all [the flies] she could make." This story we know because of a letter written in the 1930s by her son Joseph, then in his eighties. The letter was subsequently uncovered by fly-fishing historian Austin Hogan, as described in *American Fly Fishing* by Paul Schullery.

A decade or so later, and some 150 miles to the north in western New York, a young woman named Sara McBride gained national prominence by more comprehensively connecting entomology and imitation—and by designing and tying beautiful flies. The daughter of Irish fly tyer John McBride, Sara grew up near Caledonia Creek (now known as Oatka Creek). She wrote about her new ideas on imitation in a three-part series titled "The Metaphysics of Fly Fishing," published in *Forest and Stream* in 1876. Her flies were exquisite; she won a bronze medal at the Philadelphia Centennial Exposition that same year. As her appearance in De Graff's book suggested, she had become one of fly fishing's luminaries. However, by the early 1880s she also had, like Elizabeth Butler, dropped out of sight—even as fly fishing itself continued to grow in popularity. McBride is known to us today thanks to her inclusion in *Favorite Flies and Their Histories*, published in 1892.

The author of that important text, Mary Orvis Marbury, was the most influential of the three women. Her magisterial effort began with the initial help of her father, Charles F. Orvis, who solicited the top fly fishermen around the country about their favorite patterns. More than two hundred anglers from thirty-eight states replied. Marbury then turned their responses into a comprehensive compilation of fly patterns, with beautiful plates. The book became the fly-fishing bible of its day.

The written responses leave a rich portrait of fly fishing in Victorian America. One respondent, C. B. Burnham, recalled "the old days" and explained what one did upon breaking the boat net back in the 1840s: "My chum struck a three-pound trout, a fine fellow, which gave fine sport. . . . A shot-gun, which was a component of our outfit, was loaded and in the boat; at the proper moment, I saluted the trout by discharging a load of shot at his head, and by that means saved the fish."

And since fishing was supposed to be joyful more than anything else, the responses included intentional humor as well. In response to Adirondack

Murray's contention that blackflies were a myth, author Henry Guy Carleton wrote, "There is not a single black fly in the Adirondacks. All black flies there are born married and have large families."

Favorite Flies and Their Histories provided a moment in the sun to talented local anglers of the day. The dearly departed Lorenzo Prouty (the "genial Prouty," as he was called), who ran the tackle section of the famous Bradford's of Boston for twenty-seven years then died suddenly, and did so much to help other fly fishers—he got a shout-out. The book spoke back to other books. De Graff wrote of the "Hamlin," named for his pal, and that fly made an appearance in the plates and descriptions in Marbury's book.

Marbury began the organization of American fly fishing into systems of patterns and imitations. She raised fly-tying and fly-fishing experiences from the discrete and local and transformed them into recognizable and national. There is something democratic about the way that "field" authors wrote in about their favorite fly patterns. Authority rested less in canon and more in experience. Every man was a fisheries researcher. Fortunately, certain women knew how to make sense of the findings.

It was one thing for women to do the work in the home so that men would have a better angling experience. That was the story of the sexes in the early and mid-nineteenth century. It was quite another when they wanted to come along. Nineteenth-century stories (written by men) had not been kind. Earlier in the century women's presence (or aura) in a story had generally led to the angler's downfall, which certified the experience as masculine, as in Frank Forester's romantic tale of Jasper St. Aubyn. Perhaps the most important of these stories was one by Scotsman Andrew Lang called "The Lady or the Salmon," in which poor old Houghton Grannom faced exactly that dilemma. The stakes were high—it was his wedding day and, wouldn't you know it, but there was one big salmon on his line.

Grannom never really decided to stay and fight the salmon, so much as he never could bring himself to leave. Many of his fellow anglers would have protested that the latter was less egregious, but his fiancée, Olive Dunne, a lady "for whom her dignity is her idol," had deaf ears for such nuance. Grannom went fishing on the biggest day of her life, and there was little to understand, let alone forgive. His only remaining move is finding an honorable way out. Which he does of course.

But fly fishing's forward-looking orientation posed a challenge to such a mentality as women took to the streams (and fields) in increasing—some would say, alarming—numbers. Victorian convention may have ruled the institutions of the land, but the American outdoors had always been a place with fewer restrictions, where social conventions seemed less oppressive and where, most importantly, proof lay not in the bravado but in the creel, as the experiences of Ms. Savory and Ms. Roberts so clearly showed. Fly fishing, with its gentility and decorum, appealed to women participants even more.

In "A Fatal Success" by Henry Van Dyke, a certain Mr. McTurk discovered (ironically on the great pool that fly tyer Carrie Stevens made so famous but a generation later) that it is a mistake to assume women inferior anglers.

Author Van Dyke (not to be confused with T. S. Van Dyke, who wrote hunting stories) was one of the top angling writers of his day. Like Bliss Perry, he was a poster boy for the genteel tradition—minister, Princeton professor, ambassador to the Netherlands—with a sly sense of humor. The main character in this story, Beekman DePeyster, was a successful stockbroker and the best fly fisherman in his prestigious angling club, the high rod on any expedition. He met life head on, delighting in its challenges, and he married Cornelia Cochrane, a strong-willed woman who carried her beauty "like the family plate." Their union promised bliss and achievement, except for one detail: As much as he lived to fish, she hated it.

He tried to convert her. He dragged her up to the Adirondacks, but clouds of mosquitoes greeted them, and the trip, uh, didn't go so well. Next up, Maine's

Moosehead Lake. Old Testament–style rain dampened everyone's spirits. Interestingly, though, Cornelia began to take an interest in the fish that came into the dock. Moreover, she straightened out a certain Mrs. Minot Peabody of Boston on the matter of whose husband landed the biggest fish, for "Cornelia was not a person to be contented with the back seat even in fish stories."

Beekman sensed the wheel of life turning. The next September at Upper Dam Pool on Richardson Lake, Cornelia overheard the crotchety Mr. McTurk opine, "Women have no sporting instinct. They only fish because they see men doing it. They are imitative animals." Cornelia said nothing, but she was peeved. She convinced Beekman to show her how to wield a rod, the intent being to show "that old Bear McTurk, what kind of animal woman is." Her first night out she insisted on fishing late through the rain and finally, just before midnight, hooked and landed an eight-pound, fourteen-ounce brookie, the best in camp. She struggled up to the yellow light of the main house lugging the trout, inquiring politely of McTurk, his opinion of her fish.

From that point on it was Katy, bar the door. Cornelia wanted only to fish. When Beekman grew tired, she let him snooze and hired a guide to go out with her and net her fish. She arranged for a six-week vacation to fish for brookies on Lake Pharaoh in Canada. She was always the first up and out. When they returned, someone asked Beekman how the fishing was. Three hundred pounds, he answered. "To your own rod?" "No-o-o, there were two of us." The next year found them in Labrador for salmon, and magazine articles appeared about her, one which, titled "The Equivalence of Women" she believed sold short her achievements.

Cornelia became "a 'record' angler of the most virulent type." She intended to fish 'em all. As for Beekman, "well for him there were no more long separations," that's for sure. He was last seen following Cornelia along the Beaverkill. In response to congratulations on having made "an angler of Mrs. DePeyster," he responded, "Do you know, I'm not quite so sure as I used to be that fishing is the best of all sports. I sometimes think of giving it up and going in for croquet."

The problem was not women themselves but how to stop them once they got started—at least if Beekman DePeyster's domestication is any measure. His dilemma offered a comment on the social anxiety resulting from suffragists marching in the streets and the Nineteenth Amendment looming on the horizon. Although humorous in tone, the piece reflected the worry that women's gains came at the expense of male freedom. Cornelia Cochrane DePeyster's "preferences . . . became law." She won the fight, in other words, and it wasn't even much of a contest. Careful, boys.

"No Incident . . . Unworthy of His Attention"
GEORGE LA BRANCHE

The Dry Fly and Fast Water, 1914

Times were changing. Wider participation in sporting hunting and fishing was a fact. White upper-class men, after all, had argued long and loud that fishing and hunting were good for the character, better for the soul. They couldn't then turn around and say, "but it's just for our characters and souls, you know."

Ideas such as the equivalence of women filled the air in the first part of the twentieth century, but other, less-apparent forces also helped open up fly-fishing participation. One was an increase in consumerism and commerce—both of which were promoted in the general sporting press in publications such as *American Angler, American Field, Forest and Stream, Field and Stream, Outers, Outing,* and others. These magazines included articles on how to cast, fish, tie and select flies, and whatnot, and this information was in turn broadcast throughout the land. These magazines carried articles about and by authors such as John Harrington Keene, Louis Rhead, Theodore Gordon, and F. M. Halford—all of which developed further the idea of fly-fishing strategies, particularly one of growing popularity, dry-fly fishing.

Moreover, the access to these articles expanded. Magazine articles were often picked up and reprinted in local newspapers. In this way, people in remote areas of the country learn how to fly fish. Not everyone was as lucky as Lewis France to have a "fish-hungry" neighbor, who taught him how to skitter his flies. The following is an example of how that literary sort of transmission may have worked. In the July 1886 issue of *St. Nicholas Magazine,* a New York City publication targeting wealthy youth and intent on putting them on the path to righteousness, Ripley Hitchcock published a brief instructional article: "Fly Casting: How to Acquire a Practical Knowledge of this Accomplishment." He advised there is no need for access to water to learn to cast. You can use "a house-top, door-yard, or even the spacious floor of an old-fashioned barn." And from that he proceeded to explain the technique of fly casting. Good information for would-be young fly fishermen (and women) living in New York. But what if you lived on the other side of the country from the Beaverkill and Neversink?

The solution lay in the power of the press, as shown in an article titled "Fly Casting Instruction Reaches the American Frontier," which appeared in the spring 1994 issue of *The American Fly Fisher*. Authors Warren Vander Hill and David Wheeler explain that the *St. Nicholas Magazine* piece somehow impressed the editor of the *Oklahoma War Chief*, a newspaper published in Kansas and hardly claiming a genteel readership. The editor, Colonel Samuel Crocker, printed the article in its entirety for his frontier audience in the July 29, 1886, issue of the paper. That sort of transmission of information occurred every day, and increased with the rise of mass media and consumerism. Kansas fly fishermen were hardly legion—though future president Dwight Eisenhower, an avid fly fisherman throughout his life, grew up in 1890s Kansas. Could an article like this have awakened his unconscious inner angler? In any case, any Kansas fly rod enthusiasts alive at the time of the article were no doubt relieved to be kept in the loop.

But wherever an angler lived, he (or she) had access to sporting equipment through advertisements in magazines and catalogs such as Sears and Roebuck, Montgomery Ward, and others that reached some two million households by the turn of the twentieth century.

An additional boost for new fly fishers came with the introduction of brown trout into the United States, the introduction of rainbow trout to Eastern waters, and the expansion of smallmouth bass into the lower stretches of trout rivers (and their earlier stocking in other waters), all of which occurred during the 1880s. With brook trout unable to withstand the pressures of fishing and deforestation, these new fish became the main quarry for fly fishermen. And they called for new and different angling techniques and resulted in different angling experiences.

The lower Beaverkill River, for instance, largely the domain of smallmouth bass, began to hold trout again, as Theodore Gordon's 1907 letter reflected. Brown trout were considerably more difficult to catch than native brook trout, and this began to change notions of a good-size trout from something unusual and rare and twelve inches long to something complicated and challenging and twenty inches long. As writer Louis Rhead observed in "Bass in the Beaverkill" regarding the brown trout in the smallmouth water below Junction Pool, "it is quite possible, indeed very likely, that the angler will strike and land one of the large brown trout which were planted in this section some years ago. They have grown large and fat, but rise to the fly only in the evening and have grown very wary."

Together with the ideas of fly fishing becoming accessible to all, this line of thinking opened up the idea that fly-fishing success depended less on having access to trout—either through fishing private water or being able to afford the trips that Cornelia and Beekman took—and more on developing the initiative and talent to become a good fly fisherman. Since fly fishing carried at least a hint of gentility as well, it became a way of "becoming someone," as the saying went, through the recreation you pursued.

A good example of such self-improvement shows up in the person of George La Branche who, following his Paul-off-the-horse moment at the junction of Mongaup and Willowemoc Creeks began studying and promoting dry fly fishing with a passion. A young man on the rise in all aspects of his life, La Branche's reputation as a financier, yachtsman, golfer, and wing-shot preceded him. He had no compunctions at using his social class standing as a way to claim an entrance to the American publishing scene, but once astream, his persona seemed much more like the guy next door. He regularly won casting tournaments sponsored by the Angler's Club of New York—and won them in numerous categories. *The New York Times*, for instance, reported that "for two years previously, Mr. La Branche has shown himself to be far and away the best caster for accuracy with the half-ounce bait." Nice to know, somehow, that the father of American dry fly fishing not only could thumb a level wind but also enjoyed doing so publicly.

In the years following his conversion experience, the fly fisherman La Branche came to fish only dry flies and followed the very strategy he invoked that first night; that is, he searched out problems and tried to figure out how to solve them. Anglers such as Thaddeus Norris, Lewis France, and others had been fishing the floating fly on American waters at least since the 1860s, likely before that. Correspondence between anglers, articles, and books had begun to describe tying and using dry flies. What remained was to codify how to fish them on American streams. Enter La Branche.

La Branche eventually published *The Dry Fly and Fast Water* in 1914. Two other dry-fly books—by Emlyn Gill (1912) and Samuel Camp (1913), respectively—had piqued public interest, but La Branche's was the one that captured the public's fancy. La Branche's "matinee idol charisma," in the words of *Esquire* editor and fly-fishing author Arnold Gingrich, social-class connections, and a six-part serialization in *Field & Stream* resulted in a wonderful publishing launch. But the book was more than fortunate. It was a brilliant original work, which explains its lasting influence on how we fish dry flies today.

It was good also because of how it was written. La Branche put his all into writing, as he did into any task he faced. His children would remember how he would ". . . bore us to death. . . . He'd come over every night and read each sentence to us, asking us 'Is that clear?'" He did not write down to his readers.

The authority, in other words, lay not in some man-made pseudo canon, but in the *trout*. They were the masters, and he and the readers were trying to figure them out. In many ways he offered a reframing similar to one that went on in other sports, much as Grinnell and Roosevelt did when they recast rare as elusive. In this case hard-to-catch was good; it didn't mean an angler should go to another stream that hadn't been fished (or dig in the bank like a bass fisherman).

La Branche argued that fly fishing was a sport, and "to him who realizes that it is a sport—a sport that is also an art—there is no incident, complex or simple, that is unworthy of his attention and consideration." La Branche basically showed us how to do so. His anecdotes, like *Trout* author Ray Bergman's a quarter century later, revealed a man who learned through experience; it was easy to imagine doing what he did.

The Dry Fly and Fast Water explored how to observe, respond to rise types, analyze and fish rivers, approach imitation—even how to feel about the sport. La Branche saw dry fly fishing as an active enterprise. He argued against waiting for a rise and wasting fishing time; he argued for studying the rivers and the fish, determining the best lies, and making the best presentation and drifts possible. Repeated casts were not only possible but desirable—create-a-hatch was his idea. Accurate casting was essential. The Americanization of standard dry fly practice had been codified.

Due in part to his emphasis on casting and his casual attitude toward a large selection of flies ("If I were compelled to do so I could get along with one—the Whirling Dun."), La Branche has long been accused of a general indifference to imitation. But that is a myth. In fact, "The Imitation of the Natural Insect" is the title of a chapter. As Paul Schullery points out, La Branche was indifferent not to imitation but to *pattern*, which he saw as imitation's least-important element. He believed that placement, followed by the fly's behavior—what we would call presentation—were more critical.

Over time, imitation and presentation evolved into opposing dry-fly realms, each with its own stereotypical personalities. The "studious" imitators led by Preston Jennings, author of *A Book of Trout Flies*, became associated with "bug studying," while the lineage of the "practical" presenters could be traced back to La Branche or, to put a finer point on matters, to Thaddeus Norris in his debate with Robert Barnwell Roosevelt. La Branche and Norris were problem solvers and possessed fishing's physical skills. Athletic (often Western) fishermen like brother Paul in *A River Runs Through It* became their angling legacies. Paul carried only twenty to twenty-five flies in his hatband, and these were more or less five patterns in different sizes. Paul stands as the remarkable caster, the resourceful angler, the impulsive doer—the dry-fly fisher activated.

Today La Branche steps out of photographs as a dressed up, stiff-collar sort of fellow, but he had some of Paul's fire too. He was nothing if not resourceful. *The New York Times* reported that he was arrested for driving without a license on the evening before his wedding (with his fiancée), but the judge let him off because he was to be married later that day. His success in various sporting contests suggests an edge. Like Paul, he fished hard.

"George is a dualist," one of La Branche's fishing friends told writer Sparse Grey Hackle. "The fish is his antagonist, his adversary. He'll return it to the water after he has conquered it, but he attacks it as furiously as if he were fighting for his life."

La Branche fished like it matters in his book too. That competitiveness and intensity may have been at the heart of his commitment to self-improvement in (and through) the art of dry-fly fishing, which in a sense was the theme of his book: Because of the inherent challenge, there is no greater joy than in becoming a proficient dry-fly fisherman. His interest in trout fishing centered on a rather new idea at the time: fooling the trout, made all the more interesting given the changes in species and fishing pressure. In a sense it was the application of the question of what does elusive confer upon the captor.

La Branche did not deny "the excitement attending the playing of a good trout nor the skill required in its handling." But he also added that in most cases, "the rod will kill nine out of ten fish hooked." Playing a trout "is but secondary to the pleasure derived from casting the fly and deluding that old trout into mistaking it for a bit of living food." The fly-fishing world, however anglers did it—by dry fly, wet fly, nymph—was laying claim to a new source of satisfaction, one that had nothing to do with how many pounds of trout were in your basket.

For this reason fly fishing epitomized sport: None other "requires in its pursuit a greater knowledge of the game, more skill, more perseverance." It so happened that La Branche saw a sort of stages-of-fly-fishing approach to why the dry fly was the "premier method," which was probably part of what made people label him a snob. And certainly that only confirmed what people who didn't fly fish would say about those who did. But it also opened an avenue to the top of fishing's challenges; meeting them could do a lot for a person. It was all a matter of how hard you tried.

CHAPTER 7

"What a Godsend This Sport of Hunting"

UPLAND BIRDS, 1887–1914

By the turn of the twentieth century American young men were learning to play nicer. College football was all the rage. President Roosevelt hosted several meetings to do what he could to temper the violence and limit the casualties on the scholastic playing fields. As for guns, the duels with pistols that occurred in the early part of the nineteenth century, in which men occasionally killed one another, most famously when Vice President Aaron Burr killed former Secretary of the Treasury Alexander Hamilton, had definitely fallen out of favor. But duels with shotguns, with birds as the targets, most definitely remained "in." Americans did love a contest, as described in "A Match at Chickens," a chapter from *Upland Game Birds (1904)* by Edwyn Sandys and T. S. Van Dyke, both well-known outdoors editors and writers. Sandys was the author of this story.

Mr. Sandys, it seemed, had a reputation to uphold. He had landed at an exclusive club whose president, known as the colonel, was a tall and majestic man with a "long, snow-white mustache and imperial" bearing that suggested his was of Southern heritage. "Nor did his appearance belie him, for the colonel was one of the genuine old fire-eating, high-bred lot."

The colonel matched Sandys with a young man named only M—— (the anonymity an apparent courtesy from writer Sandys), described as a "handsome young fellow, straight as a rush." M—— did appear to look down on Mr. Sandys, however, prompting the latter to think, "You're a bit overfond of yourself, my bold Bucko." The talk among club members, regardless, was "that young M—— was a tearing fine shot. . . ."

The colonel explained the contest rules: ". . . in the field, any game recognized as such to count." He reminded all parties of the importance of a fair, gentlemanly contest. Sandys, appropriately reserved, tried to decline but stiffened his resolve when the colonel said, "Well, suh?—Do you desiah to—to—*back out?*"

"Then it's a go—shake!" exclaimed the colonel. As an aside to Sandys, he confided, "I know the man. Well ahead, he's a wondah; even, he's only ordinary; and once behind, he's beat. . . . It's only a dinnah for six gentlemen and a trifling side bet, but we'll win it. We'll show them that an Englishman is game off his own dunghill." The Englishman being the Canadian, Sandys'.

The next morning from the wagon, the four men (M—— brought a second) watched the colonel's magnificent pointer make game. He "drifted to his anchorage [and] loomed large above the grass—a glorious image of steadfast purpose, which might well have been carved from rarest marble by some master hand of old."

"Out with you, gentlemen," ordered the colonel. M—— had the first turn. When the bird flushed, M—— seemed to wait forever, but "at last the big gun roared, the chicken went down like a wet rag." Sandys realized that "this man understood the game, he knew he had a hard-shooting gun, and he had faced the traps. Still, his method lacked finish."

Then Sandys stepped up to "a roar of wings and half a dozen birds flushed." Two bore to the right, and to cut the head off the first and repeat on the slow follower was easy enough. From there the two "fairly settled down to work with the kills even at nine straight." Three more of Sandys's came back headless—he was trying to preserve the meat, as he'd learned to do—and he overheard the colonel: "Wish he'd hit one squarely, I'd dearly like to see what the little gun (a reference to Sandys' 12 gauge) can do." Sandys missed an easy crossing shot, and the colonel's "face [grew] very red, and . . . the white mustache was bristling in a marvelous fashion." When M—— scored on his next shot, a sneer crossed his face, and Sandys vowed to shoot like never before.

As Sandys put it, "The next one [of his] got it squarely in the back at about twenty-five yards and the works of it flew to the four winds of heaven. The next was mashed to a pulp. And the next would hardly hold together. "

The colonel cheered him on, "That's the right way to kill chickens," he said. "Meat don't count in a match!"

Each man shot well, until the colonel decided to try some thicker cover. M—— and his companion protested, but the colonel ignored them as the great white dog quivered to a point.

It was Sandys' shot, and as he approached the pointer, he thought it odd for chickens to be holding in such a thicket. Then came the familiar

Birr-birr-birr! as a covey of quail burst out of the brush. As Sandys put it, "in an instant I was at home." He'd grown up hunting the heavy cover of western Ontario, and he "felt like Wellington did when he heard Blücher's guns." He killed two of them like he was picking up the morning paper.

M—— and his companion tried to get out of shooting, saying "the match is at *chickens*, you know!" But the big white dog was again on point.

"Your turn, Mr. M——." But M—— was rattled. He "looked black as thunder." He stepped up and the covey exploded. With quail zipping off for cover, "there was no time for holding on . . . he *had* to hurry." He missed clean. Then, he missed again.

Back in the open on chickens, Sandys was on the money—no more shooting to save the meat. The next chicken "flew into four bits."

At that point, M—— said, "I—I—give it up. I'm not feeling very well."

At the club, the colonel was glowing with victory.

"Yes, suh, boo-tiful match, suh; one of the finest ever I saw, suh! They outgunned us a bit, suh, the big 'ten' against a poor little 'twelve,' but my young friend is quick, suh, ree-markably quick, suh, and that helped, especially on some quail which we accidentally found."

Later, after the festivities and settlement, the colonel explained to Sandys, "I always liked the English, Southern, you know,—I always preferred a pointer, got one, you know,—and I've always fancied a small gun, quicker, you know,—and I've never lost a match of my own making, suh, never, suh!"

"A Match at Chickens" reflected the twin themes in upland bird hunting in nineteenth-century America—first, the social facility and athletic dexterity of the participants; second, their deep attachment to the land that emerged as a regional veneration of particular game birds, in this case the southern attachment to the bob-white quail. Together these elements formed the core of the upland tradition in the American outdoors.

Wing-shooting anticipated the modern age. Gunners such as Captain Adam Bogardus and Doc Carver rose to fame through match shooting contests featuring live pigeons, and their celebrity sparked a rise in the popularity of bird hunting. Antebellum stories had emphasized the hunter's love for the chase, his manliness, his bravery. Contest shooting, with public challenges, thousands of spectators, five-figure side bets, and runs of a hundred straight passenger pigeons, called less for character than athleticism. Mastery belonged to the skillful contestant who could keep his cool amid the trash talking, a distinction in step with the fast-paced social and business culture of the new century.

The gentility that infused fly fishing also characterized the interactions of bird hunters. And it is interesting that the winner of the contest (the writer, Sandys) and the fixer of the contest (the colonel) were both careful to maintain a courtly behavior in public while sharpening blades in private. M——, the loser, became the villain when he broke the gentleman's agreement and looked down on his fellow scatter gunners.

Certainly this fit with the way Southerners came to see themselves, but in general it distinguished wing-shooting as more genteel than other hunters. Such politeness and class distinction made wing-shooting the blood sport that most appealed to women. And it provided leverage in the class war that developed over land use, or at least wealthy sports entertained the notion that it did. Wing-shooters, after all, were nearly always a guest on someone else's land, and relations ranged from cordial to hostile.

"A Match at Chickens" played off the regional identities that had roots in the pre-war American landscape. Sandys' rival stood as everything the colonel loathed: a posturing urbanite (read: Northerner), well-tutored in shooting method and inclined to gloat when ahead. The rural-born, untutored (but cultured, read: English) hero answered the challenge reluctantly, and therefore with honor. With the contest turning on a bird so common and witless as a prairie chicken, his superior character amounted to little more than wasted genes. Fortunately, the Old South's native game bird made a dramatic entrance and presented the true test of a man's dexterity and composure—and some insight into the nature of victory. As the colonel would no doubt agree, winning was that much sweeter when you beat a Yankee at his own game.

In contrast to the bobwhite quail, the prairie chicken was treated with disregard, a reflection of their abundance, which, as with any fish or game, tends to run counter to nobility. The chicken reached its peak at the end of the nineteenth century, as native grasslands became infused with farmland forage. Trains and wagons, such as the one the colonel commanded, transported hunters directly to the obliging chicken.

Initially the abundance of chickens meant that their numbers held up despite the harvest. But in time mechanized farming destroyed the chickens' habitat; numbers declined, and they were finished as a significant game bird. This development, too, told the story of America's upland game birds.

But that was in the future. The tale begins in abundance, and that had a profound impact on the way wing-shooting gained a solid leg up in the sporting world—and the way we came to feel about the upland birds we pursued.

"The Vault of Heaven"

T. S. VAN DYKE

"Days among the Plovers," *Game Birds at Home,* 1895

Whether hunting agricultural land no longer farmed or shooting birds that once had blackened the sky, American wing-shooters built their traditions on a nostalgic past.

"Days among the Plovers" offers a great example of that wistfulness—in setting and in species. The golden plover ranked among our most popular market and game birds throughout the nineteenth century. Prodigious travelers (both upland and golden plovers winter in lower South America), the plovers signaled their spring arrivals and early-autumn departures with their whistles, as if to say, the hunt is on.

Fittingly, Van Dyke takes us to an innocent place and time, nearly forty years earlier—New Jersey, summer of 1858. Princeton man and son of a congressman, Van Dyke ended up the most widely read and imitated hunting writer of the late nineteenth century. (He also wrote *The Still Hunter*; see p. 145.) He assumed a prominent role in the conservation movement and in various civic affairs, befitting a man of his station. Victorian readers loved his rhapsodies about upland hunting. In this story he recalled an agrarian, communal America that had disappeared beneath the sword of war and crush of industry.

One warm day, the sixteen-year-old Van Dyke wandered through the fields near his New Jersey home, not expecting to find much of any game, maybe "a lark or highholder (flicker) at best." Perhaps some blackberries had ripened beneath the August sun. Instead came a "triplet of melody so soft it seemed to fall through a mile of air." Van Dyke knew that sound. All was game to a boy with a shotgun, and he thrilled to "those pearls of sound that only one little throat can string." He squinted into "the vault of heaven" for "that little film of gray trailing over the late summer sky." He spied a blur, "a bit of gray flitting over some corn," and he threw his gun to his shoulder, fired, and "when the smoke cleared nothing was there but the corn waving darkly green." The "sweet call" sounded everywhere, "as if rebounding from heaven," and "a half dozen more scraps of gray" flew into the air.

Van Dyke rushed back to the house to get more shells, and upon return he flushed plover after plover from the corn, "their notes falling louder and sweeter as they fringed the clouds. He even made a couple of 'handsome doubles' in the process. This was a big deal to the young Van Dyke, for unlike the modern gunners of the 1890s, "he was not born of flame, swaddled with powder-smoke, and tutored by thunder as many 'professionals' are today."

Van Dyke elevated the birds, their beauty and their world, and demoted himself, evincing a humility that helped endear him to readers. He added the quotation marks around "handsome doubles," in recognition of its clichéd usage. He missed more plover than he hit. One, for example, surprised him, and he "wrecked the hopes of a promising pumpkin" with the first barrel and "ventilated the waving corn-leaves" with the second. The plover "climbed the summer breeze with never a feather marred, and on the wings of its silver song bore away toward the zenith."

Van Dyke told of other days, as well, when late-summer storms blew in large flights. He and his companions erected little blinds of cornstalks, tossed out a few plover decoys (bought in New York City), and added a common whistle to the hunting gear. When the crescent lines of plover appeared in the distance, one would blow the whistle, which invariably turned the flock to the decoys even at several hundred yards, and elicited a response from the plover in the form of "their tender notes, often so many at once they seemed the tremolo of some distant organ." The birds would "mass in the air and set their wings to slide down to the decoys."

Often Van Dyke and his buddies shot too soon, and their timing was complicated by the "farmer's brats" on the edges of the field with "relics from the Revolution" ready to shoot at the decoying plover from across the field. The young hunters also faced competition from others—the village parson, for one. He would be out there with an "old musket that had not been fired since he shot his annual rabbit behind his house the winter before" and he would be ready to touch it off at the first sight of plover.

But more often than not, the crescent line sailed in over the decoys in "a medley of white and black and brown and golden dots." At the sound of the first barrel, the plover rose and "sheered off" but then "close[d] for an instant into a dense cloud. . . ."

The softness in Van Dyke's tone hints at the pain he faced as an adult. Before he wrote this book, he contracted tuberculosis and had to move his young family to San Diego (where streets still bear his name) and he hunted, fished, and wrote more enthusiastically than ever. But beneath his decorum and recovery lay failure and tragedy: worthless investments, divorce, two young sons dead in the same winter. By some accounts Van Dyke eventually found peace on a ranch in the California desert, where he lived until his eightieth year. In the meantime, he wrote stories like this one.

What goes on in a writer's heart is never easy to decipher, but you do hope that his personal sadness at least could be said to account for the humility in his prose. He understates his own competence but takes quite seriously the spirituality bursting forth in nature's august beauty and abundance. In so doing he came to speak for a growing middle class, scarred by war, estranged by machine.

You sense that Van Dyke understood that wing-shooting for upland birds became the sport that appealed to this side of the sportsman's being—namely his emotional relationship with the past. Part of this had to do with his own longing for a time that existed before the war, and to a lesser extent, probably, industrialism robbed him of the future he saw himself having. By returning to the land of his youth, he could reinhabit that time when the future was still his, when a flock flitting in meant another moment of life at its fullest. The opportunities were thick, and the world around him was a song growing louder.

"The Guns Become Almost Too Hot to Hold"
FRANKLIN SATTERTHWAITE

"Snipe Shooting on the American Prairies," *Outing*, March 1887

While plover were abundant in late summer and early fall, spring brought snipe, an even more challenging target. Franklin Satterthwaite's story told of the spring shooting at Elbow Bend, recalling the halcyon days when snipe actually darkened the skies.

Challenging or not, snipe were more loopy than elegant like plover, and Satterthwaite zeroed in on abundance as the snipe's main attraction. Why else gush about riding fifty-five hours by rail and wagon and floundering through the mud—all to try to shoot a bird that zooms around the prairie like a balloon losing air and, wings folded, could fit in his watch pocket?

This is a bird-hunting tale, and, abundance or not, Satterthwaite can't wait to tell us how good the hunting used to be. That, in fact, literally became the story, beginning with the first time he ever saw Elbow Bend back in 1875, how many snipe zipped about, even as the horse was pulling the author in the buckboard out to the farm, with his gruff, silent farmer host who held the reins and only "showed signs of life . . . when the flask [was] put about."

The narrator basically considered himself a member of this little Nordic house on the prairie. He had been coming here to hunt for a decade and had seen the children grow up. He first visited Elbow Bend thanks to a "very short man by the name of Mr. Long." And jokes aside, Satterthwaite remained forever grateful, exclaiming, "may the best of luck attend him, and may his hogs never die of cholera." This story represented his chance to draw a breath and tell about that first visit.

On that trip, Long and Satterthwaite were joined by a threesome from the Midwest, two from St. Louis and a third from Cincinnati, the latter a large man who, on the first morning of the hunt, staggered across the soggy ground, toting a satchel filled with 350 shells. White splotches dotted the ground. When, after a half mile, a bird finally flushed, it corkscrewed over the big guy's head, and as he swung he toppled over beneath the weight and shot "no.1 of 350 in midair." The sound tore open the plains and snipe "in thousands . . . rose . . . alighting and re-rising, and rolling over each others as blackbirds are wont to do."

As the men slogged along, they formed a "skirmish line," and Satterthwaite's setter "settled on perpetual point." He sent the dog back to the wagon, "so as not to delay the proceedings." And with that the firing picked up, to the point that "the guns became almost too hot to hold." The man from Cincinnati was a shooting machine, killing birds left and right. He appeared to be on pace to burn through his 350 shells.

One snipe flushed and dipped back through the skirmish line. Just as it did, the Cincinnatian fired and felled a companion rather than the snipe. The Cincinnatian ran "flask in hand, toward his victim." Satterthwaite and the others joined them. "They are all in his stomach!" one yelled, in reference to the pellets.

"Either 49 or 50," said the third man, striving for accuracy.

"Have you a knife?" the Cincinnatian asked. "I guess I can pick 'em out. It won't hurt much, old fel.'" This reassurance prompted "a roar" in the negative from the fallen hunter.

Satterthwaite observed that "the pattern is excellent, [but] the penetration is not first class. The Cincinnatian was still bragging on his shotgun. He nodded to the pellet marks and whispered to Satterthwaite "No dern snipe could get through that—th' best gun in th' United States; jist put her up."

With that the Cincinnatian and the other man helped the wounded fellow back to farmhouse and from there intended to seek medical attention. The frat team out of the way, Satterthwaite brought his setter back on the field and set about enjoying some serious snipe killing. Clouds rose up at each shot, landed, and then could "be seen running like rats on the ground," only to be flushed again.

In time Mr. Long joined him and reported that the two gentlemen from St. Louis "had set sail for home" with an order courtesy of the man from

Cincinnati for more ammunition. At present he was in the kitchen loading more shells, while the "Norwegian and his frau had adjourned to the barn for safety."

It is reasonable to wonder what happened to all the snipe that gunners shot. The answer is that they were desirable table fare, particularly as populations of larger game birds declined in the late nineteenth century. We might think them "sedgy," but the nineteenth-century palate held them in esteem. George Bird Grinnell claimed that he could not tell snipe from woodcock. (I bet I could.)

Snipe proved a market favorite, particularly during the spring months when they gathered in numbers that made their pursuit profitable. Some towns used snipe as a springtime barter system, with certain men basically speculating in snipe futures by barreling, refrigerating, and stockpiling them until they could be sold at a higher profit. Satterthwaite conceded that spring hunting could destroy the species but, after seeing his longstanding protests ignored, explained that "my advice is to go and make merry, for tomorrow we die." As always, the experience in the field didn't conform to entreaties in the press.

Such abundance rendered individual birds objects, indistinguishable in the face of their numbers. Their flocks became the subject of awe. Expeditions for snipe, as with golden plover, were more a matter of shooting than hunting. There was no strategy to finding them. The challenge involved having the hand-eye coordination to pattern them with a shotgun—and that was easier said than done, the failed attempts at doing so comical. As Charles Waterman once wrote, ". . . a snipe appears to do a great many things just for the hell of it—his objectives concealed somewhere in snipe logic." Not exactly a lofty tribute—more akin to the way Wile E. Coyote thinks of the Roadrunner.

But stripping away the veneration of the quarry also reveals something elemental about the nature of wing-shooting. It is a relational sport, different from the individual quest that underlies the pursuit of big game, and that makes it great fun. Missing a ten-point buck doesn't leave any smiles; missing a snipe makes you the butt of jokes. This atmosphere infuses the hunt. In this story, a shooting accident (with fifty pellets, by the way) came across like a football injury—the price of the sport. The snipe flew the wrong way, like a halfback slipping as he makes a cut and fumbling the ball. There was little recognition of the Cincinnatian's irresponsibility—in fact, Satterthwaite mostly used it for jokes—on-field surgery, family cowering in the barn, and so forth. With its promise of great fecundity on the April land, with the timeless continental bounty of birds in flight, with the public display of a person's reputed poise and skill, a morning on Elbow Bend was nothing less than recess without a teacher.

"I Feel Like a New Woman."

The Madam

EDWYN SANDYS

"The Madam's Chicken Shoot," *Outing*, August 1893

National mythology held that in addition to the abundance of the land, the West had open vistas and big skies that promised a clean start and boundless opportunities. Eastern shooting took place on land that had once been farmed; the West's shooting took place on land that still was, or at least had no agricultural past. The West became a place where hunting identities were less recalled than created. Such a backdrop offered a welcoming setting for women's involvement in shooting.

With the prairie's openness, upland bird hunting took on some of fly fishing's gentility, with its easy pace and companionable interaction, the feeling of a picnic (popularized in the nineteenth century) with buckboard, baskets of food, and of course with a dog and gun. Such an outing allowed a woman to demonstrate poise and charm—important given the conventions of upper-middle-class Victorians. These elements—and their appeal—comprised the story in "The Madam's Chicken Shoot" by Canadian-born Edwyn Sandys, which appeared in the August 1893 issue of *Outing*.

In time, Sandys became the most famous wing-shooting writer in America, an advocate for conservation and a new way of understanding our place in the outdoors. "The Madam's Chicken Shoot" was one of his earlier stories. He portrayed the beauty in the bird hunter's natural world in scenic terms, but he was less descriptive than Van Dyke, more narrative. This story began with Mr. Sandys finding himself on the Wisconsin ranch of a friend on August 14, the eve of prairie chicken season—no ordinary time for nineteenth-century midwestern bird hunters

Early chickens held tight, flushed in sequence, and flew straight—and briefly, after which they waited to be reflushed. The young birds were more toothsome than the adults. *The Chicago Tribune*, which covered the approaching chicken season with titles like "The Slaughter of the Innocents," reported that one farm boy, apprehended for hunting before the season, defended himself by insisting, "Why it's only an ole hen." The judge, citing natural reproduction, was unimpressed. In today's management jargon, the chicken enjoyed a multiuse status—as much an agricultural commodity as a sporting proposition. Newspapers balanced notices for "five-cent chicken dishes" with parodies of Chicago hunting parties that shot their dogs and nearly one another (as though they were snipe hunting, or something).

But Sandys's host, his friend Hub, had a lot on his plate. His lovely wife had been feeling poorly, and between nursing her and helping "his man" keep up with the chores, Hub had no time for hunting, or even socializing. A gracious guest, Sandys did his best to pitch in and help. He entertained "the Madam" with stories from the city—she had been out on the prairies for a while. After a few days, she began to come around.

Hub convinced Sandys and the Madam to take the buckboard and the family pointer, Bob, a most handsome and splendid animal (whom the Madam had made a point of spoiling), and go on a chicken shoot. Sandys, after all, had come to hunt. The drive would do her good. Careful, he told Sandys, "she'll talk you to death." To her, he said, "Take him to the big prairie, Sis."

The wagon was already hitched by the time he was done talking. "The Madam . . . face glowing with pleasure" whipped up lunch, grabbed the reins, and, with Bob curled up asleep, "away [they] sped, the stout ponies pulling too hard . . . for the first couple of miles."

"Isn't this too lovely?" asked the Madam. "I feel like a new woman." The Wisconsin "rolling prairies, spangled with golden grain fields, and ringed about with rounded, forested heights" stretched out in front of them. In time Sandys and the Madam made their way into the brown prairie grass, with Bob roaming "farther and farther away, until the lemon head was indistinguishable, and merely a flying white spot."

Sandys questioned Bob's range, only to have the Madam explain politely that, no, he was not ranging too wide. "That's the grandest dog in all the world," she said. They looked out over the brown grass, in Sandys's words, "farther than I had ever looked for a dog before, when what seemed to be a toy-dog that showed whitely" suddenly stopped. They moved up, and Sandys hopped out of the buckboard, Bob quivering. The ponies were feeling left out, apparently, and so they moved up as well. "It was a most extraordinary sensation," Sandys explained, ". . . to be walking up to a point dog while a team of ponies almost stepped on my heels, and two pony muzzles almost rested on my shoulders." Bob, eyes lolling, looked around at him. The animals basically had Sandys surrounded.

The chickens flushed, and Sandys proved himself in fine fashion. As in "A Match at Chickens," Sandys never was one to understate his prowess. In this article he refers to himself as "chain lightning." (Writer Emerson Hough noted Sandys' "invariable skill and success" in an otherwise positive review of this book, *Upland Birds.*) Soon the Madam took her turn. She walked past the staunch Bob "with an easy indifference." She waited, and "up buzzed a strong bird within fifteen yards and flew rapidly low to the grass, affording quite a difficult mark." She was more than ready: "The wee figure straightened with a snap, the gun seemed to flash to the level—one instant's pause, then she tumbled that chicken like a rag in the grass—clean killed!"

Speechless, Sandys recovered his manners and congratulated her with a solid "Bully!" With her bird in hand, her face "glow[ing] with delight and her eyes snapp[ing] in triumph," Sandys thought "if some of our city ladies could have seen that shot, how soon we'd have more of them a-field. . . ."

On the ride back, the Madam "rattled merrily away, for she was a good talker." She also had some news. Her "lovely sister" would be arriving in a day or two. Sandys was wary, but what choice did he have? "A woman like the Madam always has a sister on tap somewhere," he sighed.

Sandys was charged with picking up the guest at the station, the Madam and Hub having "developed a strange weariness." The next day, Sandys taught the visiting lady to shoot. The two, plus Bob (who seemed to divide his time between prairie chickens and his feeding dish), took the buckboard on "long romantic drives over Elysian plains; good sport, good dog, good nags, and a fascinating comrade as keen for fun after the first taste as I was—could a mortal ask for more?"

Sandys extended his vacation and then in "the gathering shadows of a perfect September evening . . . drove her to the depot . . . [and] finally I—I—

"'Yes!' says a lady reader, 'you—out with it, man!' Well, I put her on board her train and bade her good-by. What did you think I said to her?'"

So it is that wing-shooting, as it became socially fashioned, allowed men to act as gentlemen *and* women an opportunity to develop competency—and both to maintain the respectability of their middle-class social roles. Madam was still feminine but no girlie girl; she could engage in activities and show her mettle. Unlike Cornelia DePeyster, the Madam and her sister achieved *and* allowed Sandys to keep his masculinity intact. They might miss the city's excitement, but hardly its urbanity. The plains had fewer restraints, physical and social; the women who inhabited this new country laughed at bawdy tales and spoke their minds.

Sandys died of heart disease in 1906, at the height of his career. He was survived by his mother and two sisters (one of whom was a magazine editor and writer), who may well have given him some insight into what it meant for women to set foot onto the doorstep of equality. His obituary in *The New York Times* included no mention of children or marriage, so it remains a mystery if there ever was a younger sister of his friend's wife and if she ever became part of his life. Sandys enjoyed the sentimental, and perhaps she was his wish for a tomorrow that never came, or even an ode to a choice not made somewhere along the way.

"No Shuten' Aloud"

MAURICE THOMPSON

"The Confessions of an Ancient Poacher," *Outing*, November 1900

Such open-sky stories unfolded with reciprocal warmth between hosts and guests. Satterthwaite virtually ended up a member of the family. Other sports reloaded shells at the kitchen table while the family hid graciously in the barn. The Madam's household operated like a nineteenth-century version of Match.com. As with other elements of the printed sporting life, such stories may not have accurately represented the reality on the ground. They are, after all, written from the point of view of the guest. And, whatever warmth existed cooled off considerably as you moved east.

Economically and socially, farming entered a general decline in the late nineteenth century. Rural land values dropped like a dead-centered quail, thanks to deflating currency and exorbitant costs. The same land that fell into agricultural disuse began to hold more game. But landowners were not so thrilled with a profusion of city hunters they didn't know, who had better guns than they had and assumed they could do whatever they wanted, whenever and wherever they felt like it. Farmers began posting land. This led to hard feelings between landowners and sportsmen, which built through the 1880s and 1890s and were further inflamed by the raging agrarian radicalism that swept through the heartland before dying in the bitter presidential election of 1896. The result was a culture war in which gentlemen sports attributed the "hirsute and humpbacked" (author Maurice Thompson's words, below) farmers' plight to inbreeding and backwardness rather than the market forces of an industrializing nation. The farmers who had epitomized the glory of American democracy and "fired the shot heard round the world" in Emerson's poem of 1836 had become the nation's embarrassing liability just fifty years later. Ministers and educators sponsored programs to modernize rural life, but those backfired: Farmers might not be able to spell "condescension," but they knew it when they felt it.

Differences in class standing and attitudes toward hunting and fishing only made matters worse. Increasing numbers of urban middle and upper-middle classes showed up in the countryside with fancy toys, clothes, and dogs, while the rural folks were there to watch, knowing they could not afford to cultivate an interest in sport hunting. Rural folks also knew on some level that the sporting involvement had social currency in the new urban middle-class culture, so the result was an ever-widening dissonance between urban sport and rural landowner. Small wonder that rural folks stopped being so friendly about sharp-dressed men shooting up their land.

As evidence of the cultural differences, and how they were meaningful in this time of Social Darwinism, urban sports pointed to the way rural folks hunted—for the pot, as if they didn't have the intelligence to wrap their heads around the idea of sport's beauty. The new sportsmen overlooked—conveniently or not—that playing by sporting arrangements required a certain economic privilege. Freed men in the South and poor farmers in the North shot game for food and didn't discriminate by species. And, they had a good deal of fun doing so—as much fun as wealthy sports did on their catered quail hunts, no doubt. Four-legged game such as squirrels, rabbits, possums, and raccoons became quarry (and pastime) for the rural underclass—which preserved the winged species for the sports. Most poor rural folk didn't have money to waste shells on activities in which the elusiveness of the quarry marked the glory of bagging it.

In time, the edges of this difference softened, and rabbit hunting, in particular with beagles, developed into one of the great twentieth-century middle-class hunts. In fact in 1897 and 1898, none other than Edwyn Sandys wrote pieces in *Outing* about hunting hares and cottontail rabbits. In the piece about the latter species, he wrote of "rabbiting," a term that (fortunately) never caught on. But the point was that as the turn of the twentieth century approached, there was less concern with the gentlemanly essence of hunters, a reflection probably of the growing acceptance of sport hunting in general. That said, there was still considerable differences in the identity a man could take from any activity. To call someone a wing-shooter was a compliment;

to call a man a rabbit hunter, well, it probably depended, first of all, where he lived. In the northern part of the country, where a winter hare hunt with hounds was the only sport, it could well be a complement, too. The question could also turn on how the hunter "complicated" the pastime—did he raise hounds? Did they perform well? Did others purchase them? If so his avocation became an indicator of industrious middle-class behavior—so long as it fit with the rest of his lifestyle.

In other locations and situations, a "rabbit hunter" probably carried the same connotations that it did in the antebellum period; that is, it could be taken in any number of ways, none of them particularly attractive. (One could imagine "Shorty" (see p.160) raising hounds as part of his entrepreneurship, for example.) For the most part, sports shot quail, woodcock, and grouse; poor whites and blacks, the rest. The point to remember, as much as anything else: Sports shot more four-legged quarry in the woods than in print.

The belief that bird hunting over pointing dogs represented a more sporting endeavor than other sorts of small game hunting is a wonderful example of one of the central axioms in the creation of American sporting traditions: Urban culture shaped the practices of hunting and fishing.

Rural folks made the hunting and fishing possible (through their land, lodging, guiding, and the creation of a services industry), and generally they were better anglers and hunters. But it was the city sports and, by extension, the writing of city sports, who decided what the activity meant. Publishers, advertisers, and retailers made most of the money off the "outdoor experience."

This tension ran through big game hunting and trout fishing, and in particular through wing-shooting—the three of the five traditions that most intimately involved the land of others (rather than the oceans, bays, lakes, big rivers, and marshes frequented by waterfowlers and bass fishermen) and, perhaps not coincidentally, were most fervently pursued by the most gentlemanly of sports.

Of the first three traditions, big game hunting was more likely to involve land without people, and trout fishing was somehow less invasive, given the use of fishing rods rather than shotguns. As Maurice Thompson explains, wild creatures are the "common property of all men." That is easy to see with bucks that trot across mountain ranges or trout that swim up and down a river. But what about a covey of quail that lives in the same overgrown field all year long? That was a tougher question to answer.

Bird hunters climbed over fences; hunted near buildings and stock; and shot their guns ten, twenty, thirty times. Their dogs often enjoyed a good chicken chase before turning their attention to quail. They hunted back and forth across agricultural land. They took up a lot of space at the table. Posting land was about the only move that farmers had—and it became the most contentious of the urban-rural sporting issues. Posting land amounted to a trump card, given the traditional primacy of rights of property in American history. Historian Daniel Herman quotes one Indiana sporting club: ". . . matters have reached such a pitch among the farmers that no matter how gentlemanly in deportment we are, we are ordered (often with curses and all kinds of foul abuse) from nearly every farm in this section."

That's basically Maurice Thompson's experience, in "The Confessions of an Ancient Poacher," which told of some farmland "whereon I had discovered some woodcock." But a scruffy looking farmer brandishing a musket was less than thrilled with Thompson's visit. "I owns this yer farm," the farmer hollered, "an' I'll jest everlastin'ly shoot the clothes clean off'n any dad ding town scallowag 'at I ketch a-trompin' 'round on it. Git, an' git quick! Ye can't do nothin' on this yer land 'ceptin' ye do it a runnin'!"

Thompson recalled the "time was when I could tramp the country openly in pursuit of the common property of all men. Now, however, 'No shuten' aloud' has destroyed my immemorial privilege, and I am compelled to poach. Amen."

From that day forward, Thompson vowed to be a poacher. A few days later he returned and waited till the farmer left for town. Then he sneaked in the woodlot, killed a passel of woodcock, and sauntered down to the house and enjoyed a cup of buttermilk with the farmer's wife. Thompson told her where he'd shot the woodcock—knowing she'd tell her husband.

After that Thompson amped up the poaching operation. He began using a bow and arrow because of its silence. He pedaled a bicycle to get on and off the property quickly and quietly. On the next visit he shot a bag of quail, barely escaping the farmer and his sons, who chased him down the lane. He fell asleep that night, thinking happily: At different "intervals all over his estate is posted the information to all to whom it may concern: 'Enny man Kotch on this farm will get the law poot to him warm.'" Not this sportsman.

In truth, Maurice Thompson was never the sort to sit on the porch and whine. Behind his lighthearted, briar-patch escape stood a man of considerable starch who gauged future victories rather than past defeats. Born in Indiana, Thompson spent his boyhood bow hunting and fishing in the old Cherokee country of northern Georgia. He fought with the South, serving as a scout with the Georgia 63rd. He returned to Indiana after the war and made his mark in engineering, law, and letters. By the 1880s he was penning a stream of essays, stories, novels, and books on topics ranging from archery (upon which he made a lasting impact) to politics. He became a voice of Main Street, breaking with the Democrats over populism (as might be anticipated from this poaching story) in 1896 and, ex-Confederate or not, supporting the Republican platform of business and expansionism.

If anything, "The Confessions of an Ancient Poacher," written as his health was failing, advanced just such a modern vision. To be sure, Thompson took on the Yankee farmer, but his enemy was the farmer not the Yankee: The story ignored "honor," "valor" and any other "Lost Cause" values and championed such corporate virtues as "enterprise" and "nerve." Admittedly, the bow was about as aboriginal as weapons get; but in function archery predicted how dexterity and challenge might come to define the sportsman's character. Finally, this cunning scout from the past found himself in need of a rather speedy exit from his place of plunder. What better than a modern convenience like a bicycle with which to achieve it?

"Like a Knight of Old"
NASH BUCKINGHAM

"The Harp That Once—," 1921?

Nowhere in the nation did land claim such eternal worth as in the Old South. As Gerald O'Hara (Scarlett's father) famously pronounces in *Gone with the Wind*: "The land is the only thing in the world worth working for, worth fighting for, worth dying for, because it's the only thing that lasts." An entire war, one in which Southern casualties ran to one in four white men killed, had been fought repelling Yankees from that land, that "mystic dirt of home," in the words of *Killer Angels* author Michael Shaara.

As the popularity of wing-shooting spread in the years following the Civil War, it became clear that the land of the old plantation system had the best quail hunting in the country. Historian Scott Giltner explains in *Hunting and Fishing in the New South* that the South as a region experienced a loss of wildlife, but it was "a relative lag in wildlife slaughter compared with other regions of the country." Sporting clubs bought up land in hopes of preserving the quail hunting. Other big parcels of land were owned by the ex-planter class—meaning that contention between small farmers and wealthy sports did not complicate access to the land. The hunting opportunity, moreover, received considerable props in the sporting press. Southern quail hunting exemplifies how sporting traditions began with accessibility to the natural resources but were ultimately created by people. A good example is the story by Wirt Howe titled "With the Quail among the Cotton," which appeared in the December 1898 issue of *Outing*.

Howe observed that in spite of the quail's diminishing numbers nationwide, it was different in the Old South, as "these plantations are natural shooting grounds." In the cotton areas, the quail "is comparatively little shot over. The negroes have no fancy for such amusement and the absence of a large market near-by has retarded the appearance of the pot-hunter." The hunt in the story began with descriptions of black servants and their proud preparations of a scrumptious dinner. The next morning the sports and their servants set out across the old plantations, which have "practically the same appearance that they did in ante-bellum days and which are operated upon methods that have been in use for many years." The author described, "the 'quarters,' parallel rows of log cabins where live the negro hands and their families, very much as they did in the days of slavery." The men had great quail hunting.

Promotion such as Howe's drew good numbers of Yankee hunters down for the quail hunting as well as an opportunity to see and walk through an Old South, one in which the farms may have fallen into disrepair but the structures remained as they had been, monuments of sorts. The war, after all, had occurred on this land and was in those years in the process of passing from memory into history, lending it a magical aura.

Other visiting sportsmen wrote similar stories, further defining the emerging tradition of Southern quail hunting as a contemporary enactment of the moonlight and magnolia days of the Old South—urban culture once again the arbiter of rural space. Emerson Hough wrote a series of articles in *Forest and Stream* in 1895 titled "The Sunny South." As Hough explained, "The negro makes a large factor in the field sports of the South." In the North sports do their own camp work, or at least share it. But "the southern idea of comfort in camp means a large tent, abundant furniture and two or three servants to the work—an idea which certainly grows upon one, and which one is not disposed to call a bad one after he has gained acquaintance with it." Giltner's study concluded as much: "Southern sportsmen felt more like aristocrats of old when accompanied by African-American attendants. . . .Tourists could feel like they had a uniquely Southern experience. . . . Slavery had passed away, but visitors could recapture the mythological, highly romanticized relationship between benevolent, honorably masters and loyal, contented slaves." Packaging and marketing, in other words, located the authenticity of Southern quail hunting in its attachment to the Old South.

Nash Buckingham, better known for his duck hunting stories, wrote a classic story in this tradition titled "The Harp That Once—." In *The Best of Nash Buckingham*, George Bird Evans notes that the story probably first appeared in some form in 1921, or thereabouts. It was included in the 1934 Derrydale edition of *De Shootinest Gent'man*. Evans explains further that unlike some of Buckingham's other quail pieces that are heavy on Civil War remembrance, "The Harp That Once—" has "a toothsome amount of butternut and Stars-and-Bars, but not so much that it smothers the bird-shooting flavor." The story's narrator (based on a young Nash) grew up a neighbor to Mister Arthur, a real hero in his eyes, who told tales of pre-war deer and bear hunts with hounds and "hairbreadth forays and brushes with Yankees." Then, out of nowhere, Mister Arthur found himself accused of embezzling money and had to sell his house and move, whether out of shame or lack of money, it was never clear, for the narrator was but a lad at the time and remained in the dark about such matters.

However, before departing, Mister Arthur bequeathed his gun and dog to the young narrator, and the boy was deeply moved and "never saw Barney [the dog] on a point or cocked an eye down that treasured gun's rib, without thinking of Mister Arthur."

Twenty years passed, and word came of a death-bed confession—it turned out that Mister Arthur hadn't embezzled the money after all. His honor restored, he returned—stooped but proud—and he and the narrator promptly arranged a quail hunt. They rode on horseback through the town where Mister Arthur's company had been mustered for service in the War against Northern Aggression. They reached the old grounds where Mister Arthur had frolicked as a youth. The narrator's dogs worked beautifully, and "Mister Arthur sat on his horse like a knight of old. At that moment he was nearly seventy-five years young."

Suddenly, Mister Arthur swept his arm forward, "P-o-i-n-t!" Some three hundred yards off, one dog (Don) had locked on point, the other honoring. They galloped over. "No mounted skirmisher could have quit his steed with the graceful alacrity of Mister Arthur's departure from that livery stable nag. He might have been taking cover from a hot corner in cavalry days." He opened his gun, dropped in two shells, and strode ahead. "The Lord was gracious," the narrator said to himself, "to have spared us both this moment."

Then, "with a dynamic buzz and swirl, a bevy exploded just beyond Don's pop-eyed stare. . . . Could he 'come back'?" Mister Arthur fell into his old form: "The same fractional pause; then up came his weapon—hitched quickly, but steadily. His eyes handled the covey, the gun itself. A husky cock bird skimming the briars for an opening higher up, wilted at the edge of mock-orange and tumbled into the weed tops. A second fugitive, arching over sassafras tippets, was sent hurtling. A clean, beautiful double."

Mister Arthur just stood there. "My boy," he managed, "my boy, I'm a very lucky old dog I have made a sure enough, old-time double." Don and Jim raced one another to his side, "each trying to nuzzle a bird into my old friend's trembling hands."

The remainder of the piece continues this ode to the Old South, with Mister Arthur reminiscing about his younger days, punctuated by exceptional hunting. Late in the afternoon the men happened upon a cabin, and an African-American woman introduced herself. In response to Mister Arthur's inquiry regarding his former slave, she said, "Yes. Landom Harris is still alive. He's my gran papa, suh!"

And with that Mister Arthur headed to the next cabin and reunited with his former slave in a tearful embrace. They reminisced, feasted, and visited the old "Big House." The narrator and Mister Arthur spent the night in the Landoms' cabin, with Landom sleeping with the children, and Mister Arthur and the narrator sharing a room made up just for them.

Stories such as this one fit in what historians call the "Lost Cause" tradition—the belief that Southerners were better soldiers and more gallant and brave than Northerners and were only defeated because their leaders betrayed them and because the North had more money and men. Such a myth allowed the South to deny the Civil War's finality and continue the fight, even if unofficially. A central element in the Lost Cause is the belief that the South fought not to preserve slavery but only to safeguard Southerners' rights—a notion that historians of the period agree remains the single biggest myth about the Civil War. According to the Lost Cause, antebellum days were filled with happy slaves and kind masters, as exemplified in the fantasy of this story: The whole party, former master and slave among them, had a big sleepover in the old slave quarters.

Buckingham's story serves as a great example of how sporting traditions of the nineteenth century ended up fitting into and strengthening the belief systems of larger nineteenth-century American culture. This story of the Old South, after all, sold very well in the North, where white citizens agreed as years passed that the Civil War's legacy had been to confirm the valor of white men rather than to secure the freedom of African-American slaves. The South, embodied in Mister Arthur, had risen again. He was not defeated in ignominy; he had been betrayed. But now he returned. He could walk through town again, reclaim the world that had been his before the war. He was always proud, but he had kept it inside—until the quail hunt brought it out.

The white South's investment in such a myth is not surprising given the racial attitudes of the day, to say nothing of the horrific toll of the war. The question for our purposes is why bird hunting, of all the sports, wrapped itself in such a gauzy, imagined past. The answer begins with the fact that bird hunting typically involved treading across old land that had once been farmed but no longer was. Hunting there was like walking through an abandoned house. You entered with a careful reverence for the place, as though the old owner might be home any moment. Or was watching somehow. This same aura infused grouse hunting in the Northeast. Western bird hunting didn't seem to have the nostalgia, as Westerners were only coming to the land.

Bird hunting, moreover, was different from big game hunting. In bird hunting, the cover "held" game. The land itself produced or grew it. The land was the birds' home. When hunting, you tried to flush game *from* it. With big game, by contrast, hunters tracked or drove animals *across* it. And much of the nineteenth-century big game was hunted in mountains or wilderness, not on land that had been farmed. Either way, the connection was between the hunter and the animal, not the hunter and the land.

At a time when corporate nationalism washed over people's daily lives, men and women understandably looked to their past and held on fiercely to the stories of who they had been, if only to confirm who they were (and were not). They looked to their communities and their regions. (In the Civil War, for instance, both North and South regiments had been mustered by community.) Writers told stories—be it "Fishin' Jimmy" or "The Harp that Once—" that allowed readers to anchor themselves in these particular places.

Of course sporting traditions weren't designed only for effect or for playacting but also because they were functional. The wagon, the horses, the servants so familiar from an earlier time, were also the most efficient way for wealthy sports to hunt over wide-ranging pointing dogs in the lands of the Old South. The quail themselves were intoxicating game birds—exhilarating flush, steady to point, handsome, strong-flying, toothsome. Quail, "Gentleman Bob," as they would be called, were the ideal game bird hunted in an idealized way.

It would be a mistake, however, to assume that quail hunting was basically a Civil War reenactment. Throughout the twentieth century, increasing numbers of middle-class hunters in the South and elsewhere would hunt them on foot through thick cover. (The bobwhite quail's range extended northward into Ontario and westward.) These hunters came to love the dog work and hunting more than anything else. They lived for the moment of "truly delicious tenseness," in the words of Edwyn Sandys, as a hunter walked in past a pointing dog and braced himself for the explosion of a "big mortar crammed with feathered balls." His November 1903 *Outing* story "Quail in Painted Covers" said a good deal about the joy that was quail hunting.

Sandys and his buddy Long Tom laid over at the hunting grounds, "the guest of one of those grand old farmers who delight in entertaining what they are graciously pleased to term 'the right sort of fellers.'" After an artery-clogging breakfast, they headed out hunting over Tom's brace of setters, sisters, a mix of the Llewellin-Laverack strains. The dogs worked through a mix of wheat stubble, standing corn, new growth, and secondary hardwood. A creek, with yellow leaves drifting on the surface, cleaves a woodlot. It is beautiful land.

The men were old friends, similar in their hunting ways except for one. Whereas Sandys was a quick shot (as we certainly know by now), Tom was a might-as-well-fill-my-pipe kind of gunner. The men busted on each other. "Cut loose you darned snip-snapper," Tom hollered, after Sandys shot twice so quickly that the shots sound as one. "Get focused, you old land-surveyor," Sandys retorted.

The dogs were the picture of style, with one holding an early "point with that satisfied air which ever hints of greater things to come." The covey burst out, "a storm of whirring missiles, with three came streaming right overhead." Sandys missed. Tom waited till they cleared, Bang! And " the bird went down full sixty yards away."

Later while following up the singles after another covey flush, each man took a different side of a substantial hedge and rail fence. Sandys had a deep furrow on his side. The birds were there, and the "following ten minutes proved the next thing to immortal bliss." With the quail scattered all along the furrow, the dogs crept forward a few yards to point after point. Sandys didn't miss.

Then it was Tom's turn. While eating lunch the men spotted a covey on the ground on the far side of the creek. "The dogs won't go over," said Tom. "If I could swim, I'd hustle over there and drive em to the brush this side—then we'd have 'em for sure."

Unfortunately for Sandys, he could swim (which Tom knew), so it was up to him to "peel down to the buff." He waded over in the freezing water, and the "first touch of it fairly frapped" him. He climbed up the bank, and just then Tom let the setters go and they leaped in the water and "came plowing across, each whining in her eagerness to outspeed the other." Then Sandys promptly fell back in, howling some curses, which flushed the quail to the other side and the dogs, "as much at home in the water as a couple of otters," sped back across and Tom shot quail after quail, over point after point.

Sandys waded back across and dressed, with shots sounding like a battlefield. But then he couldn't find his gun. (Tom had slipped it in a hollow log.) By the time he located it, the birds were gone, the shooting over. But it didn't matter, really. The day held all the adventures one might expect to find on a bird-hunting trip, where the sports are forty going on fourteen. They "trudged on though that sweet darkness which ends a day of sportsman's toil when the leaves are painted and the silver mist lies low on lonely levels."

"Allus Telling Me Never to Say a Word about [It]."

A New Hampshire farmer

C. HARRY MORSE

"Dr. Craig and another Woodcock Shooter," *Outing*, October 1899

As American game bird populations dwindled, productive hunting areas became valuable bits of land, at least in the estimation of wing-shooters. Bird hunters in the Northeast, in particular, often cultivated relationships with landowners, as Sandys and Long Tom did with their host. The hail-fellow-well-met attitude between wing-shooters, however, evolved into a more guarded attitude in general. No game bird more evinced such responses than the American woodcock. In England, gunners shot woodcock as well, and that may have given them a bit of a boost reputation-wise at first. But the European bird was bigger, a different game bird really. The American bird was smaller, a nocturnal, frog-eyed, worm-eating shorebird with a worker's bill and a capitalist's belly. Colonists didn't know what to make of the bird, and in essence they gave up. Each state gave the bird a different name.

Aside from those who hunted timberdoodles, no one really knew or cared about them. Local farmers considered them (and by extension their hunters) as puzzling as modern living. Writer Ray Holland quoted one thusly: "If you ask me, I'd say they [woodcock] all is teched in the head a little. They sit around in the daytime and are on the go all night. Still, I've known some fellers that had them habits, and they thought they was all-fired smart."

The woodcocks' mysterious comings and goings extended to hunting them, which was all about finding the birds. The secrecy element fit with the Northeast, the region of the country most closely associated with woodcock hunting and a region that had always had hunting pressure. As early as the 1840s, William Henry Herbert (Frank Forester) had been writing about the pressure that Northeast woodcock faced. From that point, the matter of "secrecy" attached itself firmly to the sport. As New England writer H. G. "Tap" Tapply wrote in the 1960s,

"When a shotgunner starts acting like the cat that ate the goldfish, you can make up your mind that he has probably stumbled on a new woodcock cover."

What Tap left unsaid was that other than finding them, woodcock were not the challenge of quail or grouse. Tight-sitters, woodcock turned mediocre dogs into champions, and their fluttering flight did the same for many mediocre wing-shooters as well. Where you found one, you often found many. The trick was finding them in the first place or, short of that, someone who had; one man's secret, in other words, became another's mission.

This was essence of an 1899 *Outing* story, "Dr. Craig and another Woodcock Shooter." Author C. Harry Morse told of a certain Boston physician, one Dr. Craig, who had two dear interests in life. For one, he was "a fastidious burner of the fragrant weed." He treated his pipes like "old and tried friends." For another, he adored his woodcock shooting. Dr. Craig, in fact, had developed a reputation as New England's finest woodcock hunter, though he was extremely secretive about where he hunted. He always returned from New Hampshire with plenty of woodcock but remained mum on the location of his covers. He occasionally brought along a friend, but he too became as "dumb as oysters" when queried about the L word.

It turned out, location was on the mind of another hunter—a man named Ezra Benton. He too was quite the woodcock hunter, with a reputation second only to Dr. Craig's. He knew of Dr. Craig and had developed an obsession about discovering his covers. A traveling salesman for a nursery from New York City, Ezra knew the lower 40s of the state of New Hampshire like no one else. But he never could find Craig's favorite spots.

One afternoon while hunting with his setter, Ned, Benton flushed a woodcock—and missed his shot. Benton had had good luck that morning, with eleven woodcock, and he was annoyed that he left the circle unbroken on Ned's nice point. He reflushed the bird, did so numerous times, but each time the woodcock whistled merrily off—out of sight or range. Or, he uncharacteristically missed. The bird took him several miles across ridges and valley, until finally Ned and Benton stopped for lunch.

Benton's gaze fell upon a russet form in the grass. The woodcock. He must have hit it and not known it. He walked over and bent down to pick it up—and the bird twittered off. Such duplicity prompted "but one means of relief," and Ezra ". . . availed himself of it in the most vigorous manner until his quite extensive vocabulary was exhausted."

Ned and Benton picked up the pursuit, flushing and reflushing the bird. Oddly, he realized, he hadn't jumped another since he began the chase. He crossed a stream and knelt down to take a drink when he noticed a pipe stem—probably from some other hunter—sticking out of the mud. He picked it up, dropped it in his pocket, and continued the chase.

A short time later he got a twenty-five-yard crossing shot on the woodcock, and this time he didn't miss: "You would have thought a feather pillow had been ripped open." When Ned went over to retrieve it, however, there was nothing there. No sign. Ezra searched—nothing.

He looked around and realized that he was quite a ways from his starting point. But he saw a farmer with his team working in the woods, walked over, and learned that he was six miles from his own team. He convinced the farmer with an offer of $2 and some tobacco to give him a lift back. On the way, Ezra showed him the pipe, and the farmer replied, "Why the doctor's pipe—Dr. Craig—ye know."

Ezra brightened like he had been goosed. "Dr. Craig? Oh, yes, of course. . . . Hunts up here some, I believe, doesn't he?"

"Yaas, every fall; stops daown to my house, end o' this rud. Brings up his guns an' dawgs. Mother don't do nuthin' but cook all the times they're here. Never seen men eat so 'n all my born days."

"Kills a good many birds, doesn't he?"

"Waal, a considabl number o' patriges; not enny more'n sum ova our own hunters, tho. But, say, them air swamp robins, Jehu; they kill the tarnalest sit o' them tings, ha'f a bushel baskit of 'em a day. I wouldn't eat one o' the pesky things no more'n pizen. Doctor says th' won't nawthin touch 'em anyway 'cept hunters an hawgs. But they keep on killen' 'em."

The farmer allowed that the Doctor was "dumbed skart" that someone would find out where he hunted and "is allus telling me never to say a word about [it]." Benton reassured the farmer, as he gave him the pipe to return. Tell the Doctor that "I'll try to get through with my shooting here before he comes."

In truth, woodcock cover itself tended to be the sort that made eloquent waxing difficult at best—no Elysian fields, or Old South, or abandoned orchards. Artists have always liked to paint pictures of woodcock flying across open meadow brooks or through clearings in birches, but most woodcock flush from alders or other dark, damp places where they have little ground growth and access to worms, not exactly the cornerstones of landscape romance. The main and, ultimately, fun fact was that certain alder runs held woodcock every fall; others that looked just as good, did not. All of which fit with the woodcock's mysterious reputation.

In a place like northern New England, with long fingers of alders and aspen, where soil was thin at best, woodcock gave the land a new meaning for those who searched for them. There is something humble and satisfying in woodcock hunting that may derive from the awareness that your success has mostly to do with being in the right place at the right time, and little to do with your own brilliant strategy. Most woodcock hunters learn to count their blessings—and move on to the next cover.

"Good, Stout, Honest Birds"
MAX FOSTER

"After Grouse with Hiram," *Outing*, October 1906

Woodcock hunters generally didn't know where woodcock were, and half the time, it seems, the woodcock didn't know where they were either. Ruffed grouse, their companion game bird of the Midwest and East, had no such problem. Grouse had always been considered "crafty," which can be seen as a sign of respect or disrepute, depending on which side of the Mason-Dixon Line you are referencing.

But whether it was a matter of avoiding flight, or initiating flight at the least opportune (for the hunter) time, or a matter of craftiness once forced to flush, grouse could outwit hunters at every stage of the hunt. They also had physical gifts that, at the least, put them on a par with quail as a sporting bird. Their flight speed and agility—to say nothing of their roaring takeoff—left all who chased after them humbled, and occasionally gratified.

Sportsmen pursued grouse throughout the North, Midwest, and East, and their reputations in the minds of Yankee hunters was a mirror of the quail for Southerners. Grouse hunters, like their quail hunting counterparts, saw their sport as bringing out the best of their idealized selves, as in Max Foster's 1906 story.

Foster was on his annual trip to Pennsylvania's Alleghenies. The structure of the tale resembles the quail stories—early awakening, cooking already going on, cajoling by the host (minus the servants). The old gray horse drew the wagon into the covers, but Max and Hiram took it from there on foot for these "good, stout, honest birds that twist and dodge and rocket among the trees in flights to try the keenest hand and eye." There was no swinging or tracking the birds, no open shots, "no time to fish about at ease, dwelling on the flying bundle like a punter potting rails." Just as quail elicited the courtly, honor-bound sensibility of the South that created such a chivalrous culture, the grouse seems to bring out the industrious, competitive ingenuity of the

North that led to the world's most productive democracy. Myth versus myth, in other words, with all the comforts of home.

Foster missed the morning's first grouse—one he had seen "mincing" along a fallen tree—getting flummoxed on the flush, for it was less the grouse's top speed (35 miles per hour) that vexed hunters than how immediately they attained it. His host, Hiram, a crack shot, killed a bird after some fine dog work, and not long after missed an open shot when, "at the crack of the gun, the grouse dodged sideways."

"Why, look a-here!" he explained. I was a-holdin' right straight to the heft o' him. I jest a-couldn't missed."

Max chuckled as Hiram broke his gun. "Durn it," Hiram said, "ye needn't look so cussed funny about it, anyhow!"

Later Hiram redeemed himself. In the afternoon sun on a sidehill, two birds flushed. Foster dumped his—an easy open shot—then watched Hiram. His bird was "a wise one [that] screwed into the trees at the first jump, dodging behind the nearest trunk. . . ." Hiram held his fire until the "bird show[ed] itself a hand's breadth" and then connected. By the time the sun had dropped behind the mountains, the dogs had pointed more birds than they bumped, even if the two men had missed more than they hit. The day had been a fine one.

At the end of the hunt, when Hiram responded "fair to middlin" to his wife's inquiry on the luck, Foster added, "to me it was more than that. I had my share of birds and had missed nothing—save here and there a bird."

As with hunting other birds, hunting grouse conferred a new value on the land. Once the site of intensive logging, as indicated by the presence of an old charcoal camp, Hiram's covers appeared to be at a perfect stage of forest succession, given the thickness of the growth. In time New England farms overgrew too and, in the eyes of many, represented the aesthetic ideal of American grouse hunting. But early in the twentieth century that designation belonged to the mountains of Pennsylvania. Grouse hunters see land with different eyes; to them there is nothing like popple (poplar) with a perfect stem density. Maybe a stone wall and a few apple trees mixed in, with a corner of spruce and a side hill of thorn apple.

Grouse hunting also offered a human connection with land, though in this particular case in the mountains of Pennsylvania, the relationship seemed less about region and more about the national perspective afforded by such a vantage. Edwyn Sandys, for what it's worth, thought the mountain hunting grand, with uncommon sport in the downhill grouse shot (". . . to swing a gun three ways at once is a serious task for ordinary hands . . .") and with moving vistas, from which "you can see ever so far south, the great storied ground— the battlefields."

Grouse numbers bounced around in the Northeast during the first few years of the twentieth century. Pennsylvania's mountains held their populations, but elsewhere the peaks and valleys that even today characterize grouse populations showed up more prominently. This only made the birds "craftier" and "more challenging"—similar to the way other sorts of hunting (and fishing) had been reframed. Edward Cave's "Our Geared-up Grouse Shooting," which appeared in the December 1913 issue of *Outdoor World & Recreation*, is a good example.

Cave's story portrayed the essence of the grouse's challenge—and what that element of the hunting came to mean. Southern writer Havileah Babcock describes *the* moment in quail hunting, when "a big covey explodes under my very garters," and how he "sometimes forgets to release the safety catch," how he "stands there with a look of imbecilic ecstacy on my face, dazedly squeezing a dead trigger until the covey fades into the distant landscape." Here's what happened to grouse hunters on one afternoon.

Cave and his wife were approaching a birdy-looking patch of woods when Cave decided to wait out on the road. His wife, inside the cover, followed the dog as it made game along a hedge. Just then, "out of the hedge, on [Cave's] side scuttled a fat partridge, directly in line with them. He saw [Cave] and stopped."

From inside the cover, Cave's wife called "Mark!" The dog "was standing the bird, who likewise was standing me." Cave, who was munching on an apple, froze so that his wife might get the shot. "At least I want it understood that way."

Meanwhile, the bird was looking at him, stretching his neck, and Cave was planning on how he would nail him as soon as he took flight. His wife called to him from inside the brush, and just then the grouse roared into flight—right toward his head. "It was like dodging a projectile!" Cave wrote. "For some unaccountable reason I held on to the apple. No, I didn't throw the gun away. I clubbed at him with it." The swing knocked the apple to ground, Cave stepped on it, and being on a hill, it sent his feet flying and knocked the breath "out of me as completely as if the grouse had struck me head-on in the softests spot of my anatomy." The grouse, meanwhile, was last seen ripping "down the hillside like a brown streak."

This was—and is—the classic grouse anecdote, which begins with hunters being outsmarted even when they've got the bird cornered. If the default response of the startled quail hunter was to freeze, the partridge hunter generally cinched himself in a knot. The quail moment nearly always involved a covey, grouse nearly always an individual bird. As Cave wrote, "When you pick up at last, as you have often pictured yourself doing, a wise old cock partridge that you have hunted with malice aforethought for three or four consecutive seasons, you have the whole upland game bird family by the legs." At this point, grouse had been almost elevated to big game, and Cave sounded like he was deer hunting more than bird hunting. What made the grouse special was the challenge of the individual birds—at every stage of the hunt.

This ode to grouse derived some of its poignancy from their uncertain future. Hunters had been aware of grouse cycles at least since the mid-nineteenth century, but the decline that occurred at the beginning of the twentieth century appeared to be permanent. Game animal populations, large and small, were disappearing every year; white-tailed deer, for instance, were but a decade gone from the very Sullivan County (New York) habitats Cave and his wife hunted. Nationwide, grouse numbers had fallen to a low point—a reflection of denuded habitat and decades of snaring and unregulated hunting. The cycling accentuated these low numbers and would do so until the fourth decade of the twentieth century. For New Yorkers the bottom came in that bleakest of autumns—1929—when the grouse season never opened at all.

Edward Cave was a well-known magazine editor and an ardent conservationist. In this piece, he and Mrs. Cave come off as a pair of poor man's Edwardians, a Yankee shooting party. They picnicked afield and gunned for grouse. But their bag was modest. Cave seemed delighted to emerge from the woods in one piece, forget actually shooting a bird. It is difficult to imagine a writer according such standing to prairie chicken, woodcock, or even quail, but grouse, as Cave insists, are in a class of their own. The hunter who has been grouse hunting emerges from the cover scratched and humbled—as though he had just returned from climbing mountains in search of white goats.

"The Original Game Bird"

ERNEST RUSSELL

"The Secret of Getting Grouse,"
Recreation & Outdoor World, November 1913

The challenge of grouse, and how it created a middle-class sporting community, is the theme of "The Secret of Getting Grouse." The boys, life-long grouse
hunters all, were sitting around the hearth at the hotel, presumably after a full
day's hunt. A visiting Chicagoan was packing up and taking his leave. He did
so with deep appreciation for the grouse shooting—he had bagged four birds
out of sixty flushes—he loudly proclaimed it the most challenging shooting
he'd ever had. "Boys, I've been here just a week and I'm sorry to go for you've
given me a bully good time. Suppose I've tramped fifty miles, lost twenty
pounds of fat, shot about sixty shells and reduced your local bird-supply by
just four fat grouse." But he explained that he doesn't measure his sport here
by the size of the bag.

"I take off my hat to the New England grouse. He's the original game bird
all right."

The story continues the resemblance to quail stories, in this case in its
veneration of the entire system of the hunt. The setting was an open hearth
in the evening. The amenities were considerably less aristocratic in this
hardscrabble heartland of American democracy—10 cent cigars along with
cider and apples. But the aura had a similar function, which was to imbue
the hunting with an authenticity derived from an imagined past. The fellows
all waved good-bye to their midwestern visitor. They hoped to see him again,
they told him.

About the cider and apples and hearth, the regionally authentic props:
"All these preparations were accepted in silence, as time-honored preliminar-
ies to a sort of nightly hunters' council which was in session in that hotel, and
in nearly every other country hotel in New England, from the opening to the
closing of the hunting season. It had been so for more than a hundred years."

Well, not exactly. That would have had the boys trying to figure out partridge hunting while the rest of New England was contemplating secession from the Union—and the army under General Jackson was trying to throw the British the hell out of Louisiana at the end of the War of 1812. But the point is, like their quail hunting compatriots, these grouse hunters wanted to see themselves as carrying out a tradition rather than creating one (unlike fly fishermen, who all wanted to be the *first* to do things). Bird hunters strained to situate themselves in history, decorate their experience with nostalgia, and celebrate the relationships that had developed around their pursuit of their regionally venerated game bird.

In truth, these hunters-in-residence were actually the first generation to find much sport in such matters. Their fathers pot-shot their birds out of trees, snared them along trails. Gathered around the hearth, these modern New Englanders saluted the grouse for its elusiveness, the complexity of its pursuit. To them the thunder king was the perfect bird—for reasons their fathers never would have understood.

But the visitor from Chicago—and other visiting sports (it's never clear from the story about the relationship between visiting sports and resident hunters)—expected a grouse hunt in "real" New England. The participants acted their parts, much as did quail hunters from the South. Both were selling an experience made real through its connection with an imagined past.

When the Chicagoan caught his train for home, it prompted the remaining hunters to reflect on what they had. The story unfolded like a college seminar, with the grouse sort of feathered professors. The first speaker, a thin fellow who had been hunting for nearly forty years (which would have started him just about 1875 or so), said, "I don't believe I never hunted a season that I didn't tuck away something' new about their habits or learn a new wrinkle in hunting a cover."

A man named Bradshaw, "a grizzled veteran of nearly seventy years," agreed, adding that true, "you've to know your bird's habits and all that," but the key was teamwork because different covers need different approaches.

Then everyone highlighted the brilliance of everyone else's dog—which took another glass of cider to get through.

The seminar moved on to the tough part of grouse hunting, the shooting, and Ezra chimed in. "A pa'tridge knows as much about the game as anybody, and the way she'll put a scrub pine 'tween you and her when she does git up, or wait till you've passed her and git up behind you, is proof of it." You had to be ready all the time. "Why only the other day I was over huntin' the Cassidy run with that Pennsylvania feller you sent me out with, Jon." We were huntin the cart path, and "I was inside with old Dan." He started making game, and I hollered out to the Pennsylvania feller "Git up ahead! Dan's got symptoms." Sure enough the bird flushed out and would have given him a clear shot. But he never came up. "Which way did she go?" he asked.

Hubbard, the owner who had been doing some paperwork, swung his chair around and said, more or less definitively, it's what the Chicago fellow said, the system—the covers, the dogs, the men. Most of all, "we have the men—you're the kind I mean. . . . You played 'hookey' from school—country school, too—when you were kids, and you spent most of the time right here in these very covers. You know every inch of them. . . . When you got older, you played 'hookey' from work—whether it was on the farm or in the shop. You carried a gun, got a dog. . . . Trouble is, he explained, lighting his pipe, "you don't appreciate how lucky you are to have been born and raised in the natural home of the finest all-'round game-bird on the continent."

The boys had a day of hunting ahead of them tomorrow. Fire dying, cider finished, they shuffled to bed, well aware of "what a godsend this sport of hunting is to us fellows 'round here . . . keeps us all young . . . keeps us going . . . keeps the old human machinery from rusting up and going out of business . . . a college education is a great thing . . . even in grouse hunting."

Modernity may have produced studious, enlightened sportsmen, but it also brought increased hunting pressure. Five months after this article appeared, Massachusetts held its first pheasant season in hopes that it might serve as a buffer species for native grouse and woodcock; its main effect appears to have been a further increase in the numbers of hunters. In time, grouse populations would rebuild as deserted farms continued to grow over; and the ideas on hunting strategy, dog work, shooting, and guns that emerged from this early seminar at the hotel hearth would form the modern canon for hunters.

The warmth and camaraderie in Russell's article would certainly flourish in the voices of Foster, Spiller, Woolner, Tapply, Ford, and others. The rules remain the same. No bragging, unless someone else is foolish enough to bring up the story first. Understatement is preferred: The bumbling city sport was given a "detailed explanation," for instance, or on a dog getting birdy, "Dan's got symptoms!" The store owner gets final word (c.f. Perk, Uncle, the "Lower Forty" voice of reason). There's grouse hunting, and hunting for everything else. Time passes, covers grow up. Keep going. Treasure the moments.

The hunters at Hotel U, like those who would follow, certainly knew how to do that.

In this respect they are like bird hunters everywhere: They see their dogs dying, their guns slowing; their own history recedes with each flush, fades into the larger ancestral past of the deserted New England hills.

Perhaps this story was that sum: Humor, the response to failure; camaraderie, the stalwart against evanescence; loss, the measure of gain. It's the October tale bird hunters have been telling ever since.

CHAPTER 8

"The Whisper of Wings"

WATERFOWL, 1866–1923

A s so often happens with duck hunting tragedies, the mistakes start small and acquire their consequence incrementally— small boat, lots of ice, late start, lost oar, and then a big one: floe, not shore.

Pete Wiessen has been trying to convince his younger friend Joe Marsh, with whom he works at a machine shop, to go duck hunting for several years, and Joe keeps putting him off. Finally he agrees.

It is "the winter season," i.e., January 20. The pair plan to hunt on the upper Niagara River above the falls. They will row out through the floe ice to one of the islands, chop a V-shaped hole in the ice next to the island, wedge the boat, and set the decoys in the open water in the current.

Ice clogged the river that morning, as Marsh later told Orrin E. Dunlap, who wrote "An Escape from Niagara Falls" for the May 1901 issue of *The Wide World Magazine*. Marsh remembers telling Wiessen "that he didn't quite like it." But "Wiessen . . . laughed at his fears in a friendly way," and off they went.

The first two spots already have hunting parties, because "ardent sportsmen leave their homes in the city and go to the boat-houses or adjacent hotels to pass the night in order to get out on the river as soon after five o'clock as possible." Marsh and Wiessen are not the only nut-jobs, in other words.

Wiessen suggests "a landing on the outer side of the island, looking towards Navy Island." They arrive at the edge of the ice, and Marsh, in the bow, uses a "pike pole" to pry aside ice cakes so they can burrow farther into the shore ice. Wiessen holds the boat with the bow pointed toward the island by feathering the oars. On one stroke, however, he misses the water (which can happen with all the layers of clothes) and the oars skim across the top of the ice; he topples back, nearly tipping the boat. He loses an oar.

But the boat is embedded in the ice, so they are still good. Marsh keeps pushing aside ice to jam in the boat securely. That's when Wiessen "quietly told him" that they are moving. The boat is not snugged into shore ice but floe ice. He might have used different words.

At that point they are about a mile and a half above the falls. Drifting. They try to attract attention. Wiessen fires his shotgun until his hands and the action freeze.

They float downriver, several hundred yards from the American shore. Between them and land is floe ice, slush ice, open water, and then shore ice and shore. People gather along the bank. Marsh and Wiessen are now a half-mile above the falls.

They pull off each other's clothes, weep, shout. Marsh climbs out of the boat, trying to reach open water, but his wool socks stick to the ice. As Marsh remembers, "the ice was about ⅞ of an inch deep." (Who else but a machinist would preface ⅞ inch with "about"?). He keeps edging toward the open water; the ice begins to crumble around him as the wind and current push the flow toward shore. The falls roar.

People on shore yell that it's not that deep, and Marsh goes for it, leaping into the open water. He smacks his head on the ice but flounders onto the next floe, pulls himself up, and guys on shore reach out with a pole. He grabs it, and they haul him in—and hustle him off to the house. Orrin doesn't mention the crowd reaction. I imagine them cheering.

Wiessen can't swim. But now, with the thunder of the falls downstream, the cacophony of pleas from the shore, he tries. He jumps in and "battled with the water and ice . . . [and after] a brief thrilling struggle" disappears.

"Another river fatality must be added to the already horrible record the Niagara has made," began the accident's front-page coverage in *The New York Times*, "the result of boating accidents above the falls. John Wiesen leaves a wife and three children to mourn . . . his foolhardiness in going duck hunting on such a dangerous stream as the Upper Niagara in mid-winter."

In a nation that couldn't get enough public hangings, going over the falls was a sight that drew a crowd down on the shore. It was certainly a newsworthy event. The general understanding of the Niagara as deeply haunting, as one nineteenth-century visitor noted, "the very emblem . . . of unchanging inevitable death," allowed Dunlap the luxury of building drama through narrative restraint. He has only to let us know that Wiessen and Marsh are in fact attached to an ice floe—and we will do the rest.

One question we might have (as *The New York Times* implied) about winter duck hunting on the Niagara is: above or below the falls?

You can imagine that question crossing Marsh's mind (after all, he's been avoiding the trip for several years). But like so many duck hunters who die in accidents, Wiessen is lulled by the assurance of having done this before. Everybody hunts those islands! You wouldn't believe the birds out there. We'd better get out early to get a spot. (They were probably headed out to the island known today as Buckhorn; Interstate 90 crosses over it.) As is often the case in duck hunting accidents, death is not immediate. But seldom does it seem so inevitable. Wiessen and Marsh see their fate approaching, quickening.

Nineteenth-century Americans were obsessed with what would happen at the moment of death. Christianity emphasized the importance of the "good death"—that a person's countenance was a key to how eternity might go for him. How would it go for these two?

The story also raises a number of questions about the emergence of a duck hunting tradition in America, beginning with the most elemental question of why anyone would go to such lengths, take such risks, endure such hardship, to shoot what were, in all likelihood, "less desirable" ducks—whistlers (goldeneyes), buffleheads, maybe some broadbills, perhaps a snail-eating black duck or two. Moreover, the two men couldn't even get the spots they wanted because other hunters were already out there. Duck hunting must have meant something significant, must have taken hold of its participants in a way that can only be called intoxicating. The accident itself happened in the very midst of a community—does that say anything about the meaning waterfowling would come to claim? In short, how did the traditions of American waterfowling develop and change in the half century following the Civil War?

In 1855 in *The American Sportsman,* author Elisha Lewis had fretted about the indifference of Americans to the sport of waterfowling. A "few of the New York sportsmen occasionally sally forth," he observed, ". . . but the sport is not considered sufficiently enticing to carry them very often on such expeditions."

He needn't have worried.

"One Steady Stream and Whirr of Wings"

ROBERT BARNWELL ROOSEVELT

The Game Birds of the Coasts and
Lakes of the Norththen States of America, 1866

Yes, that name again.

Peter Hawker notwithstanding, American waterfowl hunting had little in the way of English canon to claim as foundational. The pastime emerged as a sporting venture alongside an already established system of market hunting in both the Chesapeake Bay area and the Northeast. Sport hunting for waterfowl began in abundance, harkening to the days of Audubon. A good example comes from Robert Barnwell Roosevelt and his literate, exciting writing about hunting on the marshes at the edge of western Lake Erie. This was waterfowling's frontier in the 1860s, when Roosevelt visited and wrote about his experience.

As always, Roosevelt had an opinion—in this case about hunting practices, namely gunning from batteries, or sinkboxes as they were called. As he explained, "In stationing a battery—that imitation coffin, which should be a veritable one, if justice had its way, to every man who enters it—and in lying prone in it through the cold days of winter, the market man may find his pecuniary profit, but the gentleman can receive no pleasure. . . ." His peeve was that the batteries drove away ducks and that it wasn't sport, only "the wearisome endurance of cold and tedium to obtain game that might be killed more handsomely and in the long run more abundantly by other methods."

You wonder: Was this simply Roosevelt being his prickly self? Or had enduring cold and hardship yet to become part of the duck hunting experience? Did waterfowling need the softness of modernity to make hardship masculine rather than simply dim-witted? His disdain for sinkboxes suggested that their hunting operations had probably deprived him of some sport. Put another way, at least as early as the 1860s, duck hunting was going great guns on the coastal waters near Long Island where he lived.

In Roosevelt's waterfowling world the "shooter [should] confine himself to points of land or sedge where he uses decoys or awaits the accidental passage of the birds." This setup allowed the shooter "sufficient motion to keep his blood in circulation," and also permitted ducks a refuge on the open water.

With these practices in operation, in the sort of authoritative voice of the outdoors that he and his family personified, Roosevelt explained, "Wild-fowl shooting, as pursued at the West, or even at the South, is glorious and exhilarating; there the sportsman has exercise, or the assistance of his faithful and intelligent retriever, and is required to bring into play the higher powers of his nature. He manages his own boat, or he stands squarely on his ground, and if he has not a canine companion, chases his own crippled birds and retrieves the dead ones by his own unaided efforts."

RBR himself, however, had a guide (or "friend," as he called him) to set decoys the night before. After an afternoon of snipe hunting, the two men "pulled [at the oars] with the utmost vigor down the channel of Mud Creek, and in a short time were again hidden among the high reeds, awaiting the ducks in a favorite roosting place." Not to put too fine a point on matters, but shooting ducks on the roost has never been known to encourage their return. Perhaps it was the last day of Roosevelt's stay.

At first there was little sign of game, with "the sun . . . leisurely dropping down the western sky, throwing his slanting rays across the broad bay, and lighting up the distant club-house as by a fire." The wind died, and only occasional guns sounded in the distance. Things were not looking good for team Roosevelt.

Then, as darkness closed in, the ducks "began to arrive, at first one or two at a time, then more rapidly and in larger flocks, till at last it was one steady stream and whirr of wings." The men were limited only by how quickly they could reload, "as from all quarters and of all kinds they streamed past; now the sharp whistle of the teal, then the rush of the mallard, sometimes high over our heads, at others darting close beside us; by ones, by twos, by dozens, by hundreds, crowded together in masses or stretched in open lines, in all variety of ways, but in one interrupted flight."

Roosevelt and his partner "drove down our charges as best we could, sometimes having one barrel loaded or half loaded, sometimes the other, often neither, when we were interrupted with such glorious chances." Roosevelt's regret? "That we did not possess a breech-loader." It is one thing to be a sportsman in print, but in the blind anyone possessed of the waterfowling passion can be seized by the compulsion to kill many quickly. Roosevelt was neither first nor last.

As they shot, Roosevelt and his companion left the "birds . . . where they fell," and with darkness "retrieved sixty-seven—the result of about one hour's shooting—doubtless losing numbers that were not noticed, or which, being wounded, escaped." Roosevelt allowed that "had we shot as the professionals of Long Island and each used a breech-loader, I could hardly say how many we might not have killed." But Roosevelt was happy. "As it was the sport was wonderful, and the result sufficient to satisfy our ambition. . . ."

They headed back to the clubhouse and after dinner "gathered in a circle round the fire of our parlor for improving conversation."

"How many birds have we killed this year?" asked one of the hunters.

"The record shows a goodly total of 2,351," answered the club secretary. "Almost as many already as the entire return of last season, during which we only killed 2,908."

"He observed that the species distribution seemed quite comparable to the previous season: canvasbacks, 246; redheads, 122; blue-bills, 395; mallards, 540; dusky-ducks (black ducks), 108; wood-ducks, 601; blue-winged teal, 474; green-winged teal, 39; widgeons, 204; pin-tails, 50; gadwalls, 67; spoonbills, 11; ruddy-ducks, 2; butterballs, 7; geese, 2; quail 14; cormorants, 2; turkeys, 3; great hell-diver, 1."

Roosevelt's is a familiar nineteenth-century story from the continental heartland, where men like Fred Kimble killed more ducks in a day than twenty-first-century hunters do in a decade, where the most common unit of harvest appears to have been "wagon load." The scene was different back east. As Roosevelt observed, the hunting was good there too, just not a sure thing.

"They Smelt Us on the Last Crawl"
George Henry Mackay
JOHN PHILLPS, ED.

Shooting Journal of George Henry Mackay, 1929

With the American sporting scene cranking up in the 1870s, more and more men took to the waters, marshes, and shores. But unless you were independently wealthy like Roosevelt, the golden days of waterfowling may have been more elusive than bountiful. Anybody of modest means interested in waterfowling—you can imagine yourself here—had to find his own sport.

So meet George Henry Mackay, born in 1843, a Boston merchant who sailed the seas in pursuit of his business and remained a fierce lover of birds and waterfowl. His hunting life began in the spring of Appomattox, and it is our good fortune that he not only kept a careful diary of his sporting adventures but also gave the record to writer John Phillips, who had it privately printed in 1929 under the title of The *Shooting Journal of George Henry Mackay*. A number of the entries focus on duck hunting and reveal how immersed he became in waterfowling and, even more interestingly, how little that devotion had to do with the size of his hunting bags.

A good example is the hunt Mackay took to High Gate Springs, Vermont, on Lake Champlain in early April 1871. The hunting was slow the first day. As he noted in his diary, "Wash, George and myself lay in Big Marsh Slough in the afternoon, in the morning at Willow Point" and killed "1 Sheldrake, 1 Buffle Head [and] 7 Black Ducks."

The spring flight was brief, but more concentrated than the fall migration. After a long winter, fowlers like Mackay anticipated ice-out with an enthusiasm akin to twentieth-century landlocked salmon trollers—only they were waiting to hunt. Young duck killers, Wash, George, and Mackay (age twenty-eight) probably planned the next morning shoot while lying in the grass that afternoon. You can almost hear them across the century:

"Well, if we got seven ducks here in the afternoon, think how many we'll get here if we're lying in the grasses at sunup." They probably went to bed worrying about how they'd tote all the ducks home. "Gunny sacks, that's it; we'll each bring a gunny sack. No, we'll each bring two, wad them up, stuff them in our coats."

The next day the glorious party had at them. They all "lay in Big Marsh Slough. No fowl flying . . . killed only one duck."

The day after that, the guys were hanging out, maybe debating where to go, when a man named Mr. Chappel stopped by and reported "that 80 or 90 Golden Eyed Widgeon were 'wonted' in Barr's Pond." Mackay et al. "hitched up and drove up there." They didn't see eighty or ninety whistlers, closer to a dozen, plus a pair of black ducks, which they shot.

But there was good news, as Mackay reported: "Mr. Chappel told us that we had better go to Cutler's pond, as it was full of Ducks and was not more than three quarters of a mile off." They left the team and "walked the longest four miles I ever saw and over very bad ground." They made it to the pond, but the cover was so thick "that it [would have been] almost impossible to get a duck out of it had it been full." But it didn't matter because "there was only one Sheldrake in it [and] we went away thoroughly disgusted."

Mackay had the fire in his belly, and the next day he was back at the marsh he had hunted two days earlier. You wonder how, after killing one duck on the previous trip, the three men convinced themselves that "laying" in that marsh for the day was the go-to move. Perhaps the wind changed. "We saw about 15 geese, but got no shot at them. . . . We had poor luck as the result shows. . . . I think we came up too late, as it was a very early spring." There was no mention of Mr. Chappel.

Mackay certainly put his time in. The next morning he rose at 4 a.m. "It was very blowy," he wrote, "and I had tough time with the canoe." That's all. No ducks, but no regrets either.

That was an easy attitude to maintain, of course, if there was no closed season and you could basically go duck hunting whenever you got the green light. Some four years later, in August of 1875, Mackay was visiting Nantucket Island. And since he was out there anyway, and since August beachgoing wasn't the carnival of flesh that it is today, and since he did happen to have his shotgun, and, well, you know how it goes. The next thing he knew, he was duck hunting.

"I went out to the Hummock Pond. It rained hard with wind S. There were no birds moving. However, I shot some Black Ducks and a few other birds." His bag: "4 Black Ducks; 1 Willet; 2 Summer Yellow-legs; 4 Winter Yellow-legs; 11 (total)."

The idea of a hunting *season* was only beginning to emerge; hunters killed waterfowl whenever the opportunity arose. That generally meant either end of the migration. Spring season included February through May; fall, August through January. June and July was the growing season.

From today's vantage, it is interesting seeing Mackay in March, when he was out on Long Island for brant. There was the waterfowler's timeless battle with the wind, which was "round to the North, blowing hard and cold. No chance to shoot . . . I trust next week will be an improvement on the last. I have only had two days and a half out of the whole of it. Such is the result of a gunner's luck. There are plenty of fowl in the bay but not a very great many Brant. . . . Towards 6 o'clock p.m. it began to snow and continued a good share of the night with the wind N.E."

Live by the wind, die by the wind. No brant hunting the next day either, it being the Sabbath. "Not a very pleasant morning early, and pretty cold," he wrote. "We took a walk on the beach but saw nothing, and amused ourselves as best we could around the house. It looks now as if we should have a fair day to shoot tomorrow and no one hopes for such a result more than myself." He did have a bag to report: "1 Crow, shot from the window."

The next morning Mackay was ready: "We got up at the usual time and went down to the shore, only to find the Bay closed with ice a mile from shore. . . . We were very much discouraged and came back to the house to wait, wait, wait, what I have been employed at all last week. I could have cussed pretty hard, but had reached that state when my feelings were better expressed by silence. So I sit in our comfortable room and look out of the window and speculate on the chances of the ice breaking . . . about six o'clock p.m. it began to snow and at nine p.m. continues. . . . Shall not set clock for tomorrow morning."

But as duck hunters know more than anyone, it is darkest before dawn. The following September (1878) Mackay was back out on Nantucket. He had come "down from Boston [the previous] evening [having] learned there had been quite a flight of Green-heads (golden plover) on the afternoon of the 12th and 13th. I learned some 300 to 400 birds were shot. . . ."

Mackay and a certain Captain Wyer took the team "first to Quaise Point, saw nothing; then to Pocomo, saw only one Winter Yellowleg and about 15 Green-heads in the distance." After that they "drove across to Gibb's Pond, saw nothing; then to Touchee Pond, where I crawled up to what I supposed were four or five ducks." Instead "about 40 Black Ducks jumped up and I . . . knocked down seven in all and got six. Felt good."

Maybe he was on a roll. No date accompanies the next entry, but it appears to be not long after the above incident, and once again on Nantucket. Returning on their boat, Mackay and his buddy glassed "some forty or fifty Black Ducks, sitting on the beach where [he] thought we could get near them." They pulled up to shore and started to sneak 'em.

They couldn't see over the dunes, so they had to "crawl up three times before I could locate them." Even then they ended up "about fifty yards too much to the windward of them on our last crawl." The ducks jumped at the edge of shotgun range. Mackay and his friend "gave them two guns each, but only shot down five dead, and by the time we had gone back to our boat the cripples and one of the dead ones had disappeared, so we only bagged four."

Mackay added, "We earned them, with the work we did," but "I was considerably disappointed, for it was one of those chances one seldom gets." Had he not been to the windward, they could have had the first shot "as they sat on the sand and as they were close together it [would] have been a big one." But, Mackay admitted, "we were tired out trying to get exactly opposite them, and they smelt us on the last crawl. Too bad, too bad."

So much for the golden days of waterfowling. Certainly some areas did have clouds of ducks, the marshes along the Mississippi being one. But that abundance did not characterize the entire country, particularly in the Northeast. The relative scarcity of ducks only deepened this hunter's involvement and made him treasure his moments of success. In the formula that Grinnell, Roosevelt, and other conservationists drew up about reframing scarcity, this innateness of waterfowling desire proved absolutely critical.

"An Instantaneous Symphony"
HAMBLEN SEARS

"Henry's Birds," *Fur and Feather Tales*, 1897

The passion for waterfowl, in other words, not only existed apart from their actual abundance but seemed more something a person created or perhaps more precisely, contracted. The passion could take many forms. Initially, when a hunter was young, it demanded numbers of ducks killed. But in time, it prompted a sportsman to seek ways to use the hunting's complexity to enrich his involvement and draw more meaning from the enterprise. (Grinnell and both Roosevelts counted on the development of this stage for it led many to advance conservationist causes.) Bird hunters trained dogs. Duck hunters also trained dogs—not only retrievers but also trolling dogs. The enterprise that proved definitive, however, was decoy carving. The decoys that flew off the workbenches of North American hunters became folk art, the most beautiful in the world.

The great carvers, whose surviving work commands small fortunes today (as of this printing, two of Elmer Crowell's decoys—*Preening Pintail* and *Sleeping Goose*—each topped the $1 million mark), did most of the whittling in the late nineteenth and early twentieth centuries. Many of these men, Albert Laing and Elmer Crowell, for example, had been market hunters who began careers hunting over live decoys, which also became popular in the late nineteenth and early twentieth centuries, particularly for goose and puddle-duck hunting, in which realism counted for more than did the density and breadth of the wooden fleet.

As in every other element of the sporting life, some guys were better than others at raising and training decoys. Some seemed to be naturals, a good example being Henry Eldrige, the subject of Hamblen Sears' memorable portrait, "Henry's Birds."

A sometimes wheelwright, sometimes builder, full-time duck raiser and trainer, Henry Eldridge lived on Cape Cod, with his family of eight. He maintained a shooting stand on Cliff Pond, which Sears and some other city friends helped finance. Henry was "practically speaking . . . a genius," one of those talented individuals whose "lines," had they "been cast in smoother places, . . . no doubt would have astounded humanity by his inexhaustible resources." He had a nineteenth-century streak of independence about him. When the mood struck, he would cease building a carriage or house and sit down and play a bull fiddle for a half hour, or pour himself a tumbler of his elderberry wine or Jamaican rum, drink it off, and "sit upon a barrel-head and gaze with unswerving thoughtfulness upon the cheeses and rafters of the roof."

His work shut down entirely when "the first black duck [of the season came] sailing over the dunes of Cape Cod." Henry loved ducks. In addition to hunting them, he maintained a highly trained flock of thirty that saw service as his live decoys. His ducks trusted "him so thoroughly that he could pick them up and put them in his pocket head downward at any time." The trust resulted from the fact that they knew that corn was coming. He'd toss a duck into the air, and it would land, preen, quack, and head over to him for corn. His ducks figured out early in their web-footed lives that Henry's quacking was their cue to start quacking in reply. As soon as they quacked, they received corn, which basically meant that if you were one of Henry's ducks, you stayed close and quacked whenever he did. The overall result would be "an instantaneous symphony" across the barnyard. .

When Sears received "a missive" from Henry one January day to come over from New York to Cape Cod because the birds were thick on the "pawn'd," he did so without hesitation. He arrived, and was greeted like a head of state. Sears reports that Henry's family was of common means, but they saw themselves as the equal of any folks. "Here were his seven children and wife within one room talking to me on all sides. Yet none was sent away. He had built the house, carriage himself." Henry and Sears pound some elderberry wine and hit the hay; 2 a.m. comes early.

In darkness they took the team on a six-mile sleigh ride, walking in silence as they approached the pond, with "Henry [taking] the ducks on his shoulders, [while Sears] carried the four guns and cartridges." As dawn spread Henry pointed "at something which in time resolved itself into a black line on the water." Ten black ducks.

Once light came on full, "Henry became a duck—that is to say, he emitted quacks by the dozen." And with that, the tame decoys opened up, and they let 'er rip. Henry and the author began tossing single ducks out of the blind, and they quickly circled and hit the water "shrieking" in duck talk. It took quite a bit of convincing, every bit of showmanship that could be mustered in—and front of—that duck blind. Eventually "the mystic ten" began paddling in to see what all the fuss was about. In all, the operation required a couple of hours— even with the vociferous quacking and flapping of Henry's birds.

Henry and the author split up the ten for the shot on the water. Henry delivered a three-count. When the smoke cleared eight drifted dead. They'd crippled two more. They eventually got them all.

Sears anticipated the reader's reaction: "If you are a sportsman, you are saying at this moment, 'This is no sport; it is slaughter.' In a measure, judged by the highest standards, that is true; but you deceived the duck when you crawled up on him, and I deceived him when I made him crawl up on me. . . . And the study, preparation, time, money, and excitement of it all far surpass the practice of crawling up on the bird or of shooting over wooden 'coys."

The live-decoy "stands" of New England remained the last bastion of shooting ducks on the water. Duck hunters in the Great Lakes areas and the mid-Atlantic coastal areas were shooting flying ducks by the late 1860s. Herbert and his contemporaries jumped ducks in the 1840s, and hunters in the sneak boats of Barnegat and the batteries of Long Island Sound and Chesapeake Bay nearly always shot their waterfowl on the wing, though they often took the first shot at them on the water if the birds landed before they got a shot off.

The determining element appears to be the numbers of ducks available. New Englanders not only shot ducks on the water but also did their best to kill as many as possible on the first shot because ducks were few, and if you didn't get them, someone else would. In general, the more revered the game—as the black ducks and geese ordinarily killed in stands undoubtedly were—the more certain hunters wanted to be of a successful shot. The nineteenth-century methods of killing deer in the Adirondacks—crusting, jacklighting, and shooting them from canoes while guides held their tails—offers a different example of the same point.

But the modern sporting code advanced by Grinnell, Roosevelt, and others called for applying only the most sporting measures to the most sporting quarry. Doing so conferred the most upon the hunter. This idea took a while to catch on. "First shot on the water" represented a common practice for brant, geese, and "big ducks" even in print, to say nothing of in practice, where it was no doubt much more common and would remain so through the twentieth century, regardless of how much it was discouraged in the press.

The live-decoy operations provided a way for hunters in the Northeast to create engaging sport with fewer ducks than their fellow hunters elsewhere in the country. A good example comes from a letter published in George Grinnell's *American Duck Shooting* (1901). "There is a certain charm about shooting in a thickly settled region which one does not get anywhere else. The game is scarce and hard to circumvent, and when a pair or two of shy old black ducks are successfully brought to bag, the satisfaction is often greater than the killing of ten times the number in a more favorable locality. . . . For two days a northwester has been doing its best to remove the few remaining leaves, until at last the wind has died away and the evening is calm and wonderfully clear. It is likely to be the coldest night of the season, and we go to bed in the best of spirits, almost certain of a shot in the morning. . . ."

It almost sounds like the writer was going deer hunting in the morning. The language suggests as much: "A shy old" black duck. He has done his scouting; he might not get a duck, but he'll get a shot at one. The excitement of birds swimming in was palpable. "You will scarcely believe that we have been in the stand two hours," he exclaimed. "Game was in sight nearly all the time." Now the game was on. The challenge of black ducks resided in their sagacity. Figuring out how to entice them was the fun of the hunt, not unlike turkey hunting today. No one's shooting *them* on the wing.

Henry's thrill was less about "deceiving" the ducks—that would emerge with decoys men carved—and more about getting his tame ducks to perform in collusion with him. If anything, it seems like falconry, without the nobility. The major shift from Robert Barnwell Roosevelt's experience to that of Mackay and Sears was that waterfowling now had little to do with composure in the face of abundance and everything to do with losing yourself in the world of the waterfowl. It almost didn't matter that the hunts took place in non-wilderness, social worlds; the hunter had to go to the duck's world—that was the joy of waterfowling. If you weren't careful, it could become your life.

"The Grand Swinging Ocean"
ROBERT T. MORRIS

"Watching the Brant Grow Big,"
Hopkins's Pond and Other Sketches, 1896

All hunters love their sport, but few exist at its mercy like waterfowlers. And the water has a good deal to do with that. Safety for the fowl, risk for the hunter, bond for both, water created the ultimate equal sign. The water shaped the memories of the sports; it called like a friend to those who ran the boats and did the guiding. The water led sports to see their guides as talented, not shiftless but "independent," but enviable and heroic. Science was beginning to make a mark in the late nineteenth century, but knowledge still resided in experience and observation. What better excuse for both than a spring trip with a man who has lived on the water all his life?

Nineteenth-century waterfowling happened not when the law allowed but when the ocean or lake or marsh became providential, even if it meant sneaking one's fowling piece in with the beach furniture, as Mackay may have been forced to do on Nantucket. Many hunters spelled spring b-r-a-n-t, in deference to the delectable three-pound, flock-challenged sea goose noted for an open-water habitat and an uncritical attraction to decoys. While brant showed little interest in stopping once they turned on the jets for fall migration, their trip north included some significant layovers, most notably in the lees of Long Island and Cape Cod, where the birds gathered before the final leg of their journey. As a result, brant hunting emerged as a spring sport, though it might be a stretch to call March on the North Atlantic the season of poets.

Imagine Henry David Thoreau going brant hunting, and you have the essence of a bold little essay called "Watching the Brant Grow Big" by Robert T. Morris. The east wind was "shiver-laden," when Morris's guide, "Captain Jack," woke him on the schooner, where they had spent the night. Sleet popped on the cabin window as Morris ventured out on the deck. "Golly," said Captain Jack as he "hitched up one suspender" and "expectorated" over the side. "Tide runs like a hoss, don't it." Morris agreed that indeed it did, and drew a deep breath, "find[ing] in distending lungfuls of it the peace of the infusoria of the flats and the power of the grand swinging ocean."

The two had their hearts set on a certain sandbar with a box blind already dug in place. They arrived just as the tide started to fall. "The jets of forty clams" greeted them, as they stepped off the boat on to the sand. Morris made a note of the salute—the bounty of the sea, "where all life multiplies, and in abundance, and forever."

Morris cleaned out the blind and snuggled in, while Captain Jack set up the decoys then sailed the sloop off a ways. A "jingle of wings" sounded overhead. In the words of Grinnell, Morris was "moved by emotions he but half understands." He was so moved, in fact, that he fantasized how good the pair of whistlers might be in a stew. But he had an empathy for the birds too, and because "they were so happy with each other," he let them fly through.

Not long after, a flock of four brant materialized, "winnowing along low over the water." Morris raised a boot at them, and the flock slowed. They saw the decoys, towered to get a better view, then faded away from the blind—except for one bird. The rest of the flock turned and followed him into the decoys, and Morris killed two, the final hitting the surface with such force that it "causes the clams to squirt for rods around."

A flock of twenty appeared. They got the old boot trick, this time with a hand. The older birds flared, but the younger ones beat it for the decoys—and then the wary followed, for "good judgment doesn't count among friends." Closer they came, and bigger they got. Morris loved their spectacle: "They have a great clamor, some rising, some settling, some hoarse, some clear voiced, some curving their wings to sail in, some fluttering and wavering and giving cries of warning. The whole flock huddles and separates, huddles and rises and wheels to go away." They skirted the edge of the decoys and Morris scratched down one.

All the while the tide had been falling, turning the sandbar into an island and finally, now, putting the kibosh on the hunting. But the ocean equals life, and the change brought new bounty. The razor clams, for one, which

Morris gathered and Captain Jack fried in pork. The eels for another, which they speared in the sand. The crabs, for yet another, then the soft-shells, and finally the flounder, which were just the right size and "shape to fit the bottom of a frying-pan and become nicely browned on both sides when the fins curl up in a crisp." They sailed for home. There was some eating to do.

Waterfowling stories can move us in many ways, though I can't recall another one that has made me want to order in seafood.

A man of means and integrity, Robert T. Morris exemplified the Victorian sportsman. His father, to whom he dedicated this book, served a term as governor of Connecticut. As a youth, Morris repaired, whenever permitted, to the woods and waters around New Haven. He later took his undergraduate degree at Cornell and eventually rose to prominence as a surgeon and professor in New York City. His labors increased with his years, and, as in this story, he depended on the sporting life to lift his soul. He loved the sea and, like most duck hunters, loved it most when it was wild with wind and storm. Such is his ecstasy on this morning that the sound of fowl overhead gave rise to thoughts about the mouth-watering stew one might make with these late-winter whistlers. (I'll wait for the fried flounder, thanks.)

A half century later, decoys crated in the attic, Morris wrote his memoirs, *Fifty Years A Surgeon*, and holds forth on matters medical before devoting the last two chapters to the outdoors, ending with ". . . at times, when all is still, I seem to hear loud surf—but that is only memory, for one who loves the sea." It is nice to know that youthful mornings on that "grand, swinging ocean" stay with us forever.

"And the Noble Bird Fell"

GEORGE BIRD GRINNELL

American Duck Shooting, 1901

As the twentieth century dawned, American duck hunting, like other outdoor sports, began to change more rapidly. The increasing anonymity of daily life meant that wealthy sports could no longer rely on friendship for their duck hunts. But other changes, more ominous, loomed as well. The same threats facing big game faced waterfowl too.

As the country's leading conservationists sought to anchor the hunting experience in sportsmanship and in an appreciation of the natural world (as a precursor to the responsibility for stewardship), George Grinnell did his part, and then some, for the future of American waterfowl. In 1901, five years after Morris's book appeared, Grinnell published *American Duck Shooting,* which became waterfowling's bible. The book profiled the various waterfowl species, their habitat, and then the methods for hunting them. Throughout the book, Grinnell emphasized the need for conservation and, as always, he relied upon his remarkable capacity for finding the story in his own experience to model how a person might duck hunt in a responsible fashion..

The following excerpt from *American Duck Shooting* reflects a conservationist ideal, but even more interestingly it portrays a modern waterfowl hunt, one that was replacing the old-school hunts conducted by Henry Eldridge and Captain Jack. The modern guide was very skilled, with a well-trained dog and well-trained live decoys (to supplement the artificial ones). But the guide was an employee of the client (Grinnell), not an old friend putting together a companionable hunt. The atmosphere in the blind was cordial, encouraging. But there were no terms of endearment, no "chords of memory". More than anything else, the excerpt shows how much wing-shooting proficiency was beginning to matter in the world of modern waterfowling.

Grinnell and his guide, John, headed out through the dark North Carolina marsh in a sail-powered skiff, the predawn "overcast and black; wind northeast, temperature 28 degrees; prospect of snow or rain during the day." Leaving the lee of the point, they flushed squawking flocks of waterfowl, and "the skiff heeled over and darted forward like a good horse touched with the spur."

Clouds of ducks rose, but as Grinnell wrote, "still the guns remained in their cases and still I smoked my pipe . . . for the law of North Carolina provides that birds shall not be shot except after sunrise and before sunset, and we respect the law." Not "obey." Interesting; one step at a time, I guess.

They arrived at a point, and John set out some seventy-five wood decoys and three live ones, while the retriever splashed about in the shallows. Grinnell thatched the blind and finished up a bit of housekeeping, which he described as follows: "My two guns, loaded and cocked, lay across their rests, muzzles to the left. Behind me was my chair, into which I would crouch if birds appeared. My clothing was yellowish gray, harmonizing well with the surrounding vegetation. The top of the cane which formed the blind was broken off about breast high, so as not to interfere with the shooting." All was ready, with "wedges of canvas-backs and redheads winging their flight north or south to the feeding grounds which please them best, while through the quivering air flies the ringing whistle of a thousand wings." They waited. Grinnell smoked his pipe and "watched the live decoys enjoy the water and their freedom from the coop."

"Mark to the east," said John. A single coming right in. John quacked, the single quacked back, and then the live decoys "lifted up their voices in sonorous calls." Such an invitation proved "too much for the lone black duck." Wings cupped, he passed over the set. Grinnell rose, "put the gun on him and pulled. Bang, went the first barrel and bang the second; the duck climbed and climbed, and kept climbing." Nothing but air. "Gunner [the retriever] tore through the cane to what had fallen and to bring in the bird; John made no comment and I said nothing, either, though I had missed a shot that a ten-year-old boy ought to have killed."

Grinnell thought: "I let him get too far over the decoys and past me, and shot at him as he was going away, and . . . shot behind him . . . a disgraceful miss."

Grinnell was beside himself: "I do not know how other men feel about missing, especially about missing easy shots, but it plunges me into an abyss of shame and mortification from which I do not easily emerge. At the best of times I am a very bad shot, and often my missing makes me declare that I will give up shooting altogether." But like an experienced ball player, he had learned not to carry over the poor performance to the next game. "When however the time comes for me to get an outing again, I forget all about my past misses and start forward as hopeful and as free from anxiety about missing as if I were a good shot instead of being a villainously bad one."

Silence filled the blind, and he "mourned over this miss, and felt horribly ashamed that John and even that Gunner, had been witness of my disgrace." I imagine the movie *The Godfather*, Marlon Brando/Don Corleone calling him aside and slapping him, saying, "What's wrong with you? Be a man!"

Just then a pair of mallards slipped in from behind, surprising everyone (even Gunner), and Grinnell promptly shot behind them. Both barrels. Gunner again splashed out into the shallows, looking "in vain for something to bring in." But the mallards flew off "like a pair of disjointed parentheses and melt[ed] into the gray sky."

"Those two came badly, sir," said John.

Before long, another single showed up, "coming in as gently as one could wish." This time Grinnell would do it right. He remembered that I "very slowly bent to get my gun. . . . On the bird came, looking only at the decoys; I rose up slowly . . . followed him, but gave the gun a little too much swing, and shot over him. Another miss."

This was not how it was supposed to go. "Again despair seized me," wrote Grinnell. Then he missed a pair of pintails that "were alighting among the decoys." Despair "tightened its grip." More silence. "The trouble was too deep for words."

As a modern guide, John was apparently used to city hunters who couldn't shoot. He had a stock response. After Grinnell perforated the air around some more birds, John wondered aloud if there were not "something the matter with [the] cartridges . . . if the shells were not old ones. . . ." Grinnell said, no, declining to "excuse [his] lack of skill on the plea of poor ammunition."

A short time later, three ducks stole in and landed in the decoys. Those birds he "missed on the water with the right barrel, and on the wing when they flew not 25 yards from me."

John was still encouraging, and though discouraged himself, Grinnell couldn't exactly say he had a stomachache and walk home. As he wrote, "It was still early in the day—only 2 o'clock—and there was time yet to kill a lot of birds if they kept coming and—if I could only hit them. But there did not seem to be much chance of my doing that."

Grinnell resolved to shoot earlier and lead the ducks more (both good ideas), and "then heard from John the grating call of the canvas-back, followed by several loud honks, and sitting down I strained my eyes to see where the birds were to which he was calling. Peering through the stalks of the cane, I presently saw off to the right a single canvas-back coming with the steady flight that distinguishes these birds from almost any other ducks. He was an old male, white, and handsome, and was headed straight for the decoys. . . . Just as he was over the tail decoys, I arose, held 2 feet in front of his bill and fired, and the noble bird fell." And before he knew it, Gunner had retrieved the can and Grinnell was stroking its plumage.

Grinnell's proficiency picked up from there. He ended the day with twenty-two ducks and hoped that he had "in some small measure erased the feeling of contempt that John—and Gunner—must have had for me." Still, his own perception of himself as a hunter rested almost entirely on his shooting skill, his ability to regain his composure. The self-examination feels like mental health day in the duck blind, and surprisingly unlike the Grinnell who didn't even think about shooting while chasing around white goats. How did wing-shooting come to play such a key role in defining his—and the modern— duck hunt? The answer has to do, in a rather round-about way, with evolving notions of sportsmanship.

Nineteenth-century writers had extolled waterfowling for its excitement and toughness, and the manliness those features produced. Good fellowship and a general imperviousness to the elements mattered in the mix of what made a man a good duck hunter too. And all these qualities mattered now more than ever in the new century with the cushiness of urban and suburban life and the perceived threats to masculinity that came with the press for suffrage. But as with upland bird hunting, waterfowling proficiency came to reference an additional set of skills, namely dexterity, facility, and composure. And in this story, with the new anonymity between client and guide and the latter now providing a professional service, with decoys, dogs, and boat, there really wasn't much else a hunter could do to showcase his ability or contribute to the hunt *other* than hit the ducks hanging over the decoys. The hunter's shot at those ducks was the reason everyone and everything else was out there, and Grinnell knew it. He had no prior relationship to fall back on, or role to assume. (Geez, just like when we were kids; can't hit a bull's backside with a base fiddle. Har-har.) That he was also the most prominent sportsman in the country being patronized with "Those came in badly, sir" probably didn't help him feel any less than totally mortified.

The recollections, stories, and essays of Sears, Mackay, Roosevelt, and Grinnell reveal this gradual integration of wing-shooting skill into waterfowling competence, as the fame of Doc Carver and others entered the duck blind too. *Gradual* being the key term—Grinnell shows no hesitation in giving the swimming ducks the first barrel as they paddled about the decoys. Such transitional moments of "integration" are key to the overall organizing function that Grinnell's book served.

At the time, duck hunting methods revealed little in the way of such uniformity, in part because of the localized nature of the sport. Aside from nationally known sports and writers such as Grinnell, most late nineteenth-century hunters kept their travel within a region. Approaches to duck hunting, which depended to an extent on the species in question, depended even more on the place. It is tough to imagine Benton and his buddy throwing out a couple dozen merganser decoys and hunkering down for the day. Publisher, editor, and writer Nick Lyons, the closest figure outdoor writing has to a patron saint, once observed that fishing is remarkably localized; the same could be said of waterfowl hunting.

By drawing on letters from hunters and naturalists around the country, *American Duck Shooting* operated as a literary clearinghouse of sorts, and raised waterfowl experiences from idiosyncratic and local and transformed them into something recognizable—and national. In this respect it served the same function for duck hunting, as Mary Orvis Marbury's book did for fly fishing. Grinnell's book reviewed guns, loads, blinds, decoys, and dog (and duck) training and called that the "art" of duck hunting. "Field" authors wrote in about their experiences. Every man was a naturalist—and his findings would go into the stew.

Their efforts were part of a larger cultural movement of the day. Historian Robert Wiebe has termed this general cultural and national impulse "the search for order," and his book by that title remains an excellent lens for viewing the attempt of sportsmen of the day like Grinnell to codify how ducks should be hunted. Slowly, over the course of the first half of the twentieth century, differences in regional perceptions of how ducks should be killed would disappear, even as differences in actual methods (e.g., jump hunting versus decoying) remained. This shift in notions of sportsmanship brought new values to the duck blind, as in Grinnell's piece.

This piece becomes the archetype for the day-in-the-blind—not so much what it should mean but which activities should dictate its meaning, in this case respecting the law, the art of organizing a setup that effectively draws ducks, the responsibility of each person (and animal) to perform to the best of his ability, and, finally, shooting competence. In a sense it is not unlike the pride that Teddy Roosevelt took in building his wilderness camp. The idea in both cases was that participation in the outdoors came with the expectation of competence.

"Trash You Call Them"
PERCY CUSHING

"Shooting Ducks at New York's Back Door," *Outing*, April 1910

Such a framework outlined a general meaning for duck hunting, though different approaches to waterfowl led to different experiences. Duck hunting was different from uplands: A guy and his buddy went grouse hunting or quail hunting, but duck hunters generally didn't go mallard hunting or teal hunting. They might say, "You know there are a lot of redheads hanging around that bay." But it was not like they'd pass up a bull canvasback. Usually hunters targeted puddle ducks or divers; they each had different habits and habitats, though you could cheat and set up for both. That decision made, most hunters took what came into the decoys or what flew past their point.

Hunters generally favored males of any species of game, for reasons often attributed to wanting to propagate the species by harvesting more males than females. But there was also a psychological dimension to the matter, perhaps having to do with the idea that female animals were better eating and sportsmen should not be seen as "needing" food. When a deer was killed for "camp meat," it was (and is) nearly always a doe. The males were seen as more challenging. Killing a male somehow offered the hunter a clearer achievement, and it was somehow not as manly to kill a female. But the reasons for preferring to shoot a "husky cock bird," like Mister Arthur or "an old male, white and handsome" canvasback like Grinnell extended beyond any simple confirmation of masculinity for male hunters, as reflected in Georgia Roberts' experience with an Adirondack buck. Hunters (and anglers), regardless of gender, believed that males provided a better test of their skill (males of any species were almost always constructed as warier and tougher than females). In most species of game and fish (to some extent) males were considered more "regal" due to antlers, coloration, morphology, or size. Important exceptions such as ruffed grouse and black ducks notwithstanding, the cocks and the drakes of game birds and waterfowl are often more colorful and handsome than the drab-colored females. This preference for male quarry was probably more explicit in the nineteenth century, but it has persisted to this day and actually cuts across all fish and game. Most states permit hunters to shoot deer of either sex these days, but how frequently do outdoor magazines picture does in hunting articles? Most of the largest bass (and other fish species) are females, the fish are nearly always referred to with a masculine pronoun, as in, "You got him!"

As for waterfowl, hunters definitely preferred certain species of ducks. In general, the worth of the meat conferred an initial value on any species of fish and wildlife, but it seemed particularly true of waterfowl. The speed with which such toothsome reputations became nationalized and generalized into worth of the species is quite remarkable; it underlines the importance of magazines in the post-war era, but also the role that earlier publications such as the *Spirit of the Times* played in laying a foundation. A price listing from the market hunting days almost invariably cues the modern game status of any waterfowl: Canvasbacks and redheads at the top; mallards, black ducks, and pintails close behind, along with the slightly smaller but tasty, acorn-eating wood ducks. Brant and geese when you can get 'em.

Diet made the difference. Brant ate eelgrass; the other above-noted ducks primarily gobbled grain, corn, and grasses, the exception being the black duck's late-season affinity for bivalves on the lake and ocean shores.

Following them were the lesser and greater scaups (bluebills and broadbills, respectively, though names—black heads, for instance, could vary by region), which eat about 50/50 percent, vegetable to animal, followed by whistlers, buffleheads, and sea ducks, which fed closer to 3 to 1 animal to vegetable. Mergansers, with their sawbills, were (and are!) pretty much solid fish snatchers. As J. R. Benton's piece shows, these ducks were certainly sporty targets, which made them fun to shoot at but not necessarily desirable to hunt.

From this ranking of the best-eating flesh, hunters of the day created the pecking order of which species were the best to hunt, and repeated it as gospel. In a story titled "On the Wide Marshes of Manitoba" that appeared in the February 1905 issue of *Outing*, Edwyn Sandys explained, "The most prized of all the Northern ducks is the canvasback, the mallard ranking second, then redhead, bluebill, gadwall, pintail, widgeon, green-winged, bluewinged, and cinnamon teal, shoveller, buffle-head, etc. The black, or dusky duck, of course, is a fine fowl anywhere, but I saw nothing of him in the North, if his regular trips extend so far."

Grinnell agreed, writing, "Of all the American ducks the Canvas-back is easily the most famous. Its flesh depends for its flavor entirely on the food that the bird eats, and since for many years it was chiefly killed where the so-called wild celery abounds, the reputation of the canvas-back was made by the individuals that fed on this grass." Grinnell himself seemed aware that the reputation of the flesh influenced the "standing" of the canvasback even when not warranted. "In waters where this plant is abundant the canvasback is [no] better than . . . the redhead or the widgeon, which subsists largely on the same food. But the fame of the canvasback is now too firmly established everywhere to be shaken, and it will continue to be regarded, as it has so long been, as the king of our ducks."

Grinnell wrote of "venerable men, occupying high positions in the business or professional world," who came close to duking it out over who shot a particular duck. They "sat down side by side and laboriously plucked the fowl in dispute in order to determine—according to club rule—on which side it had been shot." It is hard to imagine them doing so if the bird were a hen whistler.

Hunters conferred elegant and challenging physical qualities on the most desirable ducks, in other words, not the other way around—though it is fun to pretend. (A drake redhead and hen whistler fly at roughly the same speed, and if anything, a whistler is warier and hardier.) Canvasbacks were "strong-flying" and "handsome," the latter something Grinnell decided when the particular drake in his story was somewhere around one hundred yards off. Black ducks were so wary, hunters believed they could smell humans. (They can't.) Decoying them was challenging, even with live decoys. It only made them more coveted. Here was Grinnell commenting on the same attributes in the "undesirable" whistler: "While the whistler is one of our most beautiful ducks, it is not highly regarded by those who have an opportunity to kill better fowl, and like the little dipper (i.e., bufflehead) and ruddy duck and the mergansers, it is often allowed to pass over the decoys without being shot at. It is not a bird that decoys readily." The difference, apparently, was that the black duck didn't decoy because it was too discerning, whereas the whistler didn't because it didn't know any better. The reasoning was close to that embraced by old George Tattersall, who complained that American brook trout didn't know enough to understand that there might be a fake bug in among the real one.

Such "social constructions" matter because they influenced what a particular quarry said about the hunter. What meaning did a hunter take from his morning spent shooting canvasbacks and redheads? Other things being equal (numbers of birds, weather, shooting success, fellowship, and so forth), was it different from shooting black ducks and mallards? Different, probably. Necessarily better? Harder to say. How about whistlers, buffleheads, old squaws, and other trash ducks, as they were called? No question. Those ducks would come to provide what was called "poor man's duck shooting."

Admittedly, we are in an imprecise area here. But it is worth thinking about. As duck numbers in the East continued to dwindle, and more men took to hunting, more hunters availed themselves of these "poor man's ducks." As Grinnell's above description explained, whistlers were "not highly regarded by those who have an opportunity to kill better fowl." But not everyone had that opportunity; not everyone could drop everything and head out for Maryland when the cans were off Havre de Grace. And hunting late-season whistlers was truly great fun and sport; when the snow was falling, the wind whipping, and the birds trading, you could burn through some ammo in short order and have great fun. As a result, "trash ducks" enjoyed a bit of a boost. If nothing else, the new hunters—and there were good numbers of them—had to have something to try and kill.

Articles such as "Shooting Ducks at New York's Back Door" began to appear more frequently and no doubt represented a printed version of ideas bouncing around at sporting goods departments in stores, clubs, and barrooms up and down the East Coast. In this article, Percy Cushing explained how it was possible to kill a good many ducks right in the suburbs; he shot his a few miles from the Larchmont Yacht Club. You just had to be prepared to do some slumming.

"You have shot canvasback on the Chesapeake or in the celery lakes of the Middle West, perhaps," Cushing wrote. "And mallards in the corn and teal in the rice sloughs of the Dakotas and red heads along the coast! Great sport! You bet; good birds, plenty of 'em, pretty shooting. Granted, every bit! I've done it, too. But ever shoot coots? What—no?

"Slow fliers? That's so. No sport? No, sir, you're dead wrong." These aren't mud hens. "Nothing of the sort, just every-day scoters—know the breed? Sea ducks—fellows that can bore down through forty feet of salt water and nail a small clam with the ease and precision of a mallard 'tipping up' for a luscious root. . . . And, say, when there are no canvas-backed gentlemen . . . coots are pretty good fun. Then, too, sometimes there's a broad bill or so, now and again a black duck, and when the ice grinds in the coves, a few golden eyes—whistlers we call them."

Like any duck hunting trip, you'd have cold and hard work, but great fun. As Cushing wrote, "Trash you call them. I called them that myself." Then he started hunting them. "I'm simply saying that if you must shoot—and every man who has shot ducks must when the leaves turn and the water gets gray— you won't have to travel half a thousand miles and spend half a thousand dollars getting a little real fun with your old double barrel."

For New York commuters, the hunting literally was at the back door. "You can get 'em forty-five minutes from Broadway, and even less now with fast trains at your service." It helped to have "friends with the gun lust who live somewhere along Long Island Sound from New Rochelle on up the Connecticut coast." To hunt, you needed a powerboat and a duck boat—a South Bay scooter was good. "Have her able, strong, and with enough free-board to stand a stiff sea. Then you need twenty or thirty stool, a pair of oilskins, a tough constitution, and a gilt-edge perseverance. That's all."

So equipped, "any fellow living at New Rochelle, at Pelham, at Larchmont, at Rye, or Harrison, or any of the towns that border the Sound close to the big city can have some real hunting, some real hard work, a little shooting, and lots of fun."

Waterfowling represented the perfect tonic for the encroaching domesticity of modern living. Hunting close to home for ducks of any sort was better than no hunting; it simply required a bit of reconfiguration about what mattered in a hunt. The species or glamour no longer made a man a hunter, in part because proving his gentlemanly decorum—his class rank—no longer mattered as much with the increasing acceptance of hunting and all the middle-class guys who wanted to go. At stake now for the duck hunter was manliness, but in a more modern, competent sense of the term that had taken on such urgency with the perceived encroachment of women.

Between slinging decoys, dragging boats, and chasing cripples, or "shoot-overs," as they were called, and negotiating the icy December waters, duck hunters stood at the very apogee of hardiness, boldness, and all that was masculine. While women fished, hunted birds and occasionally deer, duck blinds remained tree houses with "no girls allowed." For one thing, waterfowling's predawn starts often required the hunting party to spend the night in close quarters on or near the swamp or shore, and most proper folks saw waterfront, coed sleepovers as an idea whose time had yet to come. In fact, neither gender seemed particularly anxious to end the prohibition. The joy of water-fowling has always been about shedding responsibilities, not incurring them, about its capacity, in essence, for turning men into boys. And this was probably a transformation most women would just as soon hear about as witness. ("You were rescued first by the guides, then by the Coast Guard, both times while you were holding hands in head-high surf? That sounds lovely, dear.")

As Southern waterfowler Alex Hunter wrote, "The risk only gives the sport a keener flavor." And that was the trade-off with trash ducks: Their hardiness seemed inseparable from the risk of the late season. Hunting cans or mallards or pintails or other "better ducks" didn't require risk to make the enterprise exciting, in other words. Even more interesting is the literal proximity of Percy Cushing's duck hunting exploits—just a few miles from the Larchmont Yacht Club, the epitome of eastern upper-class privilege. There is something fundamentally uncouth in this "trash-duck shooting" right out in the open. It was not unlike the famous contents of Tom Sawyer's pockets—and how that made him a "real" boy.

Duck hunting for undesirable game was very different from fly fishing or wing-shooting, for instance, which seemed to cling to class attachments. This story severed them—it is almost as though Percy would like some of the club members to say, "Now what exactly is it that those men are doing out there in that skiff? Shooting? My land."

More to the point, by hunting in skiffs on the big water of the sound late in the year, upper-middle-class sports took on the very risks that their working-class guides and market hunters faced every day. In a sense it made them feel more authentic, in the same way music patrons expect some suffering in their musicians or artists. It makes the music sound real, as though it comes from the heart. The desire to be out on a skiff on the North Atlantic in January could probably be said to come from the same place.

Quite possibly such risk created a suburban wilderness. Then and now, duck hunting on big water felt like stepping into a different world, with civilization literally behind you. Whether that was fifty yards or fifty miles didn't matter much in a snowstorm with a surf roaring in your ears. Real duck hunters loved wild weather, and they delighted in it—publicly. It was less that they sought out risk than that they remained oblivious to it. They had become the duck.

That they had done it for so long and were doing it in sight of their community only rendered the situation more business as usual. Experience counted. The later the season, the greater the risk, of course, but often the greater the number of ducks available.

Midwinter duck hunting seems to have been a rather popular indulgence in the region, in spite of the average January temperature in the nineteenth century. Grinnell's book tells of hunters who clothed themselves in white and snuggled into the ice floes of Lake Ontario. Freighters often ran aground off certain shoals, depositing their grain into the waters, and waterfowl availed themselves of the feed. Waterfowlers, in turn, availed themselves of the waterfowl, but they were not always able to retrieve their ducks for, as one participant noted, ". . . launching a boat in the wintry seas is a dangerous operation and a capsize is something to be carefully avoided." Interesting. We might see shooting ducks that can't be retrieved as unsportsmanlike, but the act meant something different at the turn of the twentieth century. Removing the "worth" of the meat (or feathers) out of the equation left one reason to be out there freezing: hunting for its own sake or, put another way, for the joy of it—which is as good a reason as any to end up heading down the Niagara River on an ice floe.

"She'll Go through This All Right"

Peter Bailey

GEORGE FORTIS

"The Toll of the Sport," *Outing*, August 1913

Wind and snow kept the ducks flying and the hunting more dangerous, which infused the scene with more chaos, and gave waterfowling its peculiar and compelling authenticity and, as Alex Hunter observed, formed a central part of its appeal.

Too much love can be a bad thing.

Tom Veltman was a nineteen-year-old bayman. The Veltmans had always lived on Great South Bay. Tom was employed as a boat captain by Peter Bailey, a twenty-three-year-old insurance man, and Carl Clemons, a thirty-three-year-old physician. They had said good-byes to their wives and come down from New York for the last day of the duck season. Earlier that fall, Bailey had built a shack on Sexton Island, some six miles across the bay.

The men were pumped. The problem? It was January, below zero, with "the wind . . . roaring out of the northwest, a living gale. . . ."

Veltman knew that "[crossing] would be taking a chance," wrote George Fortis in "The Toll of the Sport." "But, nevertheless, he did not hesitate to take that chance." Veltman, it turned out, "had a bride of two weeks waiting" for him at home (on Cap Tree Island).

"We can slide across all right, Tom," Bailey said. "We can hold under Great Flat until we hit Dickson's Channel. Then we can run up under the meadows and anchor. She'll go through this all right." The "little dory-built power boat" waited at the dock, tugging at the cleats.

Veltman looked out toward the island. Whitecaps marched "out of the haze in unbroken, endless companies." He kept looking and then turned back. "All right."

At that point Veltman's father, Charles, stepped in. "You better stay ashore," he told the trio. But they loaded the boat anyway. "A little knot of old baymen watched the dory plunge away into the twilight that had already begun to descend" and then walked back to their homes.

That ended on-scene narration of the fate of the three hunters. Searchers found the dory at anchor, iced in, a few days later. So the trio did make it across the bay. The consensus of the baymen was that the men powered across the calmer shoal water but didn't motor up as close as planned to Sexton and for some reason anchored in deep water on the south edge of the channel, still a quarter mile from Sexton Island. They loaded their sharpie rowboat with groceries, guns, ammunition, and extra clothes. The three men must have then all gotten in. As Fortis wrote, "How far the three got away in her from the launch before the rough sea of Dickson's Channel swamped them no one will ever know. That the boat filled or capsized while they were trying to row her across the channel is certain." They couldn't have survived for long. "When the dawn came at last, the surface of the bay was rough no longer," wrote Fortis. "The ice, which reached from shore to shore in an unbroken sheet, had smoothed it out."

No one realized what had happened for a couple of days, until the empty dory was discovered by baymen in ice scooters—shallow skiffs with sails designed to navigate the alternate ice and open water characteristic of a South Bay winter. The whole village turned out to join with the three spouses of the men as they awaited news.

Other duck hunters had been luckier. A few had been caught out on the islands or "over on Fire Island Beach." They stayed out there, "crouching over red-hot stoves which they fed ceaselessly all through the night with driftwood." A few had come back earlier, fighting "their way across the bay in scooters as best they could."

One man named Carl Chichester had headed out in the morning (of the same day that Veltman and the two others left) and, anchored in a cove, had unbelievable hunting—so much that he was unaware of the danger he was in "until he began to notice that the breasts of the ducks he shot were covered with ice where the spray had frozen on them as they battled along close to the tops of the waves."

Chichester had a long row home, and "when he swung away from the point he found himself confronted with three miles of porridge ice—soft, leathery slush, the forerunner of hard ice and the most dangerous of all perils . . . [because] even a scooter lurches forward but a few inches to a mighty pull of the oars, and stops dead and sullen the instant the pressure is removed."

At four o'clock Chichester, a brawny bayman, started rowing. Five hours later he reached shore. But he couldn't get out of the scooter. Water and spray had half filled the boat, "and the ice had formed about Chichester, freezing him solidly in the boat." Fellow baymen came hurrying down "with oars and axes and chopped him out." Alive, presumably.

There is no evidence that Chicester considered the wisdom of the enterprise before he went. But Veltman did. He had an offshore wind, which builds away from shore, and therefore has always been the seducer. Veltman knew as much, but this was his last chance for money before spring. His clients were important men who led to other important men. And, to be sure, it wasn't *just* business. The three were a team, to the point that months later Mrs. Veltman instantly recognized the ring arrangement on Clemons's fingers when his body was discovered. But business played some part, probably a big one, *The New York Times* would later report, "All Bay Shore was interested in the trip . . . ," which can also be read as the entire town was watching how the young Veltman handled matters. And so he said the only thing he could: "All right."

The accident received considerable news coverage. In an article dated Thursday, January 11, *The New York Times* reported that the men were to have returned on Monday, and it was then that "their absence excited comment." Some twenty ice scooters zipped about in search. On Wednesday "the village became nearly hysterical" when word came that Veltman's body had washed ashore on Little Fire Island and that Clemons had been discovered alive. The news turned out to be rumor. Baymen intensified their search. Through January, February, and March, scooters crisscrossed the ice and slush. In time, Mrs. Bailey seems to have accepted her husband's fate (Bailey's body was never found.). Mrs. Clemons and Mrs. Veltman, in particular, refused. The latter woman urged "searchers to their work day after day." They did so into April, because "they did not dare to tell the women that they had abandoned hope."

Early one afternoon, a flash of metal from a pile of driftwood caught the eye of a searcher: a ring on a human hand. The body was that of Dr. Clemons. All of Bay Shore turned out to witness the arrival of the body, and "hundreds followed with bared heads while it was carried to a local undertaking establishment." The search had made him—and Bailey as well—a member of the community. Naturally, a detailed account of the day appeared in the Sunday *New York Times*, April 14, 1912.

That same night brought frantic reports of a grander, more lurid tale of death at sea: the sinking of the RMS *Titanic*, the mother of all icy mishaps. When, on April 29, Veltman's body washed ashore on Fire Island, *The New York Times* noted rather faintly that the "body is in fair condition and will be taken to the home of Veltman's widow and parents." Romantic tragedy was hot stuff in the early twentieth century, but with some 1,500 bodies recently fished from the North Atlantic, the recovery of a single bayman's body hardly seemed newsworthy.

"Have a Good Time, and Don't Worry"
REX BEACH

"Geese," *Oh Shoot! Confessions of an Agitated Sportsman,* 1921

It wasn't so much that duck hunting was a death wish. It was more that water-fowl bliss existed somewhere between nerve and foolishness, depending on the concessions a hunter made to leave his world and enters theirs. Always, hunters hoped for the bonanza that Roosevelt found, the sublime Chichester experienced—as each lost track of the world around him. They lived for the perfect moment when conditions converged to put the shooter in the perfect place at the perfect time. It would be nice to live to tell the tale.

In "Black Ducks and Barnegat," which appeared in the January 1918 issue of *Field & Stream, Van Campen* Heilner gave a good sense of what awaited the fortunate ones.

The hunting had been slow on this particular early-winter day. Heilner had just left for a walk to find his buddy Billy and warm up. He found him "at the salt-hole."

"For heaven's sake get down, Campen!" Billy said. "When I first came here I scared out about three hundred ducks and they'll all be back if you keep down."

Heilner doesn't seem like the sort of guy who needed to be told twice. He "snuggled down in the blind. . . ." The birds returned in "two and threes," creating a scene like the one that greeted old Barnwell Roosevelt sixty years earlier out on the marshes of Lake Erie.

As Heilner wrote, "That salt-hole must have been the feeding ground for thousands of black ducks. As far off as we could see they'd set their wings for that place and as they came up into the wind, we'd let them have it.

"My! How those ducks could climb! After the first shot, they'd go into the air like rockets for a tremendous height before going off. At first I tried to get them on the jump but missed them so often that I finally waited until they'd reached the top of the jump and then put it on them, which proved successful."

The ducks kept coming, "the continual s-s-s-s- of their wings and the twilight . . . constantly stabbed by the flashes of our guns." Even as he wrote months later, Heilner could still see "those great salt marshes, the lighthouse against the distant horizon." He could still hear "the whisper of wings, the far-off voice of the sea." He vowed to "cherish forever in his heart a fond memory for the lonely wastes and tides of Barnegat." That's why guys go hunting when they should stay on shore.

For every hunt that ended in such glory, many others ended as a humorous bust—to the point that in the twentieth century few sportsmen offered such predictable sources of humor as the waterfowler. It is tempting to blame that on cartoon character and avid duck hunter Elmer Fudd, but then, as we all know, he was first and foremost a wabbit hunter. The woes of the waterfowler showed up long before Fudd ever bought his first duck stamp.

A good example of high jinks in the duck blind comes in Rex Beach's story "Geese." Beach was a famous writer, hunting with his famous writer friends, Max Foster (see "After Grouse with Hiram") and Grantland Rice. (The following fall he would write about Notre Dame's "Four Horsemen," in one of the most famous sporting articles of all time.) But their goofball behavior demoted them to the ranks of any other waaaaack waterfowler.

Whatever can go wrong with a hunt, will go wrong with a hunt—that was Beach's motto. He was a sucker for every new contrivance and hunting spot. "They use rolling blinds on the sand bars," a buddy told him about North Carolina hunting. "They put down live decoys, a couple hundred yards away, then, when the geese come in, they roll the blind up to them."

Yeah, right, Beach said. The next day Beach signed on for the goose hunt, heading off to North Carolina, with visions of geese at twenty yards. He not only had returned there every year since, for longer and longer times, but had purchased a boat, which he kept there.

On this trip, upon reaching the boat he adopted his captain's voice and ordered the two men he had hired to run the boat: "Let us go away from here," and then turned in for a nap.

Shouts of profanity woke him, and he went below to find engine trouble and his intrepid crew trying to fix matters. His buddy Foster had run after the fire extinguisher. Where are the Three Stooges when you need them?

Beach had the innocence of the consumer sportsman lapped by the new technology: He had gear he couldn't operate himself—unlike, for example, Teddy Roosevelt, who would have been running the boat, or at least have advanced several theories on what was wrong with it. Beach just wanted to get there—and start hunting.

Bluebird weather greeted them when they finally did reach the marshes and had to figure out a plan of attack. There were three choices of blinds and ways of getting geese, which they already knew. One was the old "roll your blind close to the geese," which required "haze and low cloud ceiling." Second were the stilt blinds, "which are useful mainly in decoying inexperienced Northern hunters." The sinkbox was really the only way to go. Beach, aware that water would always find its way in, had "equipped [his] with a rubber mattress and pillow."

After several fruitless days, the weather worsened and birds began to move. "Field glasses revealed 'thousands, tens of thousands, or resting geese up toward Hatteras Inlet . . . and the sky was smudged with smoky streamers where we knew to be wheeling clouds of redheads." Waterfowl streamed past the three hunters. The water was on the edge of too rough. "Members of the Greely expedition doubtless suffered some discomforts, and the retreat from Serbia must have been trying," Beach wrote, "but for 100-per-cent-perfect exposure give me a battery in stormy weather."

Max and Granny got washed out, and when Beach returned to the sloop, he saw that all they had to show was "a clothesline full of steaming garments and a nice pair of congestive chills."

The next day, with Max and Granny returning to the city, the guides and Beach decided on a new approach. They had noticed a continent full of geese and ducks landing behind them in the grassy shallows, and one of guys said they should tow the sinkbox in there, dig it in, and leave it. Seeing the tortuous work involved, Beach immediately agreed. Unbelievably, the plan actually worked, and he had memorable shooting, with mallards, sprigs (pintails), and a pair of black ducks.

Then he heard geese. A line of twenty, low to the water, were winging "prettily" toward him. Just as they set their wings, one of the live decoys "a young gander in the Boy Scout class, cracked under the nervous strain and began to flap madly" and the birds flared. Beach benched the juvenile and replaced him in the lineup with a less-scrupulous Judas. The next flight came in like a charm, and he killed five.

The next morning, worming into his blind, Beach worried what he would do with all the geese he'd end up shooting. A small flock of divers buzzed toward him—and flared. He saw a powerboat heading in his direction, with the driver waving a telegram, which he knew was never a good sign. The telegram was from his wife and read: "Your secretary has forged a number of your checks and disappeared. Total amount unknown, as checks are still coming in. Presume you have given him keys to wine cellar, for they too are missing. Wire instructions quick. Am ill, but stay, have a good time, and don't worry."

The curse of modernity. Whereas the nineteenth-century sport hit the woods to cure his ills, the modern sport could only enjoy the outdoors with the reassurance that all was well on the home front. Beach was a mess, and he returned home to try to get his life in order.

Even as he did, Beach refused to take himself too seriously, and the humor in this piece exemplified its centrality in the tradition of American waterfowling. Earlier writers detailed waterfowling's hardships in order to emphasize their manliness, but the devastation of the Great War put any "heroism" a duck hunter might claim in proper perspective. Beach's humor was at his own expense and pitch-perfect. Geese certainly were big game, evident to all as they honked South, filling the autumn imagination—nothing less than desire on the wing. The desire caused men to do strange things and thereby lent itself to humor in a way that big game hunting, with its self-imposed seriousness, never could. The jackass lying on his back in the middle of the Atlantic Ocean was totally a different matter—and fair game for all.

CHAPTER 9

"Down I Went, Hat, Rod, and All . . ."

THE RISE OF THE BLACK BASS, 1881–1925

Hooked solidly, the large smallmouth bass slipped under a rock. The angler on the other end, a young man named Zane Grey, waded in up to his chin, dove in and, as he later wrote, "down I went, hat, rod, and all . . . [but] the current was just swift enough to lift my feet." He couldn't get a hold of the edge of the rock. Back up for air. On the third try Grey reached under the rock and touched . . . fish. The great bass "had gone under sidewise, turned, and wedged his dorsal fin, fixing himself as solidly as the rock itself." So went an early great fight in Zane Grey's literary career, told in "The Lord of Lackawaxen Creek," published in *Outing* in May 1909.

At the time he wrote this tale, the newly married Grey was living in a large house not far from where Lackawaxen Creek joins the Delaware River in northern Pennsylvania, and that setting framed this story. He had been fishing and camping here with his brothers for some time, and this story was about those early days. It was a rip-roaring yarn, the sort that Grey later made famous in *Riders of the Purple Sage* and a profusion of other stories and books. He described the encroachment of the bass on the terrain of the brook trout in apocalyptic terms more suitable to the frontier tales: "Wise in their generation, the black and red-spotted little beauties keep to their brooks; for, farther down, below the rush and fall, a newcomer is lord of the stream. He is an archenemy, a scorner of beauty and blood, the wolf-jawed, red-eyed, bronze-backed black bass." Grey set out to tame that ornery villain.

Grey first spotted the "great golden-bronze treasure of a bass" in "a boys' swimming hole." Grey selected a six-inch minnow for bait and flipped it out into a channel between the boulders, when "out of the amber depths started a broad bar of bronze [that] rose and flashed into gold" and whisked off with the bait "like a tiger stealing into a jungle." Grey struck back; the great fish leapt, shook itself, and threw the hook back at Grey "like a bullet."

The rude defeat got Grey thinking about his two brothers, Cedar and Reddy, and how they considered themselves such hotshots and could never "appreciate [his] superiority as a fisherman." So he hatched a scheme—he'd have them try for the fish and lose it. Then he would catch it. That ought to fix their wagons.

First, Reddy's turn. They marched along the river, with Grey smiling and Reddy scoffing at his outfit, saying, "I don't see why you've brought that heavy rod. Even a two-pound bass would be a great surprise up this stream."

"You're right," Zane replied, "but I sort of lean to possibilities."

Reddy lobbed a chub out into the pool. The huge bass was all over it, and next came a "shrieking reel, willow wand of a rod wavering like a buggy-hip in the wind . . . a foam-lashed swell, a crack of dry wood, a sound as of a banjo string snapping." With broken rod and line, Reddy snarled something, but "owing to family pride" Zane expunged the oath from the record, for "it most assuredly would not be an addition to the fishing literature of the day."

Reddy, of course, never told Cedar, whose casting, Zane explained, could only be described as something to avoid. "It was not safe to be in his vicinity," though if you must, you should face him—so as to be in position to duck. Grey just knew the big bass would again rise to the occasion, and did it ever: "He spread the waters" of his pool and "accommodatingly hooked himself." Reddy came by to watch the show, which ended with a soaking-wet Cedar "wading out with a hookless leader, a bloody shin, and a disposition utterly and irretrievably ruined."

All three boys tried again for the bass, but only Zane hung to it, losing the bass several more times. The next summer he was back again, fishing from the shore and suffering the taunts of visiting city fishermen who drifted by in their boats, calling "Hey Rube! Ketchin' any?" Or, "Do you live around here?" to which Grey responded, "modestly," yes. "Why don't you move?" Har-har.

By August the bass had apparently tired of stealing Zane's bait (and wanted more from the relationship?), which is when Zane hooked him, and when the bass camped under the rock with Zane furiously attempting to dislodge him. Zane persisted in diving. He knew he could stab it dead with a knife, but that somehow just didn't seem fair.

Zane made one more attempt to dive, reach under the rock, and grab the bass by hand, but the "gill toward me was shut tight like a trap door." Zane gripped the bass by the lip and tugged until he "saw red and my head whirled; a noise roared in my ear. . . . One more second would have made me a drowning man" and he surfaced "gasping and choking."

A better man than I, Zane realized, and he broke off the leader and vowed "never again to disturb his peace."

It's easy to attribute the tale of the fight to the two-fisted storytelling of the writer who invented Westerns. The point seems more that such a tale also crowned the black bass the hard-fighting champion of the people. The fish in Grey's tale assumed a leviathan size and power, lived in a swimming hole, and inspired a fierce competition—all this but a short walking distance from home. In many ways these themes would define the black bass in America.

How did the bass come to be seen as America's gamefish? How did certain areas of the country become bass areas? What sorts of personalities did bass fishing adopt? Bass anglers? Bass themselves? The answers to these questions begin with the original bass master.

"Plucky, Game, Brave, and Unyielding"
DR. JAMES HENSHALL

Book of the Black Bass, 1881

Bass rode the promise of the new American nation in the years after the Civil War. When Dr. James Henshall, their most prominent booster, made his famous claim ("Inch for inch, pound for pound, the gamest fish that swims."), he did so to critical applause and a growing number of bass fishermen.

As Henshall explained, basses were native to the South and to the Great Lakes watersheds, but otherwise they had forged new areas of settlement, in large part the result of the nation's burgeoning rail system. General William Shriver described how he stocked the Potomac with smallmouths in the 1850s. "I made my first trip, carrying with me my first lot of fish in a large tin bucket, perforated, and which I made to fit the opening in the water-tank attached to the locomotive, which was supplied with fresh water at the regular water stations along the line of the road, and thereby succeeded well in keeping the fish alive, fresh, and sound."

The rails transported other fish for stocking too, but few species made themselves so at home in the soul of this new machine. Americans came to imagine this native differently: The basses were not a fish that benefited from wilderness but industrialism, which warmed waters and then deposited them with efficient care. "The black bass is peculiarly adapted," Henshall wrote, "in every respect, for stocking inland waters. There is no fish that will give more abundant and satisfactory returns, and none in which the labor and expense attending its introduction is so slight." Anglers like Shriver stocked bass around the country—not only in the Potomac but also in waters up and down the rest of the eastern seaboard, including northern New England, even Maine.

For the record, Henshall denied that he ever advocated stocking bass in brook trout waters. Not that he held out much hope for the brook trout's survival: "In this utilitarian age its days are numbered and its fate irrevocably sealed. As the red man disappears before the tread of the white man, the living arrow of the mountain streams goes with him . . . iron has entered its soul. As the buffalo disappears before the iron horse, the brook trout vanishes before the axe of the lumberman." The bass was strong enough to flourish "in open waters . . . and defy . . . the causes that will . . . effect the annihilation and extinction of the brook trout."

As Henshall (and other bass promoters) noted, the bass's qualities organized around strength and fortitude, less wiles and sophistication. The black bass swam only on the continent of North America and represented the country "in his characteristics . . . asserting himself and making himself completely at home wherever he is placed. He is plucky, game, brave, and unyielding to the last when hooked." A Horatio Alger hero in fins.

The bass had movement in its soul—an all-American fish with an eye out for better opportunity, comfortable in any setting, able not only to survive the warming waters of industrialism but to thrive because of them. Already it had moved into the rivers that flowed through the nation's capital; in the capitals of the most industrialized eastern states, such as New York, Massachusetts, and Connecticut; and other lakes and rivers throughout the country.

Catching bass didn't require much in the way of strategy—they weren't fussy or shy like a trout. Bass attacked, smashed, and clobbered an angler's baits and flies. They were like characters in nineteenth century Batman cartoons. You could imagine Mrs. Trollope saying, "Why my goodness, what would you expect of a fish from the heartland of America?" Zane Grey heralded such behavior as a sign of courage. He wasn't the only angler who thought that way.

Perhaps because there were no bass in England, there was no canon to follow as far as the "proper" method for fishing them. Most anglers still-fished with bait. Others trolled with a hand line. Some "skittered" with a cane pole, short stout line, and a pork rind or frog. "Bobbing," which involved doing the same with a hunk of deer hair lashed to a hook, was a Southern strategy first described in the eighteenth century by William Bartram but still popular into middle of the twentieth century.

Tackle was American too, and it was improving, with the appearance of the original Kentucky bait-casting reels. As their name suggests they were used to cast bait, usually minnows, but also worms, frogs, crayfish and hell-grammites. Henshall's bait-casting rod was eight feet long and soft so that the bait could be lobbed. At first, lures, mostly spinners and spoons, were trolled. Casting (and retrieving) artificials caught on in the early twentieth century.

As with trout, the most "sporting" way to fish for bass involved flies, and a number of anglers did so—despite the early myth that bass did not take flies. Many of the respondents in Mary Marbury's *Favorite Flies and Their Histories* were bass fishermen who frequented largemouth ponds, lakes, and backwaters in the heartland and the South, in addition to the more predictable lower stretches of trout waters, such as the river Grey fished. Many of the larger and more colorful patterns described and illustrated in the book were intended for bass.

In time, tensions rose between bass and trout fishermen, and numerous articles and books debated the relative merits of trout and bass. One chapter in William Harris's *The Basses: Freshwater and Marine*, for example, was titled "The Black Bass and the Trout Compared." But at first many anglers in former trout territory that bass (generally smallmouths) "invaded" didn't quite know *what* to think. A good example is Louis Rhead's chapter in the above book, titled "Bass in the Beaverkill" (see p. 100). As Rhead notes, "It will probably be a great surprise to most of the anglers who yearly wade this famous trout-stream to read of bass in their favorite water. Before going any further I will say that what harm can be done to the Fontinalis is done, because bass will not ascend the stream higher than a certain point, where the temperature is lower than they like to spawn," a point that Mr. Rhead identified as the famous Junction Pool.

In fact, Rhead claimed to enjoy fishing Junction Pool *because* of the variety of fish available. He told of the evening when a fellow brother of the angle landed a double, comprising a three-pound brown and a three-and-a-half-pound smallmouth. In his description of the evening fishing, it could well be rising trout he was describing: "If a fine evening the wind usually drops, and all is calm on the surface except for the "plop-plop" of the rising bass. With a cast of two or three flies—a brown, a gray, and a red—dropped lightly, if possible, over the place where the fish are rising, the reel will probably spin to a lively tune. . . . There will be plenty of work, or play, just as the angler chooses to make it." Even at this early point that attitude set bass on a different track from trout, as the reaction of La Branche clearly showed

By most accounts, Rhead tended to be the prickly sort. And how much he was writing this to annoy trout purists is hard to say. He certainly enjoyed playing bass more than fooling them. He is glad they are in the mix. So were many other anglers. Like it or not, there was a new fish in town.

"He Can't Be Freed from Sin till He Does Stop Lyin'"
The deacon of the First Church
ELLIS PARKER BUTLER

"The Reformation of Uncle Billy," *The Century*, February 1899

Henshall was sometimes accused of favoring the smallmouth over the large-mouth. But like any parent, he denied favoritism, noting that in fact he believed that the largemouth "rose" better to the fly than the smallmouth. (Henshall was referring to wet flies fished near (or even at) the surface; poppers and bugs would not appear on a large scale and be recognized until the second decade of the twentieth century.) Henshall insisted that largemouths and smallmouths fought equally well, that smallmouths got more props because they lived in current and that "where both species inhabit the same waters, and are subject to the same conditions, I am convinced that no angler can tell whether he has hooked a large-mouth or a small-mouth bass, from their resistance and mode of fighting, provided they are of equal weight."

Throughout much of the central and southern part of the country, large-mouths did hold forth, but the northern city anglers who wrote national articles tended to have more access to smallmouth waters. Out in the country, as the saying goes, largemouths ruled the waterways. They could live right in town, beneath a bridge, under a dock, in the local frog pond. Their capacity for making a home in unimpressive water and somehow growing to formidable size while the people around them went about their business distinguished largemouths from any other gamefish on the continent, and in many ways gave them their own avenue into the American fishing psyche. When anglers said "it looks like bass water," they weren't talking about a boulder-studded smallmouth river, such as the one Zane Grey fished. They meant the kind that your sister wouldn't wade barefoot in—a slimy, lily pad–ringed pond that croaked and slithered. Largemouths became the fish that offered the cardiac surprise, amplified by their piggish table manners. They tended to show up unannounced, indiscriminately, the blessing, often as not, for an angler who could really use one.

Their larger-than-life presence within the community also had the effect of bringing some of angling's elements under serious social scrutiny. Fishing was no longer something that happened "out there" as much as "right ch'ere." That's more or less the angle, so to speak, in "The Reformation of Uncle Billy" by Ellis Parker Butler.

Uncle Billy belonged to a group of men who'd grown up together, lived in the same small town together, and now had grown old together. The others whiled away the hours on the front steps of the general store, but Uncle Billy spent his days fishing from the town bridge, where he caught very little. He never bothered anyone, although one aspect of his activities had become a cause of concern to his fellow friends—namely his chronic truth-stretching.

Every day after fishing, Billy took a place with "his cronies before the grocery" and told his "marvelous tales" of battles joined and bass lost. For Billy wasn't only a liar; he got right after it and put his whole soul into the matter, an early invocation of the George Costanza rule that it isn't a lie if you really believe it.

"Lyin' is lyin', be it about fish or money," proclaimed the deacon of the First Church one day while Billy was off a-fishin'. "[It] is forbid by Scripter, an' he can't be saved an' freed from sin till he does stop lyin'."

"It ought to be some excuse for Billy that he don't harm no one by his lyin'," replied one of the men, Ephraim. "Ef you lie about a horse you're tradin', I'll admit that's wrong, 'cause you'd do the other feller dirt; but Billy's lyin' don't fool nobody and it don't cost nobody nothin'."

Ephraim wanted to go easy on him. The deacon was having none of it. Recently a revival had swept though the town, and to him the *sitchiation* was clear as morning air: Sin is sin. "We know his sin, ef he don't, an' knowin' a sin an' not doin' our best to stop it 'mounts to the same as ef it was our sin, an I ain't goin' to everlastin' fire jest because Billy Matison lies about the fish he don't ketch."

"That sentiment does you proud, deacon," said one of the others, named Hiram. "That's lovin' your neighbor as yourself."

The deacon ignored the shot. He puffed on his pipe. Billy's getting old, he said. There's "no tellin' when he will drop off. He's got to be cured now an' at once."

Ephraim worried that the suddenness would throw Billy into shock. "Why Billy Matison's been lyin' 'bout fish off and on for nigh sixty-six year," Ephraim said. Another friend, Amos, agreed, worrying how Billy would survive the winter without lying some.

Noting how tetchy Billy could be, the deacon plowed right ahead and cautioned against letting Billy know they thought he was lying. Otherwise he'd stay away and they'd have a tougher row to hoe trying to "save" him. "Ef he lies an' says he caught a big one, we got to make him tell the truth, an' we got to do it gentle, an' not let on he's lyin'. We got to—"

At which point, enter Billy, carrying his pole, bait, and lunch bucket. Stooped, toothless, in his seventy-eighth year, he wore a big straw hat. He looked about with rheumy eyes. With the help of their canes, the men wobbled to their feet as he approached.

Billy joined them on the bench, removed his pipe and "holding it out in his shaking hand . . . said in a wavering voice: 'Deacon, I ketched the biggest bass I ever see today. I'll warrant it goes four pound.'"

Billy's friends looked at him with pity. The deacon reminded Billy that they'd been friends for years, how he had helped Billy when "you was courting Manthy" and lent him money when he lost his house in the fire.

Billy nodded, looking around at the expressionless faces of his friends.

"Billy," stated the deacon, "I'm goin' to ask a favor of you. It ain't much. Won't you say that mebby that bass only weighs three pounds an' a half?"

Billy protested, but allowed it might.

The deacon kept at it, whittlin' away at the size of the bass. He recalled the time he found Billy's lost boy, the time he'd carried Billy two miles to safety at the battle of Gettysburg, the time he gave Billy's daughter Mary Ann a place to stay after she'd left home under difficult circumstances. Billy started to cry. "Deacon, I wouldn't do it for no one but you." Billy paused. "But for you and Mary Ann I didn't ketch no fish today."

At that point, each of Billy's friends rose, if unsteadily, shook his hand, and left. They had thrown out the lifeline—and it had been grasped.

Then Billy realized what had happened: His friends considered him "a known liar! A notorious liar!"

He shuffled into the grocery with his basket and called out, "Billings, I ketched a big bass today; want you to weigh it."

Billings grasped the fish by the lower jaw and slapped it on the scale, squinting at the weight markings. "Four pound, two ounces," he announced.

At first glance, the story seems about fishing's estrangement from the community. Towns and communities had gradually come to tolerate the idea of fishing, perhaps, but expected anglers to leave their stories outside with their fishing clothes. Too bad that bass didn't snap the line and fall back into the water. At least then Billy wouldn't have wasted his fish-of-a-lifetime opportunity on a bass he couldn't even brag on to his friends.

Butler's characters have hearts, you can say that for them. The deacon carried Billy two miles, after all. Parker's attempt at reconciliation between North and South? Our hero seems like he could have been a Union soldier (Billy!), although it was likely a Reb who would have had to have been carried two miles to safety at Gettysburg. Such evenhandedness makes this small community any town, USA. And what better fish than a bass, resplendent in its American-ness (Butler never specifies largemouth or smallmouth, but we assume the former), with no particular regional meanings attached to it.

In the end, it may be that community's accommodation of angling and the passion and devotion it inspired was a work in progress. If angling were to be accepted as a seamless part of the community, perhaps it wouldn't be angling anymore. We can only hope that Billings remembered the weight correctly and let the deacon know that just because a fellow tells a few stretchers, it doesn't mean he can't catch fish.

"The Champion Angler . . . for the Season of '94"

Harry Vinton

J. E. GUNCKEL

"Fishing for Black Bass on the Maumee Rapids, Ohio,"
The American Angler, June 1896

Uncle Billy belonged to the small-town America of the nineteenth century, but by the 1890s bass fishing had also developed a national following, with tackle, gear, and flies designed specifically for them, and books and articles promoting the black bass as a fish worth traveling to catch. Fishing communities attracted increasing numbers of tourists, and they took a certain civic pride in their fishing. Florida, particularly the St. Johns River, became a popular winter fishery for vacationing northern anglers. During the summer months, the north country of Wisconsin, Minnesota, and other Great Lakes areas drew anglers seeking bass, as well as pike, walleyes, and muskies. The Thousand Islands may have been the premier summer fishing destination in the nation, and smallmouths were the chief attraction.

In other words, the same community celebration that eluded Uncle Billy became an expected part of the experience for many visiting fishermen, as in the character of Harry Vinton, the bass-fishing stranger who came to town in the 1896 story "Fishing for Black Bass on the Maumee Rapids, Ohio."

A rising middle manager from Detroit, Vinton came to Waterville, Ohio, for the expressed purpose of fishing the Maumee River, a tributary of Lake Erie. He had been directed to the home of a certain Doctor Swandown, Waterville's "representative of a true angler."

The doctor prided himself on sizing up people and liked what he saw in young Vinton. The visitor had a "full face, black hair, and eyes that bespoke the sentiments of an honest heart." He appeared to have "the necessary staying qualities of a true angler, earnest, patient and good natured." Swandown proposed that Vinton stay with his family—and that they have a try at the famous Hanford Pool, which they could see from the porch. They made for the river "with a bucket full of the choicest chub minnows." In no time, the two men "were as busy as bees fighting and caring for bass."

When they returned home with their stringer of fifty-seven bass, they learned that the doctor had to call on a sick relative in another town, which left Harry to his own devices. The next day he returned to the pool "with a bucket full of the best of minnows, a few grasshoppers and a book of assorted flies," and high hopes. He struck out.

His wretched luck continued. The following day, Vinton fished the entire stretch of river near town and again caught nothing. The doctor's two boys "rather thought that Harry could not fish, and they were not timid in introducing their beliefs at every opportunity." On the fifth day they hit the river for just an hour and "brought home a dozen fine bass." The same good luck held for other villagers. Even the local worm fishermen spanked 'em.

The next morning, Harry vowed to return in triumph, "if he was compelled to fish for bullheads in the canal." The boys giggled and jeered that they could out-fish Harry without venturing "beyond the town limits. . . ." Game on.

On the way to the river, Harry met a couple of farm boys with a stringer of bass, and had an idea. The bass weren't very big, but they were bass. So he negotiated their acquisition; or, in the vernacular, he bought 'em. Now he had a stringer *and* a bucket of bait, so he stopped at the enticing waters of Hanford pool for a cast or two. Wouldn't you know it, but he slammed the bass. He hooked a five-pounder and, hoping for witnesses, "glanced toward the green Hanford bluffs and wondered if someone was noting his wonderful success." But he saw no one. His catch from the pool totaled seventy-three, including some three- and four-pounders. He then put a final touch on the glorious day: He quickly glanced around, confirmed that he had the privacy necessary for what future generations of bassers would recognize as the legitimate art of culling, and released the purchased stringer of still lively bass.

Loaded down with his caught bass, he struggled up the bank only to run into the doctor, just back from his trip. "Well, old boy," the doctor said, "you found 'em at last. You are certainly the champion of the rapids this season." They arranged the fish side by side on the doctor's front lawn. And because "fishing news spreads in a marvelously short time in a riverside village," almost instantly "citizens came from the business houses, the residences, the alleys and from across the river, not only to see the fish but to shake hands with the successful angler." They treated Vinton like he "had been [a] friend for years."

Then, through the grinning crowd, came "a tall, lean, deep-voiced farmer" who lived across the river. "Say, Mister," he asked "but ain't you the young man what bought the bass from my sons this morning, and ain't them the fish?"

One of the boys piped up: "He's the very fellow that buyed our fish; ain't he, Jimmy?" Jimmy nodded vigorously. Harry experimented with various shades of red, which deepened "with the laughter and cruel remarks and insinuations of the crowd, which seemed to get bolder each moment." The doctor told Harry that the boys seemed to have him.

"Well, *these* fish I caught with hook and line in a pool down the river," Harry insisted.

"Nearly every person in our town is a fisherman," the doctor said, stepping carefully from word to word.. "And no one would dare to purchase bass and bring them here and claim them as being caught by him."

The farmer added, "You have been fishing . . . fur five days," and you caught "nary a fish, not even a little bullhead." Then you "bought these here fish, them fine bass" from my boys. More 'an that," he said, addressing the crowd, "you all see he cheated the boys. . . . They is worth a heap more 'n you paid fur 'em."

Harry stammered that, yes, he'd bought fish from the boys. They'd been small and he'd let them go because he had "felt ashamed of himself." (His morality curiously appearing once he caught a stringer of his own.) Doubt lingered in the crowd, although "the better class of the citizens, the older men, were inclined to believe Harry's story."

Then, Harry somehow decided "that a few dollars might have a good effect" on the farmer. (You know, from the start, Harry never struck me as all that bright.) When no one was looking he "managed to slip a ten dollar bill into the farmer's hand" and told him to skedaddle, which the farmer did, but not before showing a friend the hush money and that person announcing the transaction. Now Harry had not only stepped in it but had tracked it on the carpet. The fans were not happy.

The doctor stepped from the crowd, leading by the hand a "very pretty, modest," young woman, Miss Alice Van Dyke. She explained that, "I was on the bluff overlooking the Hanford pool this afternoon, and saw the gentleman not only catch the greater number of these bass, but saw him release the others." With that, relief reigned. Harry was "unanimously declared the champion angler of the Maumee for the season of '94."

For her honesty, Ms. Van Dyke received the largest bass. (Harry sure knows how to show a girl a good time.) And in the following year, "Harry received the summons from the good doctor, that the river was in fine condition and the bass in great fighting condition and plentiful." He was "heartily welcomed" by the entire town, to the village of Waterville. And in time, even greater joy was his, at "a quiet wedding in the village church, [when] the minister pronounced Harry Vinton and Alice Van Dyke man and wife."

Regardless of the numbers (fifty-seven? seventy-three?) Mr. Gunckel placed in front of the landed bass, his story reveals how bass fishing's simplicity and availability made it the perfect object of affection for the burgeoning tourist population that the Reverend Murray had roused a generation earlier. The Maumee smallmouths required little technique ("You found 'em at last," Dr. Swandown responded upon seeing Harry's stringer of seventy-three.) and mostly proper citizenship, with successful anglers "earnest, patient, and good natured."

The local angling had already begun to change daily life in this "tourist destination," had already created a "fishery." The townsfolk had become used to anglers, less so to new faces. Families still embraced well-heeled touring visitors—they considered them children, which made sense, as Harry was there to play. (His rivals were the doctor's and farmer's kids.) Village adults were less-enthusiastic anglers themselves, but quick to salute angling success. Fishing had become a marketable commodity.

At the same time, the community openness and celebration of bass fishing contained a skepticism as the world outside spun away. Between the Pullman

strike in Chicago and Coxey's Army heading to Washington, the Midwest con-
vulsed in social turmoil in the summer of 1894. The larger tourist industry,
moreover, only increased the anonymity of daily transactions, leading men
like the doctor to cultivate an ability to be "quick in sizing up a man" and
middle-class Victorians in general to place considerable stock in personal presentation, including speech, clothing, and behavior. Harry appeared to check
out, class-wise, compared with the farmer anyway, whose deficient character
revealed itself through speech filled with "ain't," "buy'd" and "fur."

As tourism increasingly acquired routine financial underpinnings, towns
and counties increasingly promoted the sport available to the vacationing
middle class. Railroads published pamphlets, and magazines and newspapers
included travel articles. Mr. Gunckel, for instance, was a passenger agent of
the Lake Shore and Michigan Southern Railroad at Toledo and had an interest
in promoting the recreation along the lines. His catch number are possible,
but may have benefitted from a bit of inflation (seventy-three?). I wouldn't
exactly call him a reliable narrator.

"Bass fishing on the Maumee Rapids, Ohio" shows how we made bass
into the species we needed them to be. Both Billy and Harry learn that community fishing had certain advantages, though the post-catch debriefing could
be a sticky wicket. Bass certainly seemed to take their anglers deeper into the
webs of the community—unlike the coldwater species that removed anglers
from daily lives and returned them to the woods.

In any case, the last thing Harry needed was a scandal involving some
overcharging swamp urchins. Left to his own competitive instincts, a corporate man can land in trouble in a small town too ignorant to understand modern complexities such as the relativity of truth. Enter a mysterious observer
with "a peculiar kind of womanly richness." As an index of how fishing (and
bass fishing in particular) had moved into the neighborhood, consider that the
mysterious woman who appeared on a cliff above Jasper St. Aubyn when he
was battling "A Fatal Salmon" for all intents and purposes killed him. But Miss
Van Dyke represented less the femme fatale, than a nineteenth-century incarnation of Mary Bailey, a woman of quiet substance who knows male worth

when she sees it flounder, and saves Harry from himself. One is reminded of the old ordinance—perhaps apocryphal—in Western towns in the years after the Civil War that held that a condemned man could be saved from the gallows by an unmarried woman willing to take him on as a husband. No doubt about it, Miss Van Dyke does have some work to do.

Looking ahead, the competition surrounding fishing continued to rise, with local competitions, national magazine contests, and casting tournaments routinely covered in such high-profile media as *The New York Times*. Many locate the beginnings of today's billion-dollar competitive bass fishing industry in the 1960s, but Harry's struggle to become "the champion angler of the Maumee for the season of '94" argues for earlier origins. Whereas competitions seemed anathema to the ethereal experience of trout, such festivities enhanced the bass fishing or, at the least, did it no harm. It is hard to imagine, even in the 1890s, putting up at a house in town and walking to the area's best trout fishing. Town, bridge, or local swimming hole, bass were somehow right at home.

"Ties His Casting-rod along the Top of the Gasoline Tank"

GEORGE JOHNSON

"Bass on a Motorcycle," Recreation, June 1910

Bass embodied a modern adaptability, and that quality explains their justifiable claim to the title of America's most-popular gamefish. Their proximity to population centers left them swimming in the literal shadow of the machine age, as was the story in "Bass on a Motorcycle." Bass entered the article, more or less, as an excuse to take the motorcycle out for a ride.

Johnson was a man of the new automotive century, you can say that for him. He had a new motorcycle, and he pointedly ignored the pleas from his family to increase his life insurance and get his will done. Johnson had been dreaming of strapping his hands across the engine for some time. He had an abiding interest in proving his machine superior to the automobile for traveling to and from outdoor adventures: "Although one may read in periodicals devoted to hunting, fishing and kindred sports, many enthusiastic and doubtless well-deserved encomiums of the automobile . . . the value of that humbler . . . motorcycle, seems wholly unappreciated."

Automobile camping was the new rage for trout fishing. Folks in the small towns along the Beaverkill, for instance, complained about all the city sports who showed up to "Sunday trout fish," which was considered vaguely cheating, given the unwillingness of country folks to break Sabbath. Some visitors even camped out with tarps attached to the top of the car, and they proudly showed pictures of every one in his or her sleeping bag under the tent extensions.

Johnson contended that his machine would get you wherever you want to go faster and cheaper than could a car, and certainly with less effort than "the old push-bike." But most folks, in anticipation of Dennis Hopper, continued to consider "a motorcyclist as a cross between a bank-robber and an escaped lunatic."

Johnson set out to prove them wrong. Turns out he had a farmer buddy whose land surrounded a lake filled with largemouths. When he phoned and said the bass were jumping clear out of the water, Johnson hustled outside, "tied his casting-rod along the top of the gasoline tank, strapped a market-basket on the luggage-carrier, and puffed away."

Thirty minutes later, Johnson was striding across the field toward the lake, assembling and stringing his casting rod as he walked. He had a flour sack tied to his belt to serve as creel, and tied to his silk line was a hollow, aluminum surface plug, into which he poured "a thimbleful or so of water" through "two small holes drilled in the aluminum." He "then plugged the holes with a splinter of match . . . [and] . . . the weight of the bait was increased a trifle, giving . . . better results." No plug carving in this hurry-hurry metal world.

Johnson dropped the plug in the water to confirm its floatation—and a two-pound bass crushed it. The fish were in a hurry too.

Johnson began casting and hooked bass after bass, sometimes two, on virtually every cast. One bass leapt from the water to hit the plug before it landed. Johnson was a sportsman and noted that with all the action, he "doubtless lost some fish which a little care might have secured. But I had more pleasure than a mere big string of dead fish ever brings, the pleasure that I fear too many anglers miss altogether. . . ."

The largemouth feeding chaos had been just that, and "in a little over an hour the flour sack had become a heavy drag on my belt, and to avoid cutting myself in two, I was compelled to desist." And he left, with the smacks of feeding bass sounding in his ears. He gave his friend "of hard hands and warm heart" five or six good fish, "dumped the rest without counting them into the market-basket" on his luggage carrier, and sped off.

Johnson's ride home put the cap on the day. Shortly after he headed out on the highway, "a fresh automobile tried to make [him] eat its dust." On the next straightaway, he "gently twisted the throttle control a half-inch more to the left and went past that poor old auto as if she were stuck in the mud." He concluded that other than "eating stolen watermelons" nothing beat driving "a 4-horse power motorcycle [powered] by an ambitious 40-horse power automobile."

Later Johnson reviewed his efficiency. He left his house "just before three . . . stopped fishing at five, and by six had [not only] done the 10-mile trip from the lake" but had the machine and himself cleaned—"and was ready for supper." He "took home eleven [bass] which weighed all told twenty-four pounds; the smallest being one and one-quarter; the largest, four."

In the end, he decided, "no, the motorcycle didn't catch the fish, grandpa." But when his buddy telephoned him that "the bass were eating things alive," he "got there in thirty minutes."

His new world was one of figures, time, and production. Smooth-planing bass boats remained docked in a distant future, but the desire for speed that fires those engines had George Johnson zooming straight to a certain farm pond. Well, maybe not zooming, but he got there pretty quickly.

The popularity of these you-can-do-it-too stories in the early years of the last century underscored the newly available leisure time and affordable equipment, and the growing numbers of middle-class folks like Johnson who took up rod and gun. Earlier generations of patrician sportsmen had indulged in distant destinations (as befitting rail travelers), but the new participants looked for their fish and game near home—and magazines like *Recreation* were happy to frame the outings with the excitement Americans had come to expect from their new century.

Stories like "Bass on a Motorcycle" exemplify how changing conditions—in this case, a growing interest in fishing in a suburban population—led to revisions of our sporting traditions. With a multiplying reel and a drilled-out aluminum plug, as this story indicates, you could catch a sack full. If native trout belonged to a wilderness past, the exuberant bass belonged to a Rotarian future—replete with bad fish-hogs, good farmers, and marvelous machines.

Our bass biker clearly enjoyed the fishing, but no more than he enjoyed getting there. His descendants, it is fair to say, have done him proud.

"Coming to Believe with Thoreau"
O. W. SMITH

"Bass Fishing with Frills," *Outdoor Recreation*, May 1925

But bass fishing amounted to a good deal more than vice clamps and drill presses. Bass would never be a wilderness fish like trout, but bass fishermen of the Midwest, in particular, celebrated their pastoral landscape. A good example is the story "Bronze Backs" that appeared in July 31, 1916, issue of the *Independent*. Author O. W. Smith was a preacher, and a number of the sentences in this piece would sound fine echoing down from the pulpit: "To have missed playing a bass for fifteen minutes, thru many aerial leaps and numberless soundings, rod bending double and reel shrieking in agony . . ." (I will stop there, as this sentence still has thirty-six words to go).

Smith loved bass, and he loved plug casting. He intended to leave his engraved Meek (the gold standard of bait-casting reels) to his daughter ("having no son"). As he reminded us, the smallmouth was "American to the backbone, pugnacious and resourceful as becomes his birthplace." Even in bass fishing's version of the genteel angler, it was still about the battle.

Like writers before him, Reverend Smith believed that "the glory of the black bass was his get-able-ness." Anglers "may be compelled to journey far for the winsome beauties of our brooks," but bass swam in "streams and lakes almost everywhere, within reach of every town and city, and always ready to do battle with the rodster." And he should know. As a member of his congregation, one Mrs. Grundy, was wont to say about him: "There's the preacher goin' fishin' again."

In "Bass Fishing with Frills," which appeared in the May 1925 issue of *Outdoor Recreation*, Smith assumed the literary persona of a non-clergy narrator who has a vacation. He planned to chill around the house, maybe do a bit of fishing. As he reminded the audience, he often had better fishing at home than his friends did in Canada. He found himself "coming to believe with Thoreau, that one's home locality holds all foreign countries, at least when it comes to fishing."

When the narrator's friend Bill (a preacher in the story) phoned him and suggested a float trip, he was already out the door, trying to catch the local train. A friendly competition transpired between the narrator, with his fly rod and feathered minnow, and Bill's light, split-bamboo bait-caster, with its "fine silk line" and minnow-scaled plug. Bill could put the lure on a dime at one hundred feet, with the "reel purring silently, betokening loving care on the part of the owner."

All sorts of problems awaited the pair. After all, given the "get-able-ness" of bass, something had to complicate the catching to make it a story. The most notable obstacle to piscatorial bliss was a collie that followed the drifting boat along shore and became excited, barking whenever they hooked a bass. Yipping and snapping, the pooch jumped right in when the narrator hooked a monster smallmouth. The dog actually bit through the leader, causing the men to pelt it with rocks. (They estimated the bass to be seven pounds at the time of struggle, ten over lunch.) Ever the minister, Bill worried that they lost their temper. His time was coming.

Later in the day, Bill hooked a monster bass of his own and the collie, back for season two, jumped in and bit through the line—which prompted preacher Bill into a stream of inventive invectives. The collie almost drowned in the process, but the men grudgingly saved it. Here, Lassie!

The moral of today's sermon? Your angling adventure waited next door. All you needed was a friend, a boat, and a river full of bass. As Smith observed, "No, I am not going to be more explicit about the location of the river. There are literally hundreds and thousands just like in this great country of ours, little rivers flowing through thickly settled agricultural regions, often fenced with barb-wire, it is true, though illegally for the most part, but rivers alive with small or large-mouth, as the case may be. . . ."

In the South, the home of "bobbing," the bait-casting reel, the Florida ten-pounders, largemouth reigned as king of the freshwater fish. In the Midwest, bass fishing likewise engendered a real passion. In the North you could almost track bass sentiment moving from the east to the west. Start in Maine, for instance. As late as the 1960s, outdoor writer Charlie Waterman visited that state to fish for bass and ran into a Maine resident who said, rather famously, "Oh bass are OK, I guess. There's a fellow over in Portland who eats the damn things." This was after they'd been in the state for a century or so.

Much of this attitude had to do with smallmouths being blamed for having the nerve to flourish in the same warming, industrialized waters that killed brook trout. To this day, smallmouth sentiment remains weakest where brook trout affection is strongest.

Smallmouth love heated up once you crossed Lake Champlain and got through the Adirondacks. The Thousand Islands, where Lake Ontario joined the St. Lawrence River, was such an important smallmouth fishing area that towns couldn't wait to proclaim themselves "Home of the Gamey Black Bass." In the Midwest, in the Great Lakes, and the waters to the south, smallmouths truly moved angling's soul. Often as not, the fishing centered on rivers rather than lakes.

The rivers that slipped through the Ozarks, where float fishing was an idyllic three-, four-, and five-day trip, grew to nationwide reputation in the early twentieth century. Flat boats loaded with gear, an angler and paddler to each boat, camping on the shores, bass ready to strike—the world just melted away.

"A Sweepstake of Fifteen or Twenty Dollars"
WILL DILG

"King of Kings," *Recreation*, July 1921

Fly fishing for bass had a long tradition in American sporting life, but it finally left trout fishing's shadow in the second and third decades of the twentieth century, when poppers and bass bugs hit the scene.

It's not that dry-fly fishing led to bass bugging, or vice versa, but rather that the excitement and challenge of both surface-fishing methods became in themselves *the* reason to fish. In *The Dry Fly and Fast Water*, La Branche wrote, ". . . I say that in all of angling there is no greater delight than that which comes to the dry fly man who . . . entices to the surface of the water a fish lying hidden, unseen, in the stronghold of his own selection." Could not the same be said of bass bugging? As the decade of the 1920s showed, the answer came back a resounding "yes."

The first cork bugs came out of the Midwest about the time that La Branche was writing. A number of craftsmen had their hands in the inventions, but Ernest Peckinpaugh always appears among the most frequently mentioned. Unlike developments in trout flies, which stressed connections to the British canon, bass bugs showed up with their own creation stories. They were something you built in the basement, not something you created at streamside. They were less an element of the genteel tradition than an "idea my buddy at work had."

As for inspiration, Robert Page Lincoln in *Black Bass Fishing* (1952) goes with the Peckinpaugh "dropped a cork in a stream by accident and got the idea for a cork bug" creation myth. The version in *McClane's Standard Fishing Encyclopedia* seems less apocryphal. Peckinpaugh wrote McClane in 1947 that, "I discovered that late in the afternoon, and at dusk, if I could keep a bucktail fly on top of the water, I would catch more fish. This gave me the idea of putting a cork on a hook, and tying bucktail hair to the lure and in that way making it stay on the surface."

From there it was a matter of promotion—like any other American product in the new mass culture of the 1920s. In his note to McClane, Peckinpaugh also defined the moment that bass-bug promotion found its feet. "Mr. Wilder, who was the Butterick Pattern Designer, obtained some of these [cork] bugs, and he showed him to his friend, Will Dilg." And from there Dilg took care of convincing the public that these bugs made of cork and feathers were the future.

An impassioned, driven conservationist who brought the Isaac Walton League into national awareness, Dilg lived to catch smallmouth bass on the surface and wrote emotional articles about doing so. As he explained, "Since boyhood, the call of the black bass waters has been my weakness." In this instance, anyway, weakness was strength, and certainly Dilg's fusion of conservation, sportsmanship, and surface fishing does not sound so very different at all from the way LaBranche had framed matters some seven or eight years earlier.

A strong personality, a competitive organizer, an ad man in a boat, Dilg was the most famous bass writer of his day. Dilg was at his best in the "King of Kings," which appeared in the July 1921 issue of *Recreation.*

The summer of 1920 had been a banner year for fly fishermen on the upper Mississippi, and at times "the river seemed alive with bass." Catching bass ceased to be a challenge or any fun. Dilg and his boatman decided to target big bass.

Dilg always had a touch of grandiosity about him, as in "It is quite the same type of fishing as practiced on English chalk streams. There the angler waits for a hatch and then locates a large rising trout and floats a dry fly over where it is feeding." That was his approach to smallmouths. Anglers needed to be careful, however: "Big bass will only rise once an evening, unlike smaller bass which will rise several times." Dilg's florid style derived in part from his own egotism, but he also sought to elevate the fish and the region as much as he sought to elevate himself.

He was a member in a group of fly fishers, the headquarters for which was a houseboat. Aboard the good ship Dilg, there was a rockin' time, as well as money on the table. Nothing like a fishing contest, you know. As Dilg noted, "When I have betting guests on the houseboat it is a common thing to have a sweepstake of fifteen or twenty dollars, the prize to go to the fisherman taking the largest bass over three and a half pounds."

Most of the time, Dilg noted, the prize money was turned over to the winning boatman. "It was interesting to note the solicitude of the boatmen and the importance they attached to the fly that took the big fish the day before and how careful they were to test lines and leaders. At such times wars and rumors of wars and big-business affairs faded into insignificance. . . . The boatman's and the fisherman's greatest ambition in life that day was to win the honor of being high rod."

Dilg and his boatman, Bill, finally located a fish that might win against such august competition. Dilg named him the monarch of all upper Mississippi black bass. One evening Bill maneuvered Dilg into casting position, as the great bass appeared to be rising selectively for what Dilg called a hatch of brown millers. He tried different cork bugs, his go-to fly. "My first cast was perfection itself, but my floating fly went unheeded. I made cast after cast, all of which were accurate." The great fish not only ignored the offering but emphasized his displeasure by sulking on the bottom. Eventually darkness fell and put Dilg out of his misery.

Dilg vowed to catch the fish and win the money. That night he doctored some bugs with red and brown paint. The next morning he let them dry in the midwestern sun and started thinking.

Dilg realized that most of the brown bugs were probably never even reaching the surface. He wondered if a certain river man, an old market fishermen, might be contracted to shake one of the trees near the big bass and drop a swarm of them on the surface all at once. Dilg and Bill found this river man, and he agreed to join team Dilg.

The next evening Dilg and Bill reached the "tragic spot." Dilg "whipped out the right amount of line" and "carefully shot the brown imitation miller forth on its mission of conquest." He twitched the bug. The big bass ignored it. But when a real brown miller fell from the tree branch, it was inhaled "with an indolent and sovereign-like plop, the swirl in the water always proving the great size of the bass."

As Dilg remembered, "then I decided to try out the much-planned experiment." The old man shook the tree with a crotched stick, producing a profusion of brown millers, and "instantly they were smashed at right and left." Dilg "dropped [his] floater into the midst of them," and the big bass took it instantly.

The bass zoomed "to the current with lightning speed" so that Dilg's "English reel shrieked as the mighty fish took out eighty or more feet." Then he leaped into air. "He took us downstream for nearly half a mile, occasionally coming up with a heartbreaking jump." But Dilg proved his match, for "wherever he went and whatever he did, I gave him the proper strain of the rod."

The fight continued for twenty minutes, and Dilg took in line "an inch at a time." The fish continued its resistance however, "occasionally . . . raising his head and churning the water into a foam . . ." as Dilg "ruthlessly . . . kept on the pressure." I know, quite a fight.

Bill readied the net, and in a few seconds Dilg would have had the fish in the boat. But it was not to be. The leader broke at the head of the fly. It was a dark moment for Dilg. Still, he remained ever the optimist—after all he did have him on—and the description of the fight was remarkable even by Zane Grey standards, although Dilg didn't dive in after him.

And in truth, this was only a fish story.

A far greater loss followed.

The month this story appeared in *Recreation*, the fifty-five-year old Dilg suffered an unfathomable tragedy: His only son, age four, fell from the houseboat and drowned in the upper Mississippi River. William Pohlman (probably the Bill of the story) and an angler named Fred Peet found the boy's body.

Ironically, a reader's forum titled "My Most Tragic Fishing Moment" appeared for the first time in the same July 1921 issue, with Dilg as the editor. He continued as forum editor for the next year, his grief apparently finding expression in boosterism for teaching boys to fish. In October he thanked readers for their support, published a picture of his boy in a boat, and wrote about their last fishing trip several days before the tragedy. In December he edited a spirited Christmas special that focused on boys and fishing. He didn't miss a beat.

Nor, it seems, did he intend to, ever again. In January 1922 Dilg, along with area businessmen, created the Izaak Walton League. Legend claims Dilg created the league as a living monument to his lost son. Perhaps; he'd certainly shown a similar impulse in his magazine columns. At the same time, a number of sportsmen (Dilg among them) had written of the need for river conservation before the tragedy, and some, such as businessman John Latch, had initiated efforts on the upper Mississippi. So the idea of a conservation movement was in the air. To these men, the smallmouth bass was the fish that symbolized all that was good about sportfishing. Dilg's genius was to harness the fraternal culture of the day by modeling the league after the Rotary and Kiwanis Clubs. An advertising man by profession, he knew how to dramatize his product; he strong-armed Zane Grey and other friends into writing heart-tugging conservationist articles for the league's flagship magazine, *Outdoor America*. Smallmouth was king. Membership surged.

A charismatic speaker with a drawn face and burning eyes, Dilg tore across the upper Midwest with the fury of a late-summer storm, entreating state agencies to enforce regulations, rallying supporters to pressure lawmakers, conducting conservation forums like revival meetings. Politicians turned over like autumn bass ponds as, in essence, he out-Babbitted the Babbits. Eventually he set his sights on Washington, and in 1924 he pressured Congress and President Coolidge into establishing a refuge on the upper Mississippi, his efforts offering a blueprint for future environmental campaigns. League membership topped one hundred thousand.

Dilg's sense of perspective—never his strong suit—vanished in the dust of such a meteoric rise. Some claimed he lost sight of the line between invoking God's plan and becoming it. You sense that no matter what mania he might muster, he could never drive the sadness from his soul. Ill with throat cancer, Dilg lost his position with the league in 1926, dying within the year. "King of Kings" thus remains a haunting foreshadowing of the five years to follow: The story of a magnificent campaign, one that begins with loss—and ends there too.

The campaign reflected the final point about the revision of bass fishing's sporting tradition. The bass had risen from a pugnacious newcomer to the elite club of the sporting gentlemen, had gotten noticed thanks to its hard-fighting ways and resilient physiology. The bass was the fish of the American heartland, the new twentieth-century sporting challenge. It had community approval and was technologically flexible. You could organize around it. The grandiosity of the bass, America's fish, was what Dilg always kept in mind.

It was a story that was only beginning.

Conclusion

"GREAT SPORT"

T he January 1919 issue of *Outers' Recreation* included an article titled "Great Sport: A Fishing Story" by a young woman named Aimee Morrison. The article detailed Morrison's ten-day fly-fishing trip to Colorado, where she had to fend for herself as a novice in a camp full of experts. Particularly annoying was a certain Mr. Davis, who always returned, loudly, with a basket full of trout. Morrison was on her own, nobody's wife, girlfriend, sister, or "traveling companion." And, everyone in the camp seemed inclined to keep her in the dark about fly fishing.

An Easterner, Morrison found the experience dispiriting. Vacations were different out West. Nobody offered to help. People didn't sit around and visit in the evenings. What you caught mattered more than where you were from, who you knew, or what you did before you got here. She was lonesome—but determined to catch a fish or two. And so she said to heck with it, and decided to teach herself to fly fish. And after a few embarrassing stumbles, she began to get the hang of it. And wouldn't you know it, her outlook brightened after she put a few trout in her basket. Most of us can relate.

On her final night she discovered the secret to Mr. Davis's success—the little weasel had been fishing a stocked pond. She let him have it or, as she put it, "left no word unsaid concerning the true art of fishing." One senses that she returned East with a spring in her step.

Morrison was a new woman, a traveling sport by way of the burgeoning consumer culture and the evolving notion of fly fishing as something open to all. Such boldness filled the air in 1919, with the recent war in Europe having left women to man factories and staff workplaces and the Nineteenth Amendment less than two years from ratification.

Her story seems the right way to end this book. Morrison went out west for adventure and chose fly fishing as the way to get it. In Morrison's words, "It was that picture that set me a-going . . . it looked so entrancing and so easy to land a mountain trout." She might have seen a painting, or more likely a stereoptic image, which along with the necessary "viewers" were commonplace in middle class homes during the period of this book. Surely many readers of the stories in this book were drawn into outdoor sports in the same way. In all likelihood, some read her story and decided to start fly fishing.

Morrison's confrontation with Mr. Davis exemplifies the larger theme of this book. The rules, etiquette, social playing field—the sporting code of the outdoors—were clear by 1919. They had been written and rewritten, disavowed, championed, and debated. Not everyone played by the rules, but everyone knew what they were. When Morrison caught Mr. Davis surreptitiously fishing a stocked pond—he'd always insisted on fishing alone and at night—the jig was up. He was awash in shame.

And now the story became hers to tell. Hardly a patrician or male, she nevertheless follows the path set out in this book and gets to write the story. It is a familiar tale. She complains like Irving, triumphs like Murray. She strikes out on her own, determined and confident, like so many of our writers, but admits to feeling a little lonely about the heart. She misses the old ways—that sounds familiar too. Trout caught unfairly don't count. Robert Barnwell Roosevelt and other sports would surely have approved.

As Bliss Perry insisted, what matters is your heart. And that, Morrison has. Her self-taught course in fly-fishing effort represented the enactment of George La Branche's ideas that it was the angler's own responsibility to improve and *become* a good fisherman. He notes that he has "seen golfers practicing the weak places in their game for hours with as much zeal and earnestness as if they were playing in a match." Why not fly fishers? Aimee Morrison would ask herself the same question. And answer it.

But the end of the day matters too, as we learned from Teddy Roosevelt's ode to the beautiful camp in the woods, as we know from the rise of the deer camp as an institution. That's when the day receives its meaning. Morrison is lonely not so much from the part of her past that she left back east but from the anemic social scene at the woodland domicile. But Morrison takes matters into her own hands, heads off into parts unknown along a mountain trail, and learns to fly fish. We have come a long way from Adirondack Murray's advice on what a lady should wear in the woods.

The hunting and fishing world of 1920 was very different than it is today, and then again it wasn't. The main features of the outdoor tradition—the idea of challenge as sport, civility afield, and reverence for quarry and land and water—remain centerpieces. Those are the shoulds of our world, as Mr. Davis and Ms. Morrison discussed. The particulars have evolved, thanks to some hard tweaking. We know, for instance, that the trout Ms. Morrison is intent on catching are very wary, the brainiest things in fins, even though the biggest ones are caught on nightcrawlers after a rain—much like bullheads. We know that the social world around the outdoors defines it, be it outdoor media, contests, organizations, or commercialism. We have new traditions in the process of being constructed: saltwater angling, for instance, and others that grew slowly and imperceptibly over the years like a backyard tree—rabbit and squirrel hunting—those echoes can be heard in these pieces too.

Following the trails through history shows how identity can become attached to practice—which is such a central part of our world today. One of the dangers of such an approach, however, is that it tends to put more emphasis than should be on those who have access to the power of print and leave out those who do not. Moreover, you can end up losing sight of how many people actually are involved at any point along the way. It buoys the heart to see Lewis France writing about fly fishing in 1860s Colorado, but that needs to be viewed in light of Ray Bergman, an honest man if nothing else, who owned a retail business in the years around World War I in Nyack, a small town just a couple of hours above New York City. Bergman remembered that virtually no one he knew fly fished.

The idea of narrowness shows up in other ways. Most of the hundred or so stories in this book involved men or groups of men, usually wealthy, always white—but readers extrapolated. The beauty of print is that when the words leave the writer, it no longer matters what his intentions were: The words become everyone's, and when they are read, they belong to that person who, like Ms. Morrison, perhaps feels moved by them and feels they are directed at *her*. They empower her, to borrow a saying from the world of today. As Colleen Sheehy explains in "American Angling: The Rise of Urbanism and the

Romance of the Rod and Reel," an essay that appeared in *Hard at Play: Leisure in America, 1840–1940*, most stories had men fishing with other men. "Yet other fishing experiences existed side by side with this dominant one— widely practiced traditions of families who fished together, of women who fished, of women who waded into the water with long dresses, of little girls and little boys who fished, and of women who taught little boys to fish. But these practices were not recognized or addressed to any degree in the sporting literature."

In other words, many, many other stories remain out there in the nation's woods and waters. Searching for the ones that speak back can become a sport in itself, finding them can be like opening a door to the past that you didn't know was there, and reading and thinking about them lets us better understand who we are. I am humbled by the stories in this book. For now, we should be ever thankful to the men and women of the nineteenth and early twentieth centuries who gave us an outdoor life in the stories they left behind.

Bibliography

The following books and articles informed the discussion of the primary materials, which are attributed in the text:

Aron, Cindy. *Working at Play*. Oxford University Press, 1999.

Babcock, Havilah. *My Health Is Better in November*. University of South Carolina Press, 1947.

Brinkley, Alan. *American History: A Survey*. McGraw-Hill, 2009.

Brinkley, Douglas. *The Wilderness Warrior: Theodore Roosevelt and the Crusade for America*. HarperCollins, 2009.

Brown, Dona. *Inventing New England: Regional Tourism in the Nineteenth Century*. Smithsonian Institution Press, 1995.

Campbell, A. J. *Classic & Antique Fly-Fishing Tackle: A Guide for Collectors & Anglers*. The Lyons Press, 1997.

Connery, Thomas B. *Journalism and Realism: Rendering American Life*. Northwestern University Press, 2011.

Davis, William C. *Three Roads to the Alamo: The Lives and Fortunes of David Crockett, James Bowie, and William Barret Travis*. HarperCollins, 1998.

Dizard, Jan. *Mortal Stakes: Hunters and Hunting in Contemporary America*. The University of Massachusetts Press, 2003.

Evans, George Bird, ed. *The Best of Nash Buckingham*. Winchester Press, 1973.

Foggia, Lyla. *Reel Women: The World of Women Who Fish*. Atria Books/Beyond Words, 1995.

Fox, Stephen. *The American Conservation Movement*. University of Wisconsin Press, 1981.

Francis, Austin. *Land of Little Rivers*. Skyhorse Publishing, 1999.

Giltner, Scott. *Hunting and Fishing in the New South: Black Labor and White Leisure after the Civil War*. Johns Hopkins University Press, 2008.

Grinnell, George Bird. *American Duck Shooting*. Forest and Stream Publishing Co., 1901.

———. *American Game-Bird Shooting*. Forest and Stream Publishing Co., 1910.

Herd, Andrew. *The Fly*. The Medlar Press, Ltd., 2003.

Herman, Daniel. *Hunting and the American Imagination*. Smithsonian Institution Press, 2000.

Hinman, Bob. *The Golden Age of Shotgunning*. Winchester Press, 1971.

Larkin, Jack. *The Reshaping of Everyday Life*. HarperCollins, 1988.

Lears, Jackson. *Rebirth of a Nation: The Making of Modern America, 1877–1920*. HarperCollins, 2009.

Ledlie, David. "A Brief Introduction to George Tattersall and 'Fishing in the North American Lakes and Rivers.'" *The American Fly Fisher*. Summer 2003.

Lutts, Ralph. *The Nature Fakers: Wildlife, Science, and Sentiment*. University of Virginia Press, 1990.

Lyons, Nick., ed. *The Gigantic Book of Fishing Stories*. Skyhorse Publishing, 2007.

McClane, A. J. *McClane's Standard Fishing Encyclopedia and International Angling Guide*. Holt, Rhinehart and Winston, 1965.

Mintz, Steven. *Huck's Raft: A History of American Childhood*. Belknap Press, 2004.

Monnett, John. "Lewis B. France: Outdoor Writer." *Colorado Heritage*. Summer 1993.

Morris, Edmund. *The Rise of Theodore Roosevelt*. Coward, McCann & Geoghegan, 1979.

———. *Theodore Rex*. Random House, 2001.

———. *Colonel Roosevelt*. Random House, 2010.

Mount, Nick. *When Canadian Literature Moved to New York*. University of Toronto Press, 2005.

Murray, Henry H. *Adventures in the Wilderness*. William K. Verner (ed.). Syracuse University Press, 1989.

Punke, Michael. *The Last Stand*. Smithsonian Books, 2007.

Reiger, George. *Profiles in Saltwater Angling*. Prentice-Hall, 1973

———. *The Wings of Dawn*. Madison Books Inc, 1979.

Reiger, John. *American Sportsman and the Origins of Conservations*. Oregon State University Press, 2001.

Rourke, Constance. *American Humor: A Study in the National Character*. Harcourt, Inc., 1931.

Schlereth, Thomas. *Victorian America: Transformations in Everyday Life*. HarperCollins, 1991.

Schullery, Paul. *American Fly Fishing: A History*. The Lyons Press, 1987.

Sheehy, Colleen J. "American Angling: The Rise of Urbanism and the Romance of the Rod and Reel." *Hard at Play: Leisure in America, 1840–1940*. Kathryn Grover (ed.). The Strong Museum, 1992.

Tapply, H. G. *The Sportsman's Notebook*. Holt, Rinehart and Winston, 1964.

Tygiel, Jules. *Past Time: Baseball as History*. Oxford University Press, 2000.

Van Dyke, Henry. *Fisherman's Luck*. Charles Scribner's Sons, 1899.

Van Put, Edward. *Trout Fishing in the Catskills*. Skyhorse Publishing, 2007.

Warner, Sam Bass. *Street Car Suburbs*. Harvard University Press, 1962.

Waterman, Charles. *A History of Angling*. New Win Publishing, 1981.

Wiebe, Robert H. *The Search for Order 1877–1920*. Harper Collins Canada Ltd., 1967.

Index

Adams, John, 51
"Adirondack Buck, An" (Roberts), 141–42
Adirondack Mountains, ix–xiv, 89
Adirondacks Verified, The (Warner),
    52–56
Adventures in the Wilderness (Murray),
    x–xiii, xv, 51, 52–53, 55–56
Aflalo, Frederic, 127
African Americans, 71, 210–11, 213
African expeditions, 119–22
African Game Trails (Roosevelt,
    T. Jr.), 122
"After Grouse with Hiram" (Foster),
    222–23
Akeley, Carl, 119, 120, 121
American Angler's Guide, The
    (Brown), 68
"American Angling" (Sheehy), 308–9
American Angling Book (Norris), 147–48
American Duck Shooting (Grinnell),
    90–92, 247, 252–57
American Fly Fisher, The, 24, 69
American Fly Fishing (Schullery), 177
American Game-Bird Shooting
    (Grinnell), 71
American Game In Its Season
    (Herbert/Forester), 40
American Humor (Rourke), 16
American Sportsman, The (Lewis), 32,
    34, 235
"Angler, The" (Irving), 7–8
Animals I Have Known (Seton), 94
anthropomorphism, 94–95
Audubon, John James, 13, 15–16, 67, 69
auerhahn, 95

Babb, Jim, 151
Babcock, Havileah, 224
Bailey, Peter, 266–67, 268–69
Bartram, William, 15–16, 280
bass
    availability of, 96, 183

challenges, 101, 276–78
characteristics of, 280
conservation, 303
fisherman qualities, 287, 290
gender preferences, 259
lying, 284–86
methods, 281, 299–302
motorcycle travel and fishing, 293–95
popularity of, 296–98, 304
popular locations for, 287
species comparisons, 283–84
stocking, 279
tackle for, 280–81
techniques, 100, 280
tourism and competition, 287–92
trout fishing compared to, 281–82
bass bugging, 299
Basses, The (Harris), 100, 281
"Bass Fishing with Frills" (Smith), 296–98
"Bass in the Beaverkill" (Rhead), 184,
    281–82
"Bass on a Motorcycle" (Johnson),
    293–95
Beach, Rex, 271–74
"Beaverkill, The" (Van Put), 69
Benjamin, Elizabeth, 176–77
Benton, Ezra, 219–21
Benton, J. R., 97–98
"Big Buck, A" (Gillmore), 26–27
big-game fishing, 123–28
big-game hunting
    bird hunting comparisons to, 214–15
    deer, white-tailed, 96–97, 106, 133–37,
        138–40, 141–42, 143–45
    elephants, 119
    grizzly bears, 104–6
    jaguars, 107–11
    land ownership issues, 207–8
    lions, 120–22
    moose, 129–32
    rhinos, 121
    women participants, 112–18

bird hunting (wing-shooting). *See also*
    duck hunting; waterfowling
    big-game hunting comparisons to,
        214–15
    country/city relationships, 189–93
    gender preferences, 258
    grouse, craftiness and challenge, 97,
        222–26, 227–30
    land connection, 214–15, 223–24
    plovers, 194–96
    prairie chickens, 189–93
    rules, 230
    snipe, 197–200
    social behavior, 191–92
    social tensions and land
        ownership issues, 207–9
    in South, post-Civil War, 210–17
    tradition *vs.* innovation, 228
    waterfowling comparisons to, 258
    women participants, 201–4
    woodcock, location challenges,
        218–22
Birds of America (Audubon), 13
Black Bass Fishing (Lincoln), 299
"Black Ducks and Barnegat" (Heilner),
    270–71
blinds, 272
bobbing, 280, 297
Bogardus, Adam, 191
Book of the Black Bass, The (Henshall),
    279–80
Book of Trout Flies, A (Jennings), 186
Book on Angling, A (Francis), 151
Boone and Crockett Club, 89
Boy Hunters, The (Reid), 38
bragging, 230
brant, 249–51, 259
"Bronze Backs" (Smith), 296
brook trout, 25, 96, 100, 148–49, 167–70
Brown, John J., 68
brown trout, 96, 148, 168, 183–84
Buckingham, Nash, 212–14
buffalo, 73, 77–78
Burroughs, John, 83–84, 94
Butler, Ellis Parker, 284–86

camping, automobile, 293
Canfield, H. S., 93
Carolina Sports by Land and Water
    (Elliot), 31
Carver, Doc, 191
Cave, Edward, 224–26
character associations, 19, 32, 39–40
Chichester, Carl, 267–68
Civil War, 18, 19, 50, 210, 213–14
Clemons, Carl, 266–67, 268–69
Cleveland, Grover, 78
"Climbing for White Goats" (Grinnell), 78
Compleat Angler (Walton), 4
"Confessions of an Ancient Poacher"
    (Thompson), 207–9
conservation and preservation
    bass and league creation, 303
    books influencing, 78–79, 91
    concept development, 74–82
    early efforts, 40–42, 68–69, 74–75,
        78–82, 90–91, 252
    game fish of California, 127
    of land, 89
    legislation, 69–70, 91
    licensing requirements, 91
    restraint *vs.* slaughter, 9–12, 90
Cook, Jospeh, ix
Cooper, James Fenimore, 5, 9–12
cork bugs, 299–302
Crocker, Samuel, 183
Crockett, Davy, 13–16
Crowell, Elmer, 244
Cushing, Percy, 261–64

Darwin, Charles, 43, 78–79
Dawson, George, 171
"Days among the Plovers" (Van Dyke, T.
    S.), 194–96
"Death of the Red-Winged Mallard, The"
    (Canfield), 93–94
decoys, 28–30, 237, 244–48, 252, 253
deer, white-tailed, 96–97, 106, 133–45,
    247, 258, 259
deer camps, 141–42, 145
De Graff, Thad S. Up, 161–66, 178

Delineations of American Character and Society, 67
DePeyster, Beekman and Cornelia Cochrane, 179–81
Dilg, Will, 300–302
dogs, 31, 32, 207, 244
"Dr. Craig and another Woodcock Hunter" (Morse), 219–21
Dry Fly and Fast Water, The (La Branche), 184–87, 299
duck hunting
   anthropomorphic behavior stories, 93–94
   bibles on, 90–92, 247, 252–57
   conservation and restrictions on, 90–91
   danger and death, 232–35, 266–69
   decoys, 237, 244–48, 252, 253
   description, 270–71
   gender preferences, 258–59
   modern methods, 252–57
   popular hunting destinations for, 32
   shooting diaries on, 239–43
   shooting skills and manliness, 254–56
   species preferences, 259–64
   technique development, 236–38
   upland bird hunting comparisons to, 258
   winter challenges, 97–98, 232–35, 264–65
Dunlap, Orrin E., 232–35
Dunne, Olive, 179

Eldrige, Henry, 244–46
elephants, 119
Elliot, William, 31
"Equivalence of Women, The," 180
"Escape from Niagara Falls, An" (Dunlap), 232–35
Evans, George Bird, 212

"Fatal Salmon, A" (Herbert/Forester), 39
"Fatal Success, A" (Van Dyke, Henry), 179–81

Favorite Flies and Their Histories (Marbury), 177–78, 281
fellowship, 145
Fifty Years a Surgeon (Morris, R. T.), 251
"Fight with A Trout, A" (Warner), 52
"Fish Are Such Liars" (Pertwee), 93
fishing, overview. *See also specific fishing methods and species*
   equipment development, 72
   land ownership, 150
   magazines on, 182
   perceptions of, 6–7, 11, 30–31, 150
   species decimation, views of, 68–73
   sportsmanship controversies, 9–12
   standards influenced by publications about, xiii
"Fishing for Black Bass on the Maumee Rapids, Ohio" (Gunckel), 287–92
"Fishing in the North American Lakes and Rivers" (Tattersall), 24–25
Fishing Tourist, The (Hallock), 160
"Fishing with a Worm" (Perry), 168–70
"Fishin' Jimmy" (Slosson), 58–60
"Fly Casting" (Hitchcock), 182–83
"Fly Casting Instruction Reaches the American Frontier" (Hill and Wheeler), 183
fly fishing for bass, 281–82, 299–302
fly fishing for trout
   bass fishing compared to, 281–82
   books on, 171
   as class marker, 150
   in Colorado, 171–75
   country/city relationships, 160, 161–66
   culture development, 147–48
   early descriptions and conditions, 25, 100
   fly tying innovations, 176–78
   innovation *vs.* tradition, 228
   land ownership issues, 150–54, 160–61, 207–8
   literary instruction, 182–87
   popular destinations, 160
   technique development, 100–102, 148–49, 174–75

travel pieces, 155–59
women participants, 178–81, 305–7
worm fishing comparisons, 168–70
Fly-Fishing In Maine Lakes (Stevens),
 48–49, 55
fly tying, 176–77
Forester, Frank, 38–41, 218
Fortis, George, 266–67
Foster, Max, 222–23, 271–72
France, Lewis B., 55, 62–63
Francis, Francis, 151–54
*Frank Forester's Fish and Fishing of
 the United States and British
 Provinces of North America*
 (Herbert/Forester), 38

*Game Birds of the Coasts and Lakes
 of the Northern States of America*
 (Roosevelt, R. B.), 42
Game Birds of the North (Roosevelt,
 R. B.), 236–38
*Game Fish of the Northern States of
 America and the British Provinces*
 (Roosevelt, R. B.), 42
Gardner, Jim, 124
geese, 249–51, 259, 271–74
"Geese" (Beach), 271–74
gender of quarry, 258–59
*Gigantic Book of Fishing Stories,
 The*, 67
Gilded Age, The (Warner and
 Twain), 52
Gillmore, Parker, 26–27
Giltner, Scott, 210
Gingrich, Arnold, 185
goats, 78–80, 87–88
Gordon, Theodore, 171
Grannom, Houghton, 178–79
"Great Sport" (Morrison), 305–7
Great War, 131–32
Green, Seth, 74
Grey, Zane, 276–78, 303
Grinnell, George Bird
 background, 77
 clubs founded by, 89

conservation movement
 contributions, 68, 71, 74, 77–82
 duck hunting, 90–92, 247, 252–57, 260
 as magazine editor, 77
 Roosevelt meeting and partnership,
 75–76, 83
grizzly bears, 104–6
grouse, 97, 222–26, 227–30
Gun, Rod, and Saddle (Gillmore), 26–27
Gunckel, J. E., 287–92
guns, 72

habitat destruction, 40, 70, 193
Halford, Frederic M., 174–75
Hallock, Charles, 160
Hard at Play", 308
"Harp That Once—, The" (Buckingham),
 212–14
Harris, William, 100, 281
hat decorations, 70
Hawker, Peter, 20–23
Haynes, William Barber, 129–32
Heilner, Van Campen, 270–71
"Henry's Birds" (Sears), 244–46
Henshall, James, 279–80, 283
Herbert, William Henry, 38–41, 218
Herman, Daniel, 136
Hermann, Daniel, 7
Hill, Warren Vander, 183
Hitchcock, Ripley, 182–83
Holder, Charles Frederick, 123–26
Holland, Ray, 91, 218
Holmes, Oliver Wendell, Jr., 64
horses, 116–17
Hot Pot, 151–54
Hough, Emerson, 78, 211
Howard, William Willard, 107–11
Howe, Wirt, 210–11
Hunter, Alex, 263, 266
hunting, overview. *See also specific
 species*
 character associations, 19, 32, 39–40
 early perceptions of, 6–7, 30–31
 equipment developments, 72
 hunter qualities, 143

land ownership issues, 150–51
process and skills, importance of, 145
species decimation, views of, 68–73
sportsmanship controversies, 9–12
standards influenced by publications
  about, xiii
Hunting and Fishing in the New South
  (Giltner), 210
*Hunting and the American
  Imagination* (Hermann), 7
"Hunting the Jaguar in Venezuela"
  (Howard), 107–11
Hunting Trips of a Ranchman
  (Roosevelt, T., Jr.), 65, 84, 105

"Ibis Shooting in Louisiana" (anonymous
  writer), 14–16
ice fishing, 24–25
I Go-A-Fishing (Prime), 51, 52
In Africa (McCutcheon), 120–22
India expeditions, 112–18
individualism, 19
Instructions to Young Sportsmen
  (Hawker), 20
In the Heart of the Sea (Philbrick), 123
Irving, Washington, 4–5, 6, 7–8
Izaak Walton League, 303

jaguars, 107–11
Jefferson, Thomas, 51
Jennings, Preston, 186
Johnson, George, 293–95

"King of Kings" (Dilg), 300–302
Kingsley, Charles, 155
Klapp, H. Milnor, 35
knowledge, as skill, 44
Krider, John, 34–37
Krider's Sporting Anecdotes (Krider and
  Klapp), 35–37

La Branche, George, 100, 101, 184–87
Lacey Act, 91
"Lady or the Salmon, The" (Lang), 178–79
Laing, Albert, 244

land and land ownership, 150–54, 160–61,
  205–9, 214–15, 223–24
Lang, Andrew, 178–79
Lanier, Charles D., 133–37
Lardner, Ring, 129
Latch, John, 303
Latin America expeditions, 107–11
leisure time, 29, 46, 50–52
Lewis, Elijah, 32–33, 235
licensing, 91
Lincoln, Robert Page, 299
lions, 120–22
Lobo (wolf), 94
Local Color Movement, 57–58
Long, William J., 94–95
"Lord of Lackawaxen Creek, The (Grey),
  276–78
Lost Cause, 50, 213–14
"Lovely June Day, A" (Senior), 155–58
"Lucy, That Old Mallard Hen," 93
Lyell, Sir Charles, 28–30
Lyons, Nick, 256

Mackay, George Henry, 239–43
"Madam's Chicken Shoot, The" (Sandys),
  201–4
manliness (masculinity)
  bird hunting contests testing, 192
  duck hunting contributing to, 32,
    254–56, 263–64
  fishing building, 44
  fishing safety *vs.*, 39
  gender of animal preferences and,
    258–59
  species not associated with, 32
  urban domesticity and loss of, 51,
    63–64, 264
Marbury, Mary Orvis, 177–78, 281
market (commercial) hunting, 70
Marsh, Joe, 232–35
Mather, Fred, 147
Maxwell, Martha, 118
McBride, Sara, 177
McCutcheon, John, 120–22
Merrifield, Frank, 104

"Metaphysics of Fly Fishing, The" (McBride), 177
Migratory Bird Act, 69–70, 91
Mims, Edward, 137
Mitchell, David B. W., 138–40
Mitchell, Elijah, 138–40
Mitchell, Philip, 138–40
moose, 129–32
"Moose Hunter's Letters, A" (Haynes), 129–32
Morris, Robert T., 249–51
Morris, William, 150
Morrison, Aimee, 305–7
Morse, C. Harry, 219–21
Murray, William Henry Harrison, ix–xiii, xv, 51, 52–53, 55–56
Murray's fools, xii
My Angling Friends (Mather), 147
"My Most Tragic Fishing Moment" (Dilg), 302

Narrative of the Life of Davy Crockett, A (Crockett), 13
National Park Protective Act, 78
Native Americans, 73, 85
Nature Fakers, 94–95
Norris, Thaddeus, 147–48, 161
Northern Trails (Long), 95
nostalgia, 50

Oneida Society, 31
On the Origin of the Species (Darwin), 43, 78–79
"On the Wide Marshes of Manitoba" (Sandys), 259–60
Ornithological Biography (Audubon), 67
Orvis, Charles F., 177
"Our Geared Up Grouse Hunting" (Cave), 224–26

Patton, George, Jr., 127
Payne-Gallwey, Sir Ralph, 20
Peckinpaugh, Ernest, 299
Perry, Bliss, 168–70, 307
Pertwee, Roland, 93

pheasants, 229
Philbrick, Nathan, 123
Phillips, Wendell, xiii
pigeons, 69
Pinchot, Gifford, 124–26, 127
Pioneers, The (Cooper), 9–12
plantations, 210–17
Pleasures of Angling, The (Dawson), 171
plovers, 69–70, 194–96
poaching, 151–54, 205–9
Pole, Edward, 34
prairie chickens, 192–93, 201–4
Prime, W. C., 51, 52, 58
Prouty, Lorenzo, 178

quail, 71, 210–17, 224
"Quail in Painted Covers" (Sandys), 215–17

rabbit hunting, 32, 206–7
racism, 71
railroads, 57, 155–56
rainbow trout, 168, 183
Reade, James, 20, 22–23
Reagan, Ronald, 95
Recreations of a Sportsman on the Pacific Coast (Holder), 124–26
"Reformation of Uncle Billy, The" (Butler), 284–86
Reid, Mayne, 38
religion, 60–61, 71
restraint, 9–12, 90
Rhead, Louis, 184, 281–82
rhinos, 121
Rhodes, Cecil Springs, 87
Rice, Grantland, 271–72
Roberts, Georgia, 141–43, 145
Rod and Line in Colorado (France), 62–63
Roosevelt, Elliot, 64–65
Roosevelt, Robert Barnwell, 42–46, 74–75, 148, 236–38
Roosevelt, Theodore, Jr.
    animal behavior, 94
    background, 84

books influencing, 78–79
childhood, 42–43, 64
clubs founded by, 89
conservation movement
    contributions, 68, 74
description and personality, 83, 87
elephant hunting, 119
game fish club memberships, 127
Grinnell meeting and partnership,
    75–76, 83
grizzly bear hunting, 104–6
history books by, 85, 105
hunting books by, 65, 84–88,
    105, 122
influences on, 83–84
on Latin American cultures, 107
nature books read to children, 95
Roosevelt, Theodore, Sr., 64, 65, 105
Rourke, Constance, 16
Russell, Ernest, 227–30

Sandys, Edwyn, 189–93, 201–4, 206,
    215–17, 224, 259–60
Satterthwaite, Franklin, 197–200
Savory, Isabel, 112–18
"Sawney's Deer Lick" (Lanier), 133–37
Schullery, Paul, 177
Sears, Hamblen, 244–46
Second Visit to the United States
    (Lyell), 28–29
"Secret of Getting Grouse, The"
    (Russell), 227–30
Senior, William, 155–59
Seton, Ernest Thomson, 94
Sheehy, Colleen, 308–9
Sherman, Leonard DeWitt, 143–45
Shooting Diary of Colonel Peter Hawker,
    The (Hawker), 20–23
Shooting Diary of George Henry
    Mackay, The, 239–43
"Shooting Ducks at New York's Back
    Door" (Cushing), 261–64
"Shorty: A Native Fishermen Who Takes
    'Em on a Fly" (De Graff), 161–66
Shriver, William, 279

sinkboxes, 236
Sketch Book of Geoffrey Crayon, The
    (Irving), 4, 7–8
Slosson, Annie Trumbull, 58
Smith, O. W., 296–98
snipe, 197–200
social class
    behavior expectations, 191, 192
    character associations, 19, 32, 39–40
    country *vs.* city relationships, 160,
        161–66, 189–93, 206–9
    fishing associated with, 150, 182
    hunting associated with, 19, 28, 29,
        32, 207
South, the, 210–17
species decimation, 68–73, 96–97, 106,
    193, 210, 225
sporting goods stores, 34–37
sports hunting
    character associations, 19, 32, 39–40
    conservation and preservation, 18,
        40–41, 68
    decoy ponds, 28–29
    definition and purpose, 28
    occupation *vs.* recreation, 32, 70
    rural view of, 48–49
    social class distinctions, 19, 28, 29
    sports hunters as naturalists, 95
Sportsman's Depot, The, 34
sportsmanship, 9–12, 230, 306–7
Sportswoman in India, A
    (Savory), 112
Squaring the Keeper" (Francis), 151–54
Stevens, Charles, 48, 55
Still Hunter, The (Van Dyke, T. S.), 145
stocking fish, 279–80
"Sunny South, The" (Hough), 211
Sunset Playgrounds (Aflalo), 127
Superior Fishing (Roosevelt, R. B.),
    42, 43
swordfish, 124–26

Tapply, H. G. "Tap," 218–19
Tattersall, George, 24–25, 68, 148
Terife (guide), 108–11

"Thanksgiving Deer Hunt in West
Virginia, A" (Mitchell brothers),
138–40
"That Ten-Point Buck" (Sherman),
143–45
Thompson, Maurice, 208–9
Three for the Alamo (Davis), 14
Titanic (ship), 269
"Toll of the Sport, The" (Fortis), 266–67
tourism, 57, 290–92
Transcendentalists, 31
Trollope, Frances, 24
trout
    bass fishing compared to, 281–82
    brook (worm) fishing, 167–70
    descriptions and conditions, 25, 100
    fishing locations, 148–49
    fly fishing for (*see* fly fishing for trout)
    species US introductions, 183
    supply decline, 96, 167
tuna, 124, 127–28
Tuna Club of Santa Catalina, 124, 127
Twain, Mark, 52

Upland Game Birds (Sandys and Van
Dyke, T. S.), 189–93

vacation, 50, 51–52
Van Dyke, Henry, 179–81
Van Dyke, T. S., 145, 189–93, 194–96
Van Put, Ed, 69
Van Siclen, George W., 69
Veltman, Tom, 266–67, 268–69
Victoria, Queen of England, 113

Walton, Izaac, 4, 8
Warner, Charles Dudley, 52–56
Warner, Sam Bass, 50
Warren, T. Robinson, 18–19
"Watching the Brant Grow Big" (Morris,
R. T.), 249–51

waterfowling, 28–30, 91, 236, 244, 249–51,
271–74. *See also* duck hunting
Waterman, Charles, 199, 297–98
Weeks-Maclean Bill, 91
whales, 123
Wheeler, David, 183
Whitcher, Jimmy, 58–60
Wiebe, Robert, 257
Wiessen, Pete, 232–35
Wilderness Hunter (Roosevelt, T., Jr.),
84–88
Willis, John, 84–88
wing-shooting. *See* bird hunting
Wings of Dawn (Reiger), 70–71
Winning of the West, The (Roosevelt, T.
Jr.), 85, 105
"Winter's Day with Ducks, A" (Benton),
97–98
With Rod and Line in Colorado Waters
(France), 171–74
"With the Quail among the Cotton"
(Howe), 210–11
women
    big-game hunting, 112–18, 141–43, 145
    distracting men, 39
    fishing-religion stories by, 58–61
    fly fishing, 178–81, 305–7
    fly tying innovations, 176–77
    as hunters, nineteeth-century
        perception of, 113
    saving men, 290, 291–92
    sportswomen, definition of, 116
woodcocks, 40–41, 218–22
Working At Play (Aron), 51
worm fishing, 167–70

Yellowstone Park, 78, 89
You Know Me Al (Lardner), 129